❧

Vera Kathleen Jones was born in England and lived from an early age in New Zealand where she had part of her education before returning with her family to England as a teenager.

At 17, her nursing experience began in Brighton in a convalescent home for sick children from deprived areas of London. Here she experienced diseases not familiar to nurses today – rheumatic fever, chorea, diphtheria, scarlet fever, commonly accompanied by malnutrition.

Her general training from 1935 was followed by district nursing in London. At the outbreak of war in 1939, she joined Queen Alexandra's Imperial Military Nursing Service Reserve as a Nursing Officer. Her subsequent experiences are told in this book.

After the war she joined the service as a Regular Officer, and qualified as a Registered Nurse Tutor. Further experiences followed in Egypt and Libya where she enjoyed teaching RAMC Nursing Orderlies in military hospitals.

The ill health of her father led to her decision to return to civilian life. Appointments in posts as tutor followed, including eleven years as a Principal Tutor.

In her retirement she lives in Wales.

A TIME TO REMEMBER

*A record of nursing experiences, impressions and
travels during World War II
contained in letters sent home from the East*

by

Vera Kathleen Jones

*For Jaqui
With all good wishes from
Vera.*

A TIME TO REMEMBER

A record of nursing experiences, impressions and travels during World War II contained in letters sent home from the East

by

Vera Kathleen Jones

ATHENA PRESS
LONDON

A TIME TO REMEMBER

A record of nursing experiences, impressions and travels during World War II contained in letters sent home from the East by Vera Kathleen Jones

Copyright © Vera Kathleen Jones 2005

All Rights Reserved

ISBN 1 84401 394 4

First Published 2005 by
ATHENA PRESS
Queen's House, 2 Holly Road
Twickenham TW1 4EG
United Kingdom

Printed for Athena Press

To my sister, Muriel,
without whose forethought and care
these letters would not have been saved
during the war years

The author and friends at Everleigh Manor in Wiltshire where they were assembled as a unit of eighty sisters before embarking for abroad, October 1939

QAIMNSR
2 Reserve J/766 ‧
No 12 General Hospital
c/o Army Post Office
London
23.12.39

Dear Mother and Father

I hope you have received my card and letter safely. The letter was written in haste as the post was about to be collected, so I am afraid it was only a short one.

Well, there is so little I can tell you. There is of course much I would like to write, I have had some wonderful experiences already, the places we have described, but I may not visit. We are still on the way to our destination and are having a very good journey with every comfort and consideration.

I hope you are all well at home. I think of you often, and hope I shall hear from you soon after we arrive.

Please excuse this brief letter. I shall be able to write more next time.

Give my love to all. Best love to you both.

Will write again soon.

Vera

ॐ

27.12.39

Dear Mother and Father

I am writing to you again just to let you know that I am very well.

There is, of course, nothing that I can tell you, but I know you like to have word from me as often as possible so I am writing whenever I have the opportunity.

We have enjoyed a very festive Christmas in the good old English style. I thought about you all at home and often wondered what you were doing on Christmas Day.

We hope to reach our journey's end soon, but do not know where that is to be. It is very exciting wondering where we are going to settle down to work.

It will be lovely to hear from you again. Give my love to everyone and tell Muriel I will write as soon as I can.

There is really no more in this letter than the last one, but I am sure you will not mind that too much, as long as you have heard from me.

I will write again soon. Heaps of love to you both.

Vera

∽

2 Reserve J/766
Sister V K Jones
QAIMNSR
Sarafand
Palestine
29.12.39

Dear Mother and Father

You will be very pleased to hear that I am now able to write uncensored letters, and, as you see by the above address, I am able to tell you my whereabouts.

I don't know how to start writing, as there is so much to say and such a lot has happened since I left England. It has been so difficult writing to you up to the present as the letters have been strictly censored, and many of the Sisters have had theirs returned to them for re-writing when they have really said very little of importance.

I will tell you from the beginning about our experiences. We left Southampton on the 17th December on a Channel troopship called the *Prague*. We had a most exciting crossing. It was very rough and we moved at a great speed, and the boat rolled sickeningly! We were in a convoy of course, and were escorted by a French destroyer.

We slept, or rather, tried to sleep, fully dressed, lying on our bunks, wearing lifebelts! Many I am afraid were *nearly* seasick! Many of the others were very bad. At about 3 a.m. we were in mid-Channel when there was a terrific clanging of bells all over the ship and we thought we must have been torpedoed, but were relieved to hear that it was only a signal that the flood-proof gates were being closed.

It was altogether a very rough journey, and there was quite a thick mist during the night. In the morning we were on deck very early to see the first view of the French coast. As we neared the port a French sea-plane came out to meet us and circled round the convoy until we anchored. The British plane had left us just before, to return.

We landed at Cherbourg and remained there until late that night. We stayed during the day at an Officers' Club where we had the most delicious omelettes and coffee. I had some lovely champagne also! It only cost 5 francs (about 6d).

We had two air raid warnings – one about two hours after our arrival the other at about 10 p.m. That was nice for our first day in France, wasn't it?

We did not see much of Cherbourg, as we were smuggled off to the railway station soon after tea and had to sit in the train and wait until we moved off, eight *hours* later! The town was out of bounds.

It was about 11 p.m. when we left on Monday night, and we arrived in Marseilles at midnight on Wednesday! We were travelling very fast all that time, night and day. We did not know where we were going when we left Cherbourg and just guessed it would be Marseilles.

It was a most fascinating journey and we saw such a lot of France. I think the French people are wonderful and so friendly. We stopped at several small stations and were made most welcome by the people there. As we passed through villages, peasant women leaned out of their cottage windows and waved and cheered. When we stopped once near a farm a woman gave us baskets of apples and a loaf of bread through the carriage windows.

I found myself learning French quite easily and would soon have picked it up had we stayed in France. Several of the Sisters talked fluently to the people and had quite pleasant conversations. We made friends with some French soldiers at one station and gave them handfuls of cigarettes, which pleased them greatly as they evidently do not get a good supply of them in the French army.

We saw some lovely scenery and passed several large chateaux.

We spent two nights in the train and – including the night crossing the Channel – did not undress for three nights. We felt very cramped and tired when we reached Marseilles but I was glad we had had the train journey, in spite of our weariness at the end.

The latter part of the journey was beautiful as we passed along beside the Mediterranean and saw part of the Riviera.

When we arrived in Marseilles we were taken to one of the most luxurious hotels in the city and were soon refreshed by hot baths and lunch. It was called the Hôtel de Louvre. We had separate bedrooms with every comfort and the most comfortable beds. My room was near the top of the building and had shuttered French windows, which opened into a small balcony commanding a fine view of the city and harbour. We were allowed to explore the city in parties that afternoon and did quite a lot of shopping.

Marseilles is a most fascinating city and clean and well laid out. I was most surprised as I had thought it was a dirty place. We found the shops very good and reasonable. We caused a great deal of interest amongst the people again, and everyone was most charming and helpful. Several people almost hugged us with delight when they heard we were English nurses and wished us bon voyage. The atmosphere was so friendly everywhere we went in France – it was as good as being in England.

We spent a most comfortable night at the hotel after an excellent dinner. Next morning we left at 9 a.m. for the quay and a crowd collected outside the hotel to see us off. I felt like the Prime Minister in Downing Street!

We sailed early the next morning on the *Neuralia* a ship of 9,056 tons belonging to the British India Steam Navigation Company. It was a fine boat and we had comfortable cabins and very good food.

We had an Australian destroyer in our convoy across the Mediterranean and there was one other boat a sister ship with us which went on through the Suez Canal just before we reached Haifa.

The voyage took nearly seven days and we enjoyed glorious weather all the time. Also the moon was full so it was quite light at night. On Christmas Eve we reached Malta at about 6 p.m. but were not allowed to go ashore. It is a wonderful place and I can't begin to describe it! It was just like fairyland with the little gondolas lit by coloured lights moving across the harbour and the moon shining on the white walls of the city. It was strange to come upon such a place in the middle of the ocean!

After we left Malta at 10 p.m. the sea was very rough and on Christmas Day a number of people were sick again and the boat rolled about a good deal.

We had a very happy Christmas, however. In the morning we had services with Christmas hymns and carols. At dinner at 7.30 p.m. we had a great spread, followed by speeches etc, and then dancing and music.

On Boxing Day we had a concert given by the troops in their dining saloon. It was very good and worthy of broadcasting. Gracie Fields would have loved it!

Altogether the journey was very happy and we revelled in the warm sunshine and fresh air. Was it very cold in England for Christmas?

Even on the boat, we did not know where we were bound for and heard only rumours. On the Wednesday after Christmas, however, we were told to prepare to land the next day, and the following morning, just before midday we sailed into the harbour of Haifa.

It is a modern city and very clean. We were not able to see much, however, as we were transferred from the boat to a train within a short time and soon were travelling along beside the sea on one side and the Plain of Sharon on the other.

It was wonderful to be travelling in Palestine and I felt very thrilled. It is just as I have always imagined it and one feels as if one were looking at Bible pictures! It is a most wonderful country and although, up to the present, I have only seen a small area of it, I am very impressed with all I have seen. We were four hours in the train which was rather a slow one, but I did not mind that as we saw much to take our attention.

The land is very hilly and dry. We passed groves of orange and grapefruit trees, however, which looked very fresh and green against the red sandy hills. The trees were loaded with fruit. In the fields we saw men 'ploughing the fields and scattering the good seed on the ground'. The ploughs were drawn by camels, tell Geoff! We saw veiled Arab women with children dressed in brightly coloured robes and girdles. Several times I saw women riding on asses with men walking beside them. As we passed through villages the people gathered near the line to see us and wave. They were all dressed in bright coloured clothes and headdresses and their feet were bare. I saw one little brown boy walking along trailing a palm branch behind him, and further on were women carrying earthenware water jugs on their heads! It was all so colourful and so much the same as the Palestine we read of in the Bible. The villages with their domes and minarets, are circled by stone walls and can be seen dotted on the hillsides every few miles. In some of the fields we saw flocks of sheep with shepherds, and on the hillsides were black mountain goats.

It was nearly dark when we reached Sarafand, which is a new military town about one hour's journey from Jerusalem! Here we were met and after supper were taken to our billets. We are now living in new bungalows built for families and there are three of us to each house. They are well-built houses with verandahs and French windows. We are using them unfurnished at present, except for our camp beds and camp chairs but have made them quite comfortable. We have a very nice bathroom with a shower. We have all our meals in the Mess which is about five minutes' walk down the road.

At present we are still awaiting further orders and have not started work. There is an Air Force hospital here, which we are taking over soon, but only half our staff will be needed to staff it, and the other half are going on to a place nearer Jerusalem. We do not know when the dividing up will take place or how long we shall wait here, but think we shall know in a few days. I may stay here or I may go on to the other hospital.

We are about twelve miles from Tel Aviv and the same distance from Jaffa. We hope to go to Tel Aviv by bus as they say it is an interesting town.

I have bought some interesting things here already. I have a pair of candlesticks, a camel with a hole in its back for use as an inkpot, all made of olivewood and a New Testament bound with olivewood. When I visit Jerusalem, I will buy something for all of you there. We shall be able to visit places of Biblical interest when we have local leave, as long as we go in parties.

The weather here is very hot and the sun is so dazzling that most of us wear dark glasses for part of the day. At night the temperature falls suddenly and we have to be careful not to catch cold. We sleep with plenty of blankets on the bed, but during the day we wear as few clothes as possible. This is Palestine's winter, by the way. What price the summer!

As soon as I can get to some English shops I must get some summer clothes. My 'Siegfried Line woollies' will be useful if we go to certain parts of Palestine, but not here I am afraid.

I have just heard that our letters *may* be censored before they leave Palestine but I hope you will receive this without any blackings-out, I do not think they will be subject to the strict censorship as previously, though.

Well, there still seems a lot I have not told you but the post is going soon so I must not write much more. I will write another long letter as soon as possible.

I hope you are all well at home. It seems years since I heard from you, and it will be lovely to have a letter again. Do you think you could send me the copy of H V Morton's book, *In the Steps of the Master*. It would be a good guide to see the places of interest here. We have a copy somewhere at home, and I should be very glad if you would lend it to me. There is nothing else I want.

As it is getting late I had better stop now. It has been lovely to write a real letter at last. I don't know what you must have thought of my other scrappy notes!

I will write soon and tell you where I am going to work.

Cheerio for now.

Much love to all, and heaps to you both, from

Your loving

Vera

৵

Dear Mother and Father

There is not very much more news to give you just now, as we have not yet started work and are still waiting to be divided out to our various positions. We all expect to be working before the end of this month, however.

I told you in my last letter that some of us were going to Jerusalem and the rest remaining at the hospital here. The Jerusalem Military Hospital is not yet in existence and the Sisters who go there will be pioneers, as they will help to start it and will see it improve and grow. I should love that kind of job, but I don't know whether I shall be sent there or not, as yet.

The hospital here, which is at present staffed by an RAF medical unit, and which we are taking over from them, is a well established institution situated in lovely grounds with many tropical shrubs and cypress trees. The wards are long, low buildings with shady verandahs, and the whole hospital is well equipped. At present it has about 220 beds (the size of KGH) but we are going to enlarge it to over 400 beds. In both this and the Jerusalem hospital, the experience will be very good.

The weather has been glorious here since we came although it is supposed to be the Palestine winter! We have had one terrific downpour of heavy tropical rain which drenched everything and everybody and made the gutters like miniature rivers. We are expecting more rain, as the rainy season commences about this time. There is very little warning just before it rains, and although the sky is clear blue and the sun dazzling today, we may expect a sudden change any time.

We are still living in bungalows and using our camp equipment. We have made our rooms quite comfortable, and when it becomes cold at night, we sit round a log fire just as you must be doing in England. Are you having very cold weather? I shall forget what an English winter is like, being out here!

I have just returned from a few hours' visit to Tel Aviv, which is only about ten miles away. We went by bus. This is the first time we have been allowed outside the barrier surrounding Sarafand, so we enjoyed the excursion very much. It is a fine town of about one hundred thousand inhabitants (all Jewish) and is situated on the coast. It has a fine promenade and lovely golden sand. We walked for a long way along the beach. I went with five other Sisters as we have to travel in parties. We did some shopping and had tea at a very nice café on the promenade. The shops are very good but we found most things much more expensive than in England. Fortunately, however, clothes are cheaper and of very good quality material.

About a week ago we went, by invitation, to an orchestral concert given by the Palestine Orchestra. It was really wonderful, and they played several of my favourite pieces of music. To commence the concert the National Anthem was played, followed by the Jewish National Anthem, which is a most impressive thing, and is always played after *God Save the King* – everywhere in Palestine.

We have been doing a lot of walking since we arrived here. As we have to remain within the perimeter of the town, as the order was given, we have to content ourselves with just walking *round* the outskirts of the town where we have lovely views of the surrounding districts. The sunsets here are particularly beautiful, when the sky has all the colours of the rainbow at the same time. There is hardly any dusk at all, and it is dark early.

We are two hours ahead of Greenwich Mean Time, and had to put the clocks on when we were on the boat.

We are able to buy quite good newspapers here, which give all British news, but sad to relate, we cannot tune in to BBC stations on the wireless set which we bought in England. We are hoping to be able to exchange it at a shop in Tel Aviv, for one which will pick up the English stations. At 6 p.m. a few days ago, I heard the chimes of Big Ben on a neighbours wireless set, striking 4 p.m.!

If you could send me the *Nursing Mirror* and *Weekly Illustrated*, every few weeks, I should love to have them, as English magazines seem very scarce here.

Well, I must stop now, and go to bed. It will be lovely to have a letter from you some time, but I am not hoping for one too soon as we are told the mail may only arrive very erratically and letters will take about three weeks from England by ordinary route.

I will write to you at least once a week and if you have time to do the same, we should be able to keep up a regular correspondence.

Cheerio for now,

Heaps of love to you all.

Vera

P.S. When you write would you let me know if there was much of my letter 'blacked-out' by the censor? I hope it arrived intact, as I gave descriptions of the journey here, and afterwards wondered if it would be passed!

ॐ

23.1.40

Dear All

Thank you so much for your letters received safely. My first letters since we left England, arrived on the 13th January – when I had two from Mother – one dated the 15th December, and the other the 28th. There was great rejoicing when we heard that our first mail had arrived. There were twelve sacks of letters for our unit! I had eight letters that day. On the 16th January, I had a letter from Father and it had only taken just over two weeks to arrive here. Then on the 20th, I had a letter from Mother, which had taken exactly two weeks – from Heybridge to Sarafand! I am afraid the post will not be so speedy now that my address is not 'Army Post Office', as all mails are sent overseas much quicker, when addressed that way.

I am sorry to say that the parcel you sent me before we left Everleigh, containing shoes etc, has not arrived, and as it was posted nearly six weeks ago, and parcels have already been delivered here to other people, I have come to the conclusion that it has gone to the bottom of the sea! It may have been delayed, of course, but I am inclined to think it has gone for good.

I expect you have received my first letter, by Imperial Airways, and the second one, sent by ordinary route. Was the first letter severely censored? I have a feeling it may have been as I wrote such details, and afterwards wondered if it was wise. I am looking forward to a letter from you in answer to my first from Palestine. Will you let me know how long this one takes – travelling by the

Italian airmail?

Well, at the moment I am still not working – and leading a lazy life. Out of our eighty Sisters – about fifty are at work now – some at the hospital here, and about eight are at Haifa Military Hospital. There are only about thirty of us still waiting to have our share of work. My name is on the list of Sisters to go to the new hospital at Jerusalem! I am not going to believe it until I am told definitely, however, as these lists are so often changed, and I may not go at all, which would be most disappointing. I would like to go so much – it will be quite a new undertaking as we shall be making it out of practically nothing. Did I tell you that the building is an old monastery, *on the Mount of Olives*? We shall have a wonderful view of Jerusalem on one side and of the Dead Sea on the other!

The building is still under reconstruction but should be ready very soon. It is rumoured that some of us will be going there at the end of this week.

My friend, Sister Arthur, is on night duty at this hospital in Sarafand, and she has settled down and likes it very much. The other nurse from Plaistow – Sister Bryant, who came with us, is at Haifa for a time, maybe, permanently.

We have taken over the Sarafand Hospital, from the RAF and the Sisters who are there are very busy just now as it is a large hospital, and all the beds are taken up.

We are still having lovely sunny weather, but about once a week, we have torrential rain which lasts about twenty-four hours. We are told that the rainy season starts 'in earnest' in February, when it will rain nearly all the time!

This is a most wonderful country. The fields are covered with wild flowers – lupins, anemones, and wild sweet peas. There are also some little white flowers which look like irises and later we shall have the 'lilies of the field' in bloom! The buds and leaves are just appearing. All round the outskirts of the ten foot wire barrier surrounding the town, are orange groves, laden with fruit. There is one grove within the barrier, so we are able to walk through it and pick oranges and lemons, as they are public property! Every morning for breakfast, we have huge grapefruits. I have never seen so much fruit! The little Arab children play with oranges, like balls. I believe there is great difficulty in shipping the fruit to England, so you must have a shortage.

The climate is going to suit me. I enclose a 'snap' of myself and two friends – one a Sister, and the other a donkey named *Peter*! He walked in through our garden gate and ate our few blades of grass, and then tried to walk in through the front door! On several occasions he had laid himself down on the verandahs of other houses and no power on earth can move him off! One Sister took him to the police station, when she *did* move him, and he was claimed by a little boy, a soldier's son, who had lost him.

On one other occasion, the Sister whom you can see in the background of the photo, was out walking one evening, when Peter crept up behind her and put his nose into her hand! She was petrified, until she realised what it was. He is now a great friend of ours and everyone is fond of him. It is funny that I should meet another Peter. I miss our Peter very much.

At night this is a weird place. The countryside is infested with jackals which come out of their lairs at night, and howl and wail to each other. Then the asses and donkeys lift up their tuneless voices, and sometimes a hyena joins in the chorus. What a pandemonium!

We have the most wonderful sunsets here, such as I have never seen before. It is a great sight to see the tall dark cypress trees outlined against a flame-coloured sky. The stars appear while the sun is still going down, and in a few minutes it is dark. We have a very good laundry here, and also a tailor who has cleaned my costume for me at a most reasonable price, 2/–. It really needed it after three months wearing it, and then the journey here, which made it rather grubby. It now looks very smart.

I am so glad you liked my photo. It must look very nice in the frame.

Well, there does not seem to be much more to tell you just now. I am so glad you are all well, and especially pleased to hear that Mother is sleeping better. I also hope she is not dashing about all day!

Give my love to the Fieldsteins, and Frees. Heaps of love to you all, will write again very soon, when I am working.

Your loving
Vera

᭡

2 Reserve J/766
QAIMNSR
Sarafand
Palestine
1.2.40

Dear Mother and Father

Thank you so much for the letter from Father and for the parcel containing the book and magazines. I am so pleased to have the book and have started to read it. It will be most interesting for me now that I am out here. I hope you do not mind me taking it from you.

In my last letter I told you that I had not started work and was expecting to go to Jerusalem. Well, as I half expected my name was removed from the list at the last minute and I am now at the Sarafand Military Hospital, (formerly the RAF) and have been working (at last) for the past four days! I was rather hoping to go to the new hospital on the Mount of Olives, but I am glad to say we are all going to see Jerusalem in turn and shall all be working there from time to time. There are only twenty-two Sisters there at present and the hospital is still in the hands of builders and electricians etc. We have heard from one of the Sisters there that the scenery is indescribable and they have the most glorious view to the old and new Jerusalem, and the Jordan Valley and Dead Sea! We are all so looking forward to going.

I am very glad to be working again. We moved up here to our new quarters from the temporary bungalows on Sunday (which seems to be the day for moves in the army!) Our Sisters' quarters are so nice and we have all settled down quickly. Our rooms are not furnished and we are still using our camp equipment, but I do not mind that, as my camp bed is very comfortable. We are not having any furniture supplied as we are still known as a mobile unit and may move off again at any time!

Our rooms are situated in a long, low building in the grounds, and each room opens onto a wide verandah, which surrounds the building. A lovely tropical creeper covers the verandah rails and the garden is full of tropical shrubs and plants. The trees are beautiful, and the grounds are full of tall cypresses, and palm trees grow in abundance. From our rooms and from the dining room we have a lovely view. The hospital stands rather higher than the rest of Sarafand and has the best position. We have a perfect view of a valley, covered with orange groves and cypress trees with small Arab villages here and there, while beyond that there is a long range of hills which separates us from Jerusalem. The hills are really lovely on a sunny day, when they are a study in sunlight and shadow. It is beautiful to see the sun setting behind them. We are told that the hills are inhabited by the fiercer Arab tribes and one must be well armed and escorted to pass through them. We are, of course, escorted whenever we leave Sarafand, and when we visit Tel Aviv an armed police car is driven in front of the bus! Also we never go out alone, but always make up parties.

I am sharing my room with one other Sister, and we have made it quite comfortable and homelike.

I am working in a surgical ward, and we are very busy, so the days pass quickly, and it is nice to have work to do again. We have a lot of very young men recently out from England. They are a happy crowd of patients. We have fifty-four on my ward. At present I am working with several other Sisters, but in a few days, may be nursing patients in marquees! We are erecting them rapidly, and will soon have nearly 400 beds in the hospital. There are about fifty-eight Sisters here. It is quite time the army took over this hospital as there is such a lot of work to do, and we shall never have many empty beds. It is quite different in some ways from working in an English civilian hospital, and we have to do a lot of improvising, but it is all good experience.

Our on-duty hours are from 7.30 a.m. to 8 p.m., but we have three hours off duty daily, and a half-day three times a week. We are not having a day off, but will probably be given weekends off, later on. We are given good off duty because the very hot weather will be starting soon.

In April, we are going to start wearing tropical uniform. We are ordering it now, and it consists of white overalls and veils, white shoes and stockings and for outdoor wear, light dresses and white felt hats with the QAIMNSR hatband. We are also having new capes with scarlet edges, made of thinner material than those we are wearing now. It should look nice and fresh, I think, and we shall be much cooler. We are being given an allowance of £5.00 to help to cover the cost. The uniform we wear now is very neat and attractive and everyone looks nice in it. I like our organdie caps as they are so light and comfortable.

You will be pleased to hear that we are being very well paid while on field service in a tropical country. We have an extra allowance for colonial service, and an extra allowance for living in unfurnished rooms, also laundry allowance. In all, we shall be comfortably well off, and I am going to save as much as possible. My bank account has been transferred to Barclays, of Jaffa, as it will be far more convenient, but I may still send money through the Jaffa Bank to Ilford, Barclays, if I wish.

I was so pleased to hear that Mrs Bentall's daughter is in Jerusalem. General Barker, her husband, is the Commander-in-Chief for Palestine Forces. He is a very important man and everyone speaks well of him and Mrs Barker is very well liked. There is a road in Sarafand called after General Barker! If they do visit me here, I shall be very much honoured! It would be so nice to meet them and I am sure Mrs Bentall would be pleased.

If I go to Haifa any time I will try and see Mr Norman's daughter, at the girls' school. I was also very interested to hear that the Fieldsteins have so many friends in Tel Aviv. As that is the one place we are allowed to visit without armed male escorts, we often go there on our half-days so I should have plenty of chances to meet their friends there, if they get in touch with me.

The wild flowers here are as lovely as ever and more are appearing every day. The 'lilies of the field' are now in full bloom and they are so pretty – deep scarlet in colour with black centres not white as I had imagined. I have some in vases in my room and we have put some in the ward, so that the patients can 'consider the lilies' all day long! I never thought I should be able to pick them myself! The 'Rose of Sharon' or white narcissus is also to be seen growing with the lily.

Since I started this letter yesterday, I have received a long interesting letter from Geoff, and another very nice letter from

Mother. It was such a pleasant surprise to come off duty and find them waiting for me. Your letters are so precious – I read them about six times over.

There are some very nice people in Sarafand, and they have made us very welcome. It caused a great stir when we all arrived from England or 'Blighty' as the boys call it.

We have been to two dances here already. One was for all ranks, which was a very jolly affair and went on until about 3 a.m. We left at 1 a.m. It was great fun and all the boys were falling over each other to dance with the Sisters. I had every dance! We have to go in uniform of course. Last night we went to an officers' dance at Lydda Airport, about six miles away. We had a convoy of buses to take us. It was very nice but not so jolly as the other one as it was rather too select and formal. We met a number of interesting people there, however.

Lydda, by the way, is the burial place of St George!

We have very good food here, the best I have had since I started nursing. We are waited on by Arab servants dressed in snow white gowns and wearing Fez caps! They are very good, and most polite. One of them, Mohommed, calls us in the morning – or rather he opens the door and tells us the time in Arabic – which does not have much effect upon us! My clock wakes me in time for breakfast anyway.

I was interested to hear that you are reading my letters to the Women's Institute! I will think of you that day. Have you received my last airmail letter – the one containing the snap? I will buy a camera soon and take some more. I am surprised you have received the picture I sent. I never imagined for one minute that it would reach you!

I hear from Geoff that he may join the RAF. I am sure he would like that much better than the army.

What a dreadful winter you are having. I am so sorry for you, when we are having such a mild climate here, with plenty of sunshine.

I hope you will keep free from influenza when there is so much about. Fancy people skating on the canals.

I will keep a lookout for any Heybridge boys, and hope I shall meet Connie's brother soon. It is nice to think he is also in Sarafand.

Well, I must stop now, as I don't think there is any more news just now.

Will write again soon.

Much love to you both

Vera

ॐ

Dear Muriel

Thank you so much for your two very nice letters. I received the first on the 31st January, and it had taken sixteen days to reach me. The second I received yesterday, and having been posted on the 31st January it had taken thirteen days.

It was so interesting to have all your news and I enjoyed reading both letters. I am so sorry to hear you have had flu and tonsillitis. You must have felt ill and I do hope you have now quite recovered. You are having such dreadful weather and I am so sorry to hear about the bitterly cold winds and heavy falls of snow. You are certainly having an unusually bad winter and it is no wonder there is so much illness about. Fancy the buses being marooned in the snow! I have never seen it like that before and can't imagine what Heybridge must be like. It makes me feel so greedy having all the sunshine while you have none. Also I often think of you, being rationed while we are not. I do hope you will not be rationed too severely.

As you will see by my address, I am still in Sarafand, and did not go on to Jerusalem as I had expected. At the last minute my name was removed from the list of Sisters to go to the new hospital on the Mount of Olives, and I was told to remain here. Only twenty Sisters went on, and they give us most glowing accounts of the beautiful scenery and wonderful places they have visited. We have all been promised that in time we too shall be able to go to

Jerusalem and we are looking forward to that very much.

We are quite settled down here now, and quite happy and glad to be working again. The hospital, though pleasantly situated and well built, has been much neglected in many ways by the last medical unit here, I am afraid, so we have many difficulties to contend with and have been very busy reorganising everything and trying to get the wards in good working order.

We now have about 300 patients and in time will have 600, as half the hospital will eventually be accommodated under canvas. Many large marquees have been erected in a large open space in the hospital grounds, and they are to have concrete floors. I cannot say very much about the troops out here, as you know, but I will say that there is an urgent need for a hospital of at least 600 beds in Sarafand alone, and we shall always be 'full up'. This hospital will be serving for the greater part of the Palestine Forces!

As you will have read in the papers, the Australian Imperial Forces have arrived here and we have been run off our feet with work since they came. They are a fine looking lot of men, but most of them seem to have decided to have their appendices removed, while others are being brought in with ear and eye troubles, cut limbs etc, sustained as soon as they landed. Poor lads! Their broad colonial accent causes great amusement to our Scotch, Irish, Welsh and Cockney men, while to hear a little Tommy with a broad Lancashire accent conversing with an Australian, is a most amusing thing. The New Zealand men have not come to this country as far as we know, and the boys from Essex are not here either. Mother told me that Connie's brother was in Sarafand, but I have not been able to get in touch with him, and from various reports heard, I should think he is possibly in Egypt.

Our rooms are very nice, and though unfurnished, they are quite homelike and comfortable as we have bought bright coloured oriental rugs for the floor, and one of the Arab servants made me a table. Our camp beds are very comfortable and we do not mind not having proper bedsteads. You will have read in my last letter home, I expect, all about the grounds round the hospital, and Sisters' quarters.

We are having two half-days off duty each week – and three hours a day. We may have one day off each month. We go on duty at 7.30 a.m. and come off at 8.15 p.m. It is really very hard work here just now as we have so far to walk between our wards, and the surgical block, where I am working, is separated into three wards, which are all some distance from each other, so we spend a good deal of time trotting back and forth in the garden. A military hospital is quite different in many ways from a civilian hospital, and having male orderlies to take the place of probationers, we find our time is fully taken up teaching them, as they are quite untrained, and somehow men are so different from women in the nursing profession! Of course they must find it a very hard life here after being used to clerical jobs as most of them were either in offices or shops in peacetime.

We are quite settled in now in our new sleeping quarters and find it quite strange to be stationary after so much travelling about. We are always being warned, however, that we are a mobile unit and are not here permanently. One never can tell where we may move off to! You remember the terrible earthquake in Turkey, at the beginning of the year? We had orders to go to Turkey to help with the rescue work, and were ready to leave, but the order was cancelled, and an ambulance unit was sent instead!

I have had several letters from people at KGH, and also from Sister Wood in France. She has probably gone home on leave by now, and all the other KGH nurses in France have had ten days' leave. They seem to be quite settled down in their jobs. They must be having a terrible winter too.

I have received two packages of magazines from you, and was so pleased with them. It is so nice to have the *Nursing Mirror* especially, and I was very pleased with the *Strand Magazine*. We just pounce on any English papers or books out here, as it is so refreshing to read all the home news. I have bought a neat little camera and have started taking snaps, so will send them to you as soon as they are developed.

The fields and hills are so green and fresh just now after the winter rains. Soon the heat will come and dry everything up. The fields are covered with lilies and other wild flowers, and my room is bright with flowers. The oranges and lemons and grapefruit are growing thickly on the trees for many miles. The road to Tel Aviv passes through fruit groves, and it is a most colourful sight.

I am glad to hear about Peter and Biscuit. I miss them so much and often wish I had Peter to take out for walks. Have the birds (budgerigars) survived the cold weather all right?

The parcel Mother sent me on the 12th December, has arrived safely and intact! I had given up hope of receiving it, but I was pleased when it came. I had a 5/– PO in it, and bought myself a very pretty Palestine-made rug of bright colours, showing Arabs and camels in the desert. I find it very nice to put my feet on when I get up in the morning, as the floor is of stone.

We have a cinema in Sarafand, and there is a new film on each night. We have some quite good evenings entertainment, and I have seen several films I had missed in England. A few evenings ago, I saw *The Charge of the Light Brigade*. It was most thrilling and I did enjoy it. I expect you saw it some time ago. We all got so excited, and I found myself cheering and clapping with the Tommies and getting just as excited!

Well, I must stop now and go out to church, as it is Sunday evening, and I am off duty. I will write to you again as soon as possible and tell you any more news. I will send this to you at home as I expect you will have left Colchester by the time this reaches England.

I hope you will be quite recovered by the time this letter arrives, and I also hope everyone else is 'keeping well'.

My love to all, much love to yourself,

Cheerio for the present,

Vera

∾

20.2.40

Dear Mother and Father

Thank you so much for your last letter from Mother received some days ago. I expect by now you have had my last two letters – one by airmail and the other by sea. I am going to write frequently, so that there is always a letter on the way to you.

I am so sorry you are having such a terrible winter. We have read a lot about it in the papers and have had accounts over the wireless in the overseas news bulletin. I do hope you will not get colds and flu as there is so much illness about.

We all expected to go to France and have cold weather and plenty of hardships, but instead we are in this lovely country where there is peace and calm and we do not want for anything! I feel that we have left the war behind – for the present – but we are really doing our part out here, and we have the war always in our thoughts.

We are very busy indeed, and likely to be much busier as time goes on. I must not say much about all the troops out here – but the population of Sarafand alone, has increased tremendously in the last few weeks. Now as you know, the Australians have arrived and we · are run off our feet with work and there are many 'Aussies' in all our wards. They have come in with appendicitis, ear and eye troubles, some have been kicked by horses, etc etc, so life is very exciting. They are such a jolly crowd of men – hefty and tanned, and all so free and easy. They get on well with our English boys and their colonial accent causes great amusement to all. They pass many compliments about the English Sisters, and want to know if there are a lot more like us 'over in the old country'! We are admitting patients all day long and now have over 300 beds occupied. Soon we shall be using marquees as wards, and then we shall have over 600 beds! There are only fifty Sisters here now, as ten of our number are at Haifa, and twenty at Jerusalem.

I have not met Connie's brother yet, and on making various inquiries, I have found out that the boys from Essex are probably in Egypt – or near it. The New Zealand men are also there I believe. Are you sure Connie's brother was in Sarafand?

I have not yet heard anything of Mrs Barker in Jerusalem. I often read in the paper about General Barker who travels about a lot inspecting the troops etc. I expect I shall meet them in time, but they must be very busy people.

I am hoping to go to Jerusalem when I have my monthly day off. We have great difficulty in getting transport there as one must travel in a party with two armed escorts, and as I do not know anyone with a car – it is rather difficult. Sometimes our doctors go to Jerusalem for a day and we may go with them, so I am hoping for an opportunity soon. I have heard such wonderful accounts of it, and even the journey there through the Mountains of Moab is a great experience, as the scenery is exceptionally beautiful all the way. It is so near – and yet so far. On clear days we can see part of the Holy City near the top of the hills which are visible from our rooms. The white buildings of the New City can just be seen shining in the sunlight.

We have a tiny chapel here, which was used at one time but has been neglected for some months by the RAF unit here. We have cleaned it out and furnished it with chairs again, and the altar, converted out of a white cupboard, we have covered with an altar cloth, and put a cross, candles and flowers on it. We are going to buy a blue curtain and make an altar screen – also frontals. Last Sunday we had two services there – the first for a long time. As it is situated in the hospital grounds, it is much nearer for us than the Garrison Church of Sarafand, which is about twenty minutes walk away. The Chaplain who came out here with us has been sent to Nablus, so we have the permanent Chaplain here, but as he is at present away in Cairo recovering from an illness, we now have a Chaplain from a place called Ramleh, a few miles away. (You will find it marked on a map of Palestine).

I forgot to tell you that I had a Christmas card from Queen Mary just after the New Year. It had a very good photo of her, and was signed in her own writing. All the Sisters received one, and she would have been very pleased to see our surprise, and pleasure when they came! All we want now, is an Easter Card from George RI!

Well, I must stop now and get this posted. Heaps of love to all, including Peter and Biscuit.

I will write again soon.

Lots of love to you both

Vera

P.S. You will be interested to hear that we have had the son of Lord Halifax in this hospital, with flu. He is the Hon. Peter Wood. He is now better, and I sat near him in the cinema, when we saw *The Charge of the Light Brigade*. (Very handsome, and dashing young man!)

~

Dear Geoff

Thank you so much for your very nice letter which I was so pleased to receive. It was good of you to write to me and I am sorry I have not answered your letter sooner. We are so busy here that I am not finding time to write to people so often now, but I will try and write to you as often as possible in future.

We have some very nice patients and they are so jolly and keep us laughing all day. Some of them are very young and have just joined the army, while others are older and tell us long stories of their experiences in the army in other parts of the world. We are now very busy looking after Australian soldiers who landed here recently. Many of them were brought straight to hospital to have their appendices removed. They are very amusing and all talk with a broad colonial accent. The New Zealand soldiers did not come here, so I have not had the honour of nursing any of them.

We are having glorious weather here. The rainy season has now ceased and we had one day's rain last week the last we may expect for nine months or more! Now we shall have all sunshine and later, in the months of May, June, July and August, it will be very hot and we shall be wearing all white uniform.

The soldiers who have been out here for several years, say that the temperature will be about 116 degrees in the shade, and mosquitoes buzz everywhere. We shall not have to dash about the hospital so much then, and I hope we shall not be so busy. I do not mind the heat and prefer it to intense cold, don't you?

I am sorry you have had such a dreadful winter. It must have been awful for you, getting up so early in the morning and working in the fields all day. We have read a lot about the snow, and transport difficulties because of the deep snowdrifts. Did you manage to get home from Rayne for weekends?

You asked me in your letter if there are any nightclubs or cabaret shows in Sarafand. I am afraid all we have is a cinema – not a bad place, with a different film each night. I have been several times and seen some quite good films. The nearest town is Tel Aviv, where we do our shopping. It is very modern and all the houses are of your favourite style of architecture! At present it is out of bounds for us and so is Jerusalem, as the authorities are expecting a spot of bother! You know, the usual Palestine kind of skirmish! We hope it will soon settle down as it is very dull being confined to this camp, and surrounded by a high fence with sentries on duty!

We have a very good radiogram here. We can get most stations on the radio and the 'gram' part of it is very good, as we have some nice records with plenty of dance music included. I have been to two dances in Sarafand, and I expect you read about them in one of my letters home. The only snag is that we have to go in uniform, and I am always losing my cap in the middle of a dance!

I will be careful about the Arab bazaars, as you have warned me!

Well, I must stop and feed my face with tea, as it is 4.30 p.m.

I hope you are all well at home. Give my love to Barbara. I will write again soon.

Cheerio for now.

Your loving

Vera

P.S. I thought the drawings in your letter were very good.

◈

QAIMNSR
No 12 General Hospital
Sarafand
Palestine
2.3.40

Dear Mother and Father

I hope you have received my last letter sent about the 25th February. I have received a letter from Father – a very nice long one which was started by Mother. I told you in my last letter that I had also received two packets of magazines. They are very nice and I was especially pleased with the parish magazine.

I have a lot to tell you this time. I have been to Jerusalem, and Bethlehem! From the top of the Mount of Olives I have seen the

Dead Sea – and I have walked in the Garden of Gethsemane. It was all so wonderful, and seems like a dream now. I went last Thursday, the 29th February, which was my day off for last month, and four other Sisters came with me. We went by taxi and were accompanied by one of our padres, who knows the Holy City well.

It was a glorious day, and we left here at 9 a.m. The journey there was beautiful. We travelled first across a fertile plain covered with orange groves, and passed through many small Arab villages. Then we came to the Judean Hills and the road became narrow, and twisted and turned upwards for many miles with 'devils elbows' at nearly every bend, to add to the thrills. At one place the road was especially wild and lonely with a steep hill on either side, and here the padre told us, was the favourite haunt of Arab tribes who shot down many travellers a few months ago. However, nothing happened to us!

A few miles further on we came to the 'Seven Sisters' – seven spiral turns in the road, from the top of a hill to the bottom, and then we started climbing up another hill – and so on for many miles. We passed near to Ain Karim, the birthplace of St John the Baptist, where all Arabs and Jews alike live peacefully together, and most of the inhabitants are Christian! Later we saw Emmaus, and the 'road to Emmaus'. We also passed through Ramleh, where St George is reputed to have killed the dragon.

Near Jerusalem, we came to Rachel's Tomb – the journey took nearly an hour.

We came first to the New City where there are many shops and modern buildings. As soon as possible we found a policeman and enquired if the Old City was free from trouble. It has been out of bounds for all English people, as well as Tel Aviv and Jaffa. There has been some trouble owing to the new land and emigration regulations. It has not so far been serious, however, and we were glad to hear that we could pass through the gates of the city quite safely. We went through the Jaffa Gate and left the car near the entrance. Soon we were walking down David's Street, and approaching the Church of the Holy Sepulchre. The streets of the Old City are so fascinating – they are narrow and winding and so very old they cannot have changed at all in many respects since the time of Christ.

We visited the Church of the Holy Sepulchre first. It is supported from the exterior by iron girders as it was rendered unsafe by the earthquake in 1927. Inside it is very quiet, dark and mysterious, and we were given candles to light our way. We were taken by an old Greek monk to the Tomb of Our Lord. This is a very holy and peaceful place, so wonderful that I cannot describe it well enough. We stood in the dim, silent place, lit by many gold lamps over our heads. Their glimmering lights cast soft mysterious shadows on the stone walls. We each took a flower from the vases round the Tomb, and I have mine pressed in a book. I am enclosing a picture of the Tomb.

We spent a long time in the church, wandering through the ancient passages and visiting the many chapels. On the walls we saw priceless gold icons and beautiful paintings. Later we climbed some steep stone steps, worn down by the feet of countless pilgrims, and saw the place of the Crucifixion – Golgotha. This, the holiest place on earth, has a costly mosaic floor and is marked by two altars – one at the place of the Nailing to the Cross, and the other where the Cross was raised. Here there was an atmosphere of great sanctity – but perhaps it was all too costly and too colourful. The chapel was a blaze of candlelight and glittered with golden lamps and icons. Somehow it seemed such a contrast to the bare green hill of Calvary about which we have been taught.

After leaving the Church of the Holy Sepulchre, we walked down the Via Dolorosa and saw all the Stations of the Cross marked on the ancient, crumbling walls, and we passed beneath the Ecce Homo Arch. Here we stopped and our guide led us up a flight of steps to a massive stone door on which we knocked. It was opened by a French nun and we entered the Convent of Notre Dame, which is built over the site of the Judgement Hall of Pilate. Here we saw the real courtyard where the Jews assembled and shouted for Barabbas and demanded the crucifixion of Christ. The paving stones were very old and sunken in parts. Some of them were marked out in squares and oblongs for Roman games. We saw the place of the scourging of Christ in the courtyard.

There is a beautiful church on the floor above the courtyard. It was so dignified and quietly furnished after the glittering splendour or the Holy Sepulchre. I am enclosing a photograph of it.

We walked for what must have been miles through the narrow streets in the heart of the city, and saw many ancient churches and temples. We climbed to the top of the police Headquarters – a very tall building – and stood on the flat roof to see the panorama of Jerusalem. It was most wonderful. Just below us was the Mosque of Omar, or Dome of the Rock, standing in its wide courtyard. This was built by Solomon over or near the site of the old Jewish Synagogue in which Jesus taught the priests. Christians may not enter the Mosque without a special permit. We had a grand view of the Holy Sepulchre, the Mount of Olives and the Golden Gates. These I expected to be able to walk through, and did not know that they had been sealed up well and truly by Moslems many years ago, when a prophet foresaw that the next conqueror or the Holy City would be a Christian, who, if he entered through the Golden Gates, would reign and possess Jerusalem for ever. Therefore the Moslems saw to it that no Christian conqueror *could* enter the Golden Gates!

It was just before midday when we went onto the roof to look over Jerusalem, and as the clock in the New City chimed twelve, from every minaret in view a muezzin came out on to a narrow balcony and lifted up his voice in a chant, calling the faithful to prayer. At the same time there came the sound of monks chanting from a nearby monastery!

We returned to the car soon afterwards and left the Old City and followed a road leading towards Gethsemane. Near the city walls at the place where St Stephen was stoned, we stopped and left the car again, and walked on down a dusty road into the Valley of Kedron where the waters of the Kedron brook only flow now in very rainy weather. Above us, as we climbed a steep and stony path, we could see a green sloping garden full of olive trees and tall cypresses and surrounded by a stone wall. This is Gethsemane.

We had lunch near the stone wall, sitting on the slopes of the Mount of Olives with olive trees all round us, and the Golden Gates of the city walls on the hill, just across the Kedron Valley. The grass was covered with wild flowers. It was perfect, sitting there, eating our picnic lunch with a cloudless sky above and not a sound to break the silence.

I never imagined, a few months ago when I was riding round Plaistow on a bicycle, that I should soon be looking at Jerusalem from the Mount of Olives!

We entered the Garden through a door in the wall, which was opened for us by a Franciscan monk. We found ourselves standing in perhaps the most beautiful and most genuine part of Jerusalem – a place unspoiled – simple and natural. Flowerbeds, full of fragrant violets and pansies, covered the ground beneath the olive trees. There are about six large olive trees in the Garden and the monk told us that they must be the oldest in Palestine – one in particular is about 3,000 years old. This is a wonderful tree, gnarled and solid-looking. Many people believe that most of the trees were there in the time of Christ, and that the sleeping disciples rested against this oldest tree of all. I believe it too, and if trees could talk, what a lot this one would have to tell us!

We visited the beautiful church which stands at one end of the Garden of Gethsemane – the Church of All Nations – or Church of the Agony, as it is often called. This is perhaps the most impressive building in Jerusalem, for it marks the spot on which, it is believed, Our Lord prayed. I am enclosing a picture of the interior of the church. The pillars, floor and roof are of beautiful mosaic, but the most striking parts of the building are the three huge oil paintings above and each side of the High Altar. The centre one is the most beautiful, and shows Our Lord praying in the Garden, with the disciples asleep in the shade of a tree. It is so lifelike. When we went out into the Garden for a last look round, and returned again to the church, the beautiful painting seemed to be shining through the gloom of the building.

The other two paintings showed the betrayal and the arrest of Jesus, and they too were very realistic.

I was sorry to leave the Garden of Gethsemane, but time would not stand still for us, and we wanted to see Bethlehem. There is a curfew in Jerusalem at 5 p.m., so we had to leave Gethsemane at about 3 p.m. as we still had much to see. Before setting off to Bethlehem, however, we went further on, to the top of the Mount of Olives and visited the little circular chapel of the Ascension. This is built over the place from which, it is believed, Our Lord ascended into Heaven. Afterwards we stood gazing in wonder for some time at the most amazing view I have ever seen.

Below us stretched for about twenty miles the Jordan Valley, a panorama of dry, barren waste, shimmering in the heat. Beyond, we saw the Dead Sea, blue and sparkling in the sunshine, while in the far distance another range of barren mountains could be seen. Jerusalem is so much higher than sea level, and the Dead Sea so much lower – so the view is superb!

As we came down the Mount of Olives we could see the ancient tomb of Absalom surrounded by Jewish tombs, while opposite, on the other side of the Kedron Valley, the ground is covered with Moslem tombs. Compared with those many ancient tombs with the massive wall of the Holy City towering behind them, the little Garden of Gethsemane looked so alive and fresh – as it always will be.

Bethlehem is only about three miles from Jerusalem, and the ride there only took a short time.

Bethlehem is perhaps the most peaceful place in Palestine apart from Gethsemane. This little town, with narrow cobbled streets and ancient buildings, clustered round the Church of the Nativity, is quite unspoiled, and I am sure, unchanged all down the ages. It is entirely Christian! It is just as I have imagined it to be.

We went to the Church of the Nativity, which we found after driving through a maze of narrow streets. This is quite different from the Church of the Holy Sepulchre. The latter is dim and mysterious, with a strange, sad atmosphere, but here in the Church of the Nativity there was an atmosphere of peace and stillness. I did not imagine that – for many people have said the same thing. This is the earliest Christian church in use today, and is built above a cave, which has always been recognised as the birthplace of Christ.

I am enclosing a picture of the interior of the church, showing the massive pillars of dark red stone, which have stood there for so many centuries.

We went down a steep flight of steps and found that we were standing in a small cave beneath the High Altar. Bright lamps hung from the stone ceiling, which was also dotted with silver stars. We were taken by a Greek monk to a corner of the cave, to a little shrine where it is believed Jesus lay in the straw of the manger. In the floor there is a star and round it a Latin inscription, which reads: 'Here

Jesus Christ was born of the Virgin Mary'. It was all very sweet and simple. At the entrance to the cave there is a life-size model of the Holy Family, during the flight to Egypt. This is very real and beautifully carved, and the expressions on the faces were amazingly lifelike. Even the donkey looked just like those we see in Sarafand every day, and it is hard to believe that it was not really alive!

It was strange to find that the Nativity did not take place in a stable, but in a cave beneath the inn, where the oxen and asses were housed. All the houses in Bethlehem to this day have been built above the road level, while each one has a cave, which is level with the ground, where animals are sheltered.

After leaving the Church of the Nativity we bought cards and mementoes at a shop nearby, and here I bought a Star of Bethlehem as a brooch for Mother, and a cross for Muriel, both made of mother-of-pearl. I will probably be able to enclose these in my letter. I am sending Father and Geoff something each, later.

From a hill outside Bethlehem we could see Bethany – the home of Mary, Martha and Lazarus, and we could also see the field in which the shepherds were watching their sheep when they saw the star.

To my mind, Bethany, lying below on the edge of the Jordan Valley, Gethsemane, and the courtyard beneath the Ecce Homo Arch, as well as the Via Dolorosa, are more truly marked by the Feet of Christ than any ground covered by costly shrines and magnificent altars. Bethlehem, too, seems to have a special atmosphere of its own.

We had to leave Bethlehem shortly before 5 p.m., in order to be out of Jerusalem before the curfew. The return journey was wonderful, for we were crossing the Judean Hills at sunset, and it was a sight well worth seeing. We stopped once in a small village all among the hills, and went to see an ancient church built by the Crusaders, which is now part of a monastery.

The day had been perfect and we saw so much in a short time. I don't think I have ever done so much in one day before. We were very fortunate to be able to go, as one must always have male escorts, and we do not know many people yet outside our own Unit.

I am afraid I will be making you very envious when you read my letter, but I thought you would be sure to want to know about all the places we visited. How I wish you could have gone with me!

This letter has taken two days off duty to write, and I now hope to finish it.

How glad I am that I have been to Jerusalem, as it is now out of bounds, and will be for some time. I expect you will probably have read in the papers about the rioting all over the country because of the new Regulations and Land Transfers in connection with the Jews. Tel Aviv is in an uproar, and soldiers are wearing steel helmets when on duty.

I hope you are not feeling the cold too much. Surely it will be warmer soon. Well, I must stop now, as I think I have given you all the news. I will write again soon.

Heaps of love to all,

Yours ever,

Vera

❧

The Church of All Nations

❧

Dear Mother and Father

Thank you so much for your two nice letters received on the 18th. Father's was dated the 29th February, and Mother's the 5th March, but both arrived at the same time. It was so nice to have two letters from you. I am sorry you had to wait two weeks for a letter from me, but by now you will have received two letters which were on the way to you. I will try not to keep you waiting again.

I am glad you are all keeping well, and hope that the very cold weather is over now. I was very interested to hear about you letting the ground floor of the house to the ARP. It sounds a very good idea to me, and should be a help financially, and much less trouble for you.

There is not very much news to tell you at present. Since I wrote last, when I told you about my visit to Jerusalem, we have been working very hard and the hospital has been steadily increasing in size. I have been working on a surgical block of forty-eight patients – all septic cases. Somehow I managed to pick up some infection, and developed a septic throat, so had to go off duty. I have been a patient for nearly a week, on the Families Ward, where the wives and children of soldiers and any sick Sisters are nursed. This is one of the newest buildings and is fitted up like a private nursing home. There is another Sister here, also with a septic throat, and we share a very nice room. Everyone has been very good to us and I soon felt much better. We have had a good rest, and are now up and about again and expecting to go back to work soon. We have also enjoyed the luxury of sleeping on real beds again for a change!

The trouble with the Jews has subsided now, and the country is quiet again. We were confined to Sarafand for about a fortnight while the rioting took place, and Tel Aviv was in an uproar! However, the people settled down gradually, and the curfews were lifted. We had quite a number of casualties in.

At the end of the month we shall finish with the rainy season, and the really hot weather will start in earnest. Last night we had a terrific tropical storm such as I have never seen before. The lightning was blinding, and quite blue in colour, and the thunder rolled and roared about us for hours. All night it rained in torrents, and when it rains out here you think the roof is coming down at any minute. The noise is deafening!

We are getting our tropical uniforms ready to wear next month. We shall be dressed all in white – white caps edged with scarlet and white silk dresses, shoes and stockings and white hats for outdoor wear, and on duty we are wearing white overalls, shoes and stockings and caps.

I am sending Father and Muriel birthday presents, and hope they will arrive in time, but if they are late do not be surprised as the parcel posts are slow.

I spent Palm Sunday in bed this year. I thought of you all getting your palms in church, and I could not go for mine. However, one of my friends sent one to me – an extra one she had received – it was from the Holy Sepulchre!

Well, there seems to be no more news to tell you just now.

I will write again soon.

Heaps of love to you both and everyone,

Vera

ॐ

13.4.40

Dear Mother and Father

Thank you so much for your last letter received from Mother on the 9th April and written on the 24th March. I was so pleased with the two lots of magazines received safely. I am always glad to have them as we have to pay twice as much for English books out here. It is very thoughtful of you to send them so often.

First of all I must tell you that all our letters are now liable to be censored, and as a special concession, the officers and Sisters are allowed to censor their own correspondence but other ranks have to leave letters open for inspection. We have been warned to write discreetly, and if we discuss any forbidden subjects, our letters are also going to be read each time. I shall not be able to tell you so much about my work now but I will give you as much news as possible.

I did enjoy Mother's last letter. She gave me such a lot of news and I was glad to hear that you had a happy Easter. I can just imagine what England must be like with spring coming and the snowdrops and daffodils and tulips growing. I am glad you received the telegram on Easter Sunday. It came at the right time. I was discharged from hospital on Holy Saturday. We had some nice services in our own chapel and in the Garrison Church and we tried to be as much 'at home' as possible by having daffodils and arum lilies on the altar. The wild flowers were especially lovely for Easter, the ground was covered with white daisies and anemones, lilies of the field, crocuses, and wild irises. Easter is certainly the brightest and most promising time of the year in the Holy Land, as it should be!

I am now working on another surgical ward. We have some of the nicest patients I have ever nursed, and the ward is always bright and cheerful. The men keep us laughing all day and they never complain of anything. The weather is getting hotter and we are putting up mosquito nets round the beds. We are also having them for our own beds. All the Sisters are now in tropical uniform, and I feel much cooler. It really looks very attractive. We have white overalls with low collars, white shoes and stockings and caps, and on the shoulders, Sisters have red epaulettes, and Staff nurses, plain white ones. I will send you a photo of me taken in tropical uniform. It is being developed now.

You asked me in your letter if we had good food here. Yes, you will be pleased to hear that it is the best I have ever had since I started nursing and is also well cooked. We have a very good Arab cook, and Arab servants to wait on us at table – so we are doing things in style! There is nothing I need at all. I am really thinking a lot about you having to have short rations while we have plenty. I do hope it is not too bad.

I am now sleeping in a very nice house just outside the hospital gates as there was not enough room in the Sisters' quarters, and it meant that more than two Sisters had to share a room during the hot weather. There are nine of us here and as the house is large, only a few of us are sharing rooms. I am sharing with another Sister and we have a very nice room with a French window and two other windows with pretty chintz curtains. There is also a large garden full of flowers, and a verandah all round the house. The Colonel and some officers have the house next door. We are supposed to be the quietest members of the staff who would not disturb the Colonel, and are supposed to be a chosen few. It is quite a joke among the Sisters, and we call the bungalow, 'The Mayfair Hotel'! A road nearby is named 'The Mall'.

Since I wrote and told you about my visit to Jerusalem and Bethlehem I have had another wonderful experience, for I have been to the Sea of Galilee, Tiberias, and Nazareth. It was all so beautiful and so peaceful and I don't know how to describe it to you. We had to leave here very early in the morning as we had a journey of about ninety miles. As before we were accompanied by one of our padres.

The scenery all the way was beautiful. The road, in places was really dangerous, twisting and narrow and steep, for the country is very mountainous, as all Palestine is. It reminded me of roads in New Zealand, except that the hills were barren and rocky and not covered with bush as they are in New Zealand We passed over the Plain of Esdraelon, the place of the Armageddon where many battles were fought during Old Testament history. We saw Mount Tabor, where the Transfiguration is thought to have taken place. This is truly 'a high mountain apart'. It stands alone, in the middle of a fertile plain and all round there are wild-looking hills and about four miles away in the centre of the hills, is Nazareth. We passed along at the foot of another hill which is covered with rocks, and which is said to be the Mountain of the Beatitudes, but there is a difference of opinion concerning this and many people believe that the Sermon on the Mount was preached on a hill nearer Galilee. The view from here was wonderful, for we were hundreds of feet above sea level and could see the road over which we had travelled, descending in spirals round the hills, and then stretching for miles across the Plain of Esdraelon.

Often we saw flocks of sheep and goats grazing by the roadside. The Arab shepherd wearing a flowing Bedouin head-veil, leads the flock, and never drives the sheep and goats. Sometimes we noticed a little Arab boy sitting on a rock, playing tunes on his pipe, as he watched the flock feeding. It is wonderful to think that such customs have not changed since the time of the Good Shepherd!

We did not stop in Nazareth on the way to Galilee, but visited it on the return journey. The road continued to wind upwards through the mountains. On either side of the road, the grass was covered with large white daisies and the scarlet 'lilies of the field'. The first sight of the Sea of Galilee was a strip of smooth blue water, a thousand feet below us, with a range of very high mountains beyond. To the north we could see Mount Hermon, covered with snow. This is in Syria.

The road suddenly sloped downhill and continued to do so until we reached the town of Tiberias on the edge of the lake. The Sea of Galilee is nearly seven hundred feet below sea level, and is one of the hottest parts of Palestine. Tiberias is a very picturesque town with a crumbling Roman wall.

We sat on the stones at the edge of the water and later, had our lunch there. I think out of all the places I have seen so far in Palestine, I have been quite the most impressed by Galilee. It is the most peaceful place I have ever been to. There was hardly a ripple on the surface of the water. Here and there the sails of fishing boats could be seen moving slowly along. The great thing about Galilee is that it has not been altered. No new towns have been built and there are no large hotels for tourists there, to disfigure the shore. There is only one road, which passes along near the water's edge, from Tiberias to Capernaum.

I wish you could all have been there with me to see it too, for it is difficult to describe the Sea of Galilee. It seems so apart from the rest of Palestine, and seems to be a place which has been the same all down the ages. Jerusalem is wonderful but all the sacred places have been built upon. But Galilee could never be any different from the time when Christ walked upon the water. I could just imagine the storm sweeping down from the mountains when the disciples were fishing and how the waves must have tossed the small boat. The Arabs say that Galilee is calm one minute, and a raging tempest a few minutes later.

We had a row on the water in a small boat, but could not go right across the Sea of Galilee, as it is nearly seven miles wide, and in any case, we had not the time to spare. All too soon we had to leave for Nazareth, but I should have loved to stay there much longer. It is wonderful to think that I have seen the place where the disciples, Peter, Andrew and Philip, spent so much time with their Master. We saw the present day fishermen of Galilee, and their clothes, and the nets they used, have not changed since those days!

On the way to Nazareth we passed through Cana of Galilee, the village which was the scene of Our Lord's first miracle at the marriage feast. Here we saw the women filling their water jugs at the village well – making a very picturesque scene. Their clothes were brightly coloured, and they wore white veils on their heads. Further on we met other women returning from the well, carrying their jugs on their heads! All the women out here are very upright in stature, and one never sees any with 'round' shoulders.

Nazareth is a lovely place situated on the slopes of steep hills and in the valley between them. It is clean, and the buildings are white. It is just as I have always imagined it to be like. It is even more beautiful because there are thousands of cypress, fig and olive trees growing between the buildings and on the slopes of the hills beyond.

The sun was shining brilliantly and like Galilee, Nazareth seemed quiet and undisturbed. There are many new buildings, churches and convents, but I think most of Nazareth is the same as when the Holy Family made their home there. We went to the Church of the Annunciation which is new in parts, but most of the building has a great history and was partly destroyed when the Turkish Moslems invaded the Holy Land. Franciscan Friars have charge of it and have made it a beautiful church for it is not gaudy in any way and nowhere is it over-decorated.

This church is built over, what is believed to be, the site of the carpenter's shop where the Holy Family lived, and we were shown a cave-like room in which it is thought St Joseph had his bench. There are many Christian Arabs as well as Jews in Nazareth today, and many of them are carpenters by trade. We saw some of them making yokes and ploughs. On our return journey we saw Arabs tilling the fields near Nazareth and they were using the ancient type of plough drawn by oxen with yokes upon them.

We returned via Haifa and there we had a fine view of the city and harbour from the top of Mt Carmel.

I went to an orchestral concert given by the Palestine Orchestra, about a fortnight ago. It was most enjoyable, and all the music was by Beethoven. The audience was vast, and almost entirely Jewish. At the end of each piece of music, everyone jumped to their feet and cheered and clapped for about ten minutes! At the end of the concert, they almost clamber onto the platform in their enthusiasm. The Jews certainly love music!

What a strange turn the war has taken! How and when will it all end, I wonder? I do hope you are not going to have many hardships in England.

I do hope you are all keeping well. My love to all, including Peter and Biscuit.

Heaps of love to you both
Vera

∽

5.5.40

Dear Mother and Father

I have just received two letters one from Father and the other from Muriel, for which many thanks. I do look forward to hearing from any of you at home and it is nice to have all the news. I hope you have received my last letter safely. I am very glad the parcels arrived intact. The letters from you took sixteen days to reach me – not quite so long as usual. I am wondering if our letters will take even longer to get to England now, in view of the present precarious situation in this part of the world. If you should have to wait longer for a letter in future, do not worry, as they may have to travel via the Cape! Let's hope that will not be so, after all.

I have received another big parcel of books from you. Thank you so much. They were so interesting and most acceptable as most of them are not obtainable out here.

I hope you are all keeping well now. I am sorry Muriel and Geoff have both had dealings with the war on the Home Front!

It is getting hotter and hotter here. The temperature is rising each day and it has already been between 96 and 104 degrees in the shade! We are all sleeping under mosquito nets now and are very thankful to have them as the mosquitoes and other insects are appearing in masses! The patients are much more at rest without flies buzzing round them all day. This is a country of strange creatures! I always think of that saying 'From goulies and ghosties and long leggeddy beasties and things that go bump in the night, Good Lord deliver us!' There are numbers of lizards and frogs which scuttle and jump across the ground at your feet in the dark, and SPIDERS! of all shapes and SIZES! Horrible things! You know how they give me the 'creeps'; then there are long legged green things like grasshoppers, with wings, and these fly about at a great speed and eat the mosquitoes – a good thing. There are moths as big as bats and lovely coloured butterflies.

The flowers are in full bloom all round the hospital now, but I am afraid they will all be over soon and the ground will be parched. We have some beautiful flowering tropical shrubs and trees, and the verandah rails outside the Sisters' Mess, are covered with a creeper called 'morning glory', which produces an exquisite blue flower. There are also some other trees, which, a few days ago were leafless, and have now come out in bloom, and these flowers are also pale blue. Even the coarse-looking cactus bushes, which are to be seen on both sides of nearly every road here, are producing some yellow flowers. It will seem very barren and colourless when the flowers fade.

I am still working on the same surgical ward, but may be going on night duty sometime soon. We have such a happy lot of patients and I really think most of them will be quite sorry to go out of hospital. At night they sing 'Kiss me goodnight, Sister Jones, tuck me in my little iron bed!' after the style of the song, 'Kiss me goodnight, Sergeant Major.' I like nursing soldiers very much, as they make such good and cheerful patients.

I should love to see the daffodils in the garden and churchyard. It must be most refreshing to see them after the long winter. I wish I could send you some of this lovely sunshine.

Our little chapel in the hospital grounds is now looking quite nice, and I have made some gold-coloured curtains for the windows, which have looked very bare up till now. They were covered with paper some years ago, which looked like stained glass, but this had since started to peel off, making the windows look really shabby. Now I am glad to say, the curtains have made all the difference to the chapel. It is my responsibility to change the flowers each week also, and as we have such a variety of these in the garden, I can always make the vases look nice.

I must write to Muriel again as soon as possible as she has sent me two letters recently. Please tell her she will hear from me soon. Also I am writing to Geoff.

Well, there does not seem much news just now so I will stop for this time, and write again soon. I am enclosing a 'snap' of myself in tropical uniform, as I thought you would like to see it.

Goodbye for now, take care of yourselves.

Heaps of love

Vera

᧧

19.5.40

Dear Mother and Father

Thank you so much for the nice parcel of books received safely. Also I have just received Mother's long and interesting letter, dated the 5th May. It only took twelve days to come.

I am always so delighted to have a letter and hear all the news from home.

How interesting the new 'flat' sounds. I can just imagine what it must be like – so compact and tidy. You are certainly helping in National Service by giving up the ground floor to the ARP.

Since I last wrote so much has happened near your part of the world. We were all horrified to hear of those latest developments. How terrible to think that the full force of the war has broken, and there is more destruction and death than ever! I hate to think of the fighting being so near England. We are told you can hear the gunfire from across the Channel, in East Coast towns. We all listen very often during the day to the overseas news bulletins. How we hope it will not spread any further!

I often think of all my friends from KGH who are in France; Sister Wood, Sister Tutor, S/N Insley, Robertson, and others. They must be having a terrible time, and working very hard. If I had gone to France, too, I should be with them!

The days are getting hotter and hotter here. The temperature is nearly always over 100 degrees in the shade! Often we have a khamsin – a very hot dry wind which blows up from the desert and sends the temperature up by leaps and bounds! It feels as though you are walking about in an inferno. The landscape is obliterated by dust and sand storms at the same time.

We have electric fans working in the wards and in our dining and sitting rooms. At night we often cannot even sleep with a sheet covering us, but lie on top of our beds. The patients do likewise. It used to be quite cold at night, but it is not now.

Most of the Sisters are troubled with mosquito and sandfly bites, but I am very glad to say that so far (touch wood), I have not had one severe bite. The insects leave me alone, for some unknown reason!

I heard a service broadcast from St Martin-in-the-Fields last night. It was wonderful to think we could hear a service from a church all those miles away.

We are still very busy here, and have plenty to do to keep us occupied. The Australians are a particularly jolly crowd of men. They are always so glad to have English Sisters to nurse them, as also are the English soldiers. It is good to know that we are doing some good, even though we are so far from the battlefield!

I am enclosing another photo for you, as it is rather good. You will certainly not forget what I look like if I keep sending you photos! If you have any of yourselves I should love to have them sometime.

Well, I seem to have so little news to give you just now. I am sorry that this is such a short letter, but I will write a longer one next time.

I hope you are all well, and not working too hard, especially with the vegetable gardens. I trust Father is *not* mowing the lawn (if you still have one)! Also I hope Mother is resting on the sofa, *every* afternoon.

Please give my love to everyone including Peter.

Cheerio for now.

Much love to you both

Vera

ɷ

Dear Mother and Father

Thank you very much for your last letter, sent by airmail. It took only six days. I am very sorry there seems to have been some delay in my letters reaching you, as Father said you had been waiting longer than usual for a letter. I am not surprised as we have been warned that our letters may be delayed now, especially as the Mediterranean shipping is limited, and also all our letters are delayed to a certain extent by the censor. I hope you will have received my last two letters by the time this arrives – one sent on the 6th May and the other on the 20th.

I have had a lovely long letter from Muriel, which I am answering very soon.

I am now on night duty. I have for my ward, a large tent holding twenty-four patients, all surgical cases. I am liking it very much and finding it very interesting working under canvas instead of in a building. The tent has a concrete floor and little windows cut out in the sides to make it as much like an ordinary ward as possible. We have to do quite a lot of improvising, but that is all good experience. I have one orderly 'on' with me at night.

There are only six night Sisters, including the 'Charge' Sister who superintends all the wards. We go on duty at 8 p.m. and come off at 7.45 a.m. As a pleasant change from the usual practice of not leaving our wards all night, we are able to go to our sitting room for our midnight meal, and also for tea at 4 a.m. At KGH, we could never leave the wards at all, at night.

The night Sisters have their rooms apart from the rest of the staff, so we are quite quiet during the day and can sleep well.

I believe we are only on night duty for a month at a time here, for which I am sorry as I quite like working at night.

I am so sorry to hear that Mother is sleeping badly. I do hope she rests for a long time during the day. I often think of you during the night when I am going round the ward with my storm lantern, and I wonder if you are asleep, or lying awake thinking and worrying about this rotten war.

As I sit at my table writing (it is near midnight now), I have many strange insects to keep me company. I seem to see a different one every night. There are also masses of mosquitoes humming about, and last night, with the help of the orderly, I dispatched three hornets – huge things which have a particularly poisonous sting in this country. Spiders abound! It is amazing how many different varieties of these there are in Sarafand. I am getting quite used to them and do not now, as in days gone by, run for a broom to brush them away!

We have to be careful to see that all the patients have their nets covering them, or else they would have many bites and stings. There is a lovely of the Hills of Judea view from my ward, and at four o'clock each morning I can see the sunrise. It is a beautiful sight when the gold light gradually comes up behind the hills and the sky takes on an exquisite shade, while the hills become a deep blue in colour. The sun rises very quickly here, and by 7 a.m. it is really very hot.

I expect you have heard that we have had 'practice' blackouts here. Now we are having a permanent blackout, to commence a few nights hence. It will be just like England again. We have been making many other preparations – but here, I must draw a blank!

I can't help worrying about you all – for life must be very trying just now in England, with rationing etc and now the fighting is so much nearer. I am sure you must have to give up many things, and have less of others, although you tell me so cheerfully that you do not find things so bad!

I am very sorry for Cree, having all her relations in Holland and not knowing what has happened to them. It must have been a great shock to her to hear that the Germans had occupied the districts in which her relations were living.

I went to Jaffa yesterday morning and sat on the beach in the sunshine. It is glorious there. The sand is very fine and golden and the Mediterranean as blue as ever. The air is so bracing and does you so much good after being on duty all night. We are lucky to be so near the coast.

Well, there does not seem to be any more news to tell you. To think that it is six months tomorrow, since I last saw you. Doesn't it seem years!

I do hope you are all well. Take care, and don't work too hard.

My love to all and heaps to you both,

Vera

᪐

3.6.40

Dear Mother and Father

I am sending you a cablegram tomorrow, just to let you know all is well, as I know you must be wondering why you have not heard. I hope you receive this safely.

Now that trouble is expected in the Mediterranean, I am afraid there will always be a good deal of delay in our correspondence. I will send more letters by airmail and write very often so that you are not kept waiting too long.

I am so glad you are all well and in such good spirits. We all think a lot about the people at home, and are always glad to hear that there is no depression and uncertainty about the present situation.

How you will benefit by the vegetables you are growing. I think you are all marvellous to work so hard. We heard on the wireless today that farm workers are being urgently requested to remain at their work, and an appeal for more workers has been issued. That will mean that Geoffrey will be needed indefinitely on the farm. I am very glad, and hope that he will not be called up. He can do a great deal for the country by carrying on with the farm work.

Yes, I am able to hear all the latest news, and all speeches on the wireless, as we have our own set in the Sisters' sitting room, and also a set on most of the wards. We did not hear the 'actual' speech by the King, as it was rather late at night, but we heard a recording of it the next morning. What a fine speech! I think it is quite the best he has ever made, and how perfectly he spoke! It was grand to see the convalescent soldiers sitting round the wireless listening intently, and they were all most impressed. I also heard the Prime Minister's speech, and today, a speech by Mr Anthony Eden, the new Minister for War. These were both excellent. What fine changes have been made by forming a new Cabinet, and especially by appointing a new Premier.

How nice and fresh the church must look now. You are working hard in every way.

The climate is becoming hotter every day. Yesterday we had the hottest day so far, the temperature rose to 120°F! I do not mind the heat really, except that we have difficulty in sleeping during the day. However, people say that the temperature will settle between 100 and 110 degrees during July and August.

I told you in my last letter that I am now on night duty, in charge of a large tent accommodating twenty-four surgical cases. I am on duty now and the ward is quiet so have taken the opportunity of writing to you.

We now have a blackout every night. I have a lamp on my table, covered with dark material, and just giving enough light for me to see. When I go round to see if the patients are sleeping, I have a storm lamp – also shaded. It is like old times. I expect you are quite accustomed to the blackout now, and do not feel so 'lost' at night.

We started summer time on the 31st May, for the first time in Palestine. We put the clocks on one hour at midnight much to our delight, being on night duty, as we had one hour less to work, and the day staff lost one hour's sleep. Now we have lighter evenings. The Arabs find it very strange after being used to darkness at 7 p.m. all the year round.

I sent you a photo of myself in tropical uniform, with the letter dated 6th May. Then I sent another photo with the next letter, dated 20th May. I do hope you will receive these. I have not yet had the parcel of books from you.

I have not met any boys from an Essex regiment yet, but I have one boy in my ward, who has lived in Chelmsford and knows Maldon well. He often talks to me about the various towns and villages in Essex. The other day he said, 'How would you like to be walking up the Market Hill now, Sister?'

Well, I do not seem to have any more news just at present. I will write again soon in a few days so that you are not kept waiting. I expect my other letters have gone round by the Cape.

Cheerio for now. God bless you and take care of you.

Heaps of love,

Vera

❧

11.6.40

Dear Mother and Father

Thank you so much for your letter received today by airmail. It took only five days to come! What a blessing there is an airmail, and I hope that will be carried on as usual. I am so glad you have received my wire and letters. You should by now have had another letter, sent on the 4th. I will send all my letters by air now as the shipping will probably all go round the Cape.

I am so glad to know you are all well and keeping 'your heads held high and a smile upon your faces' as the King said! You are certainly having some dark days and the tension must be acute. I am glad you are to be moved to Wales if necessary where you will be safer.

We have heard so much about the South East coast and realise how near you are to the danger. Also we usually hear about every air-raid warning you have, and were told in the news that you have been called up from your beds at least three nights in succession, when nine counties were warned. England must have changed a lot since I last saw it, with barbed wire and sentries etc. etc., everywhere.

How quickly things happen these days. As you know we now have a complete blackout and have our ARP up to standard. Yesterday, as we expected, Italy entered the war. Never mind, we shall win and we will never be discouraged!

I was interested to hear that you have started a canteen for soldiers. How well you are working! They will appreciate that so much. It was amusing to hear that you have so many Scotch boys, whom you cannot understand. I have had a great number here in my ward. They are all so humorous and seem to get a lot of fun out of teasing the Sisters. I have been given the title of 'Blackout Queen' because I am on night duty and I go round the ward with a blue-painted lantern. One Scotchman insisted that I must be Welsh as my name is Jones, so he has added 'Sister Taffy Jones – the Blackout Queen'.

They are such fine lads, and so anxious to be 'up and doing'. We may not be here very long, as there is a possibility of us moving elsewhere. We are a happy set on night duty.

There are only six Sisters so it is nicer. A few days ago, we went to Jaffa when we came off duty in the morning, and we had a glorious swim and the water was so clear and cool. The nights are almost as stifling as the days, so we were glad to go out and get some fresh sea air. Jaffa is so Eastern and the cliffs are covered with little white stones houses, and minarets, and buildings with many domes. The sand is fine and golden. We are members of an Officers' Club there, and this is right on the beach and very convenient for bathing.

I have sent Geoffrey a present for his birthday on the 18th, but cannot say when it will arrive. It will probably be several weeks on the way. Give him my love and very best wishes for his birthday. Also I must write to Muriel soon – I owe her a letter and should have written ages ago.

Would you some day, *if* you have time, write to the Manager of Barclays Bank and ask him if he has been receiving money for my account for the last three months. I am having five pounds paid in monthly so that I can have some saved up. If you are not too busy, I should be glad if you would write just to make quite sure it has been received, as I have not had a receipt.

How nice to have the church so well attended for the Day of Prayer. People always flock to church in times of trouble, but so many care so little when there is peace. We also had well attended services in Sarafand. All Christian churches in Palestine were well attended, on the Jewish Sabbath the synagogues were filled to capacity, while the Arabs, both Moslem and Christian had great gatherings for prayers for victory. You see how well the Empire has answered the King's request! How *can* we lose!

I love to get your letters and to know just how you all are. We are not receiving nearly so many letters now and the time seems long between the mails. However, we may have to wait even longer so we must not grumble. Don't worry if you do not hear from me quite so often sometimes, as letters may easily go astray now that there is trouble in the Mediterranean. Just let me know by airmail if you are anxious, and I will send you a cable.

Well, there does not seem to be any more news just now so I will close, and write again very soon. My love to Muriel and everyone else including Connie and Peter.

God bless you all.

Much love to you both,

Vera

❧

J/766
QAIMNSR
Palestine
19.6.40

Dear Mother and Father

I hope you will, by now have received my last letter, dated 11th June. It was sent by air, but we are told that it is doubtful whether any letters will be sent regularly by air now. Also the news that letters sent via the Cape will probably take six weeks or more to reach you is not very hopeful. You will find there will now be long gaps between the arrivals of my letters, but do not worry, all will be well with me. It appears to make the distance between us seem much further, doesn't it? I have just heard that no more letters can go by air, so this must be sent by ordinary route.

As you will see, I have changed my address. We are no longer in Sarafand, but I cannot say where we are. We are 'somewhere in Palestine'. Later I shall be able to give you more details.

We are all thinking such a lot about you all in England, and we follow the news closely. We hear you are all being so wonderfully calm and brave during dreadful times – air raids etc, and we often wish we could be with you. Still, we are evidently meant to have our work out here, and there is much to do in our little corner of the world. I think about you always, and hope and pray you will all be kept safe.

There is so little news to tell you just now as we are not allowed to give any details. As soon as I can write more, I will let you have another letter. I will write as often as possible and hope that you will receive the letters separately and not all together.

I hope you are all keeping well, and not losing too many nights' sleep! Has Geoffrey received his parcel yet? I thought about him yesterday – the 18th. I often wonder if you have moved away yet – may it never be necessary for you to do so.

I am keeping very well. We have very hot weather now – the sun is always shining brilliantly and the sky is a cloudless blue. We have to wear dark glasses most of the day when out, as the glare is so bright.

Well, there is no more to say just now. Take care of yourselves always. Heaps of love to you all. God bless you.

Your loving
Vera

❧

QAIMNSR
No 60 General Hospital
Palestine
23.6.40

Dear Muriel

I am so sorry I have kept you waiting such a long time for a letter. You have written several times and I am sure it must be months since I wrote.

As you see by my address we have now left Sarafand and are in another part of the country. There is a lot I should like to tell you but we are not allowed to do so as the censorship is very strict. Also we have changed our number for an unknown reason since Italy's declaration of war. Every time I write, there are things I would like to tell you, but cannot.

It is quite likely that we shall remain in this place for a time, but things are always uncertain.

You are certainly now having a very anxious and dangerous time in England. It is really incredible that events have followed so quickly upon each other during these last few weeks. We feel so far away with two enemy nations between us and England, and many of us would love to be there where there is so much to do. We shall always be very busy here, of course, but cannot help feeling 'cut off' from the major events while we are in our outpost of the Empire! I hate to think of you being awakened by the siren night after night and spending hours in a shelter. Our own blackout here is now very good. It reminds me of the early days of the war when people were scrutinising their houses for every chink of light and others were being summoned for failing to observe the blackout properly. Fortunately the public are being very careful and following all instructions carefully, so there are comparatively few offenders.

I wish I knew what has happened to all my friends who went to France to nurse. Have they returned to England now, do you think, in view of the present French situation? I have not heard from Sister Wood for such a long time. Of course she has been very busy and probably not had a moment to write even a line. I do hope nothing has happened to her hospital.

We have heard that some 'Anzacs' have arrived in England. I am so glad to know that people were much cheered by their appearance. They say, you know, that one 'Aussie' is worth two Huns!

We have not had a spot of rain since the 20th March, and shall not have any more until October at the earliest! The sun is very hot and the sky always a cloudless blue. It is strange to have days and days of brilliant sunshine, and one can hardly imagine it possible for the sun to continue to shine for so many months. I am sure we must have your share of sun as well. It would do your skin such a lot of good.

Today is Sunday, and I have been able to go to a service at the Cathedral Church of St George. It is a fine building and just like any English cathedral in any English city. It has a fine choir and organ and the congregation was very good. It reminded me very much of the Chelmsford Cathedral for it has a stone tower from which flies the flag of St George. I was thinking of Chelmsford as

I left the churchyard, but outside, the sight of a camel passing along the road, brought me back to Palestine with a bump!

I have recently read a very good book by Daphne du Maurier. It is called *Rebecca*. Have you read it before? If not, you would like it very much, as it so unusual and so well written. I am now reading a book about the life of Lawrence of Arabia, called *T E Lawrence* by Vyvyan Richards. I am going to buy *The Seven Pillars of Wisdom* some day. It is a very thick book and full of illustrations and gives all the adventures of Lawrence during his life in Arabia.

The Arabs are so fascinating and when you see them every day it is interesting to learn more about their customs and traditions. They are now most loyal to the Empire, after years of unrest in this country. The war has brought all their quarrelling to an end and united them to the British, entirely! Everywhere they speak proudly of their King and Empire. One Arab, as an example, told us that 'if Britain falls, the days of freedom and peace for the Arabs will be over' but he added 'that will not ever be, for Britain is good, and we will always fight for the British.'

Cheerio for now, and take care of yourself.

Much love from

Vera

P.S. I am glad to say, there is now an airmail service which will be much quicker than the sea route. I will send all my letters home by that way, otherwise they will take more than six weeks.

8.7.40

Dear Mother and Father

Thank you so much for your cheering cable received safely. I hope you received mine in reply. I will send you one whenever I think you have not heard from me for a long time, so that we do not lose touch with each other. It was so nice to know you were all well.

I am afraid our airmail service is going to be very irregular and the route will be long, so letters may take about three weeks to reach England. However, I am still going to use the route taken by airmail as it will surely be quicker than by sea. It is now a month since I heard from you by letter and it seems much longer. Other people have not had letters for six weeks or more, and we are all waiting as patiently as possible for our mail. When I hear from you, I will cable and let you know.

We feel so isolated now, and the distance from England seems much further. We did not know how lucky we were, when we had letters more than once a week. Still I must not grumble – other people have far worse troubles to bear.

I am still on night duty and we have settled into our new hospitals and have plenty of work to do. At present we are still living at the hotel to which we went on our arrival in Jerusalem, but in a short time we are moving into our new Sisters' Mess a short distance away, and just outside Herod's Gate in the City Wall. The Mess will consist of three nice houses with every convenience and we should be very comfortable there.

This hospital where I am now working, was in the charge of Italian nuns formerly, but they have been interned of course, and we have taken over the hospital. It is really a fine place, very spacious and clean and a pleasure to work in. The roof is flat and in the early morning we go up there to see the dawn breaking over the city. It is lovely to see the Mosque of Omar and every minaret and dome standing out against a beautifully tinted sky.

I am glad we are kept busy as our work keeps us occupied and we do not have time to brood so much over the news. All the same I cannot help feeling very anxious when I hear of raids nearly every day over England, especially the South East coast. I know you will all take care, and you would not like me to worry. I am always thinking about you.

It is very difficult for me to give you much news as we have to remember about censorship.

I often try to imagine what it must be like in England now. I am sure you are well defended, especially as there are so many soldiers on Home Service. We often hear accounts on the wireless of life in England now, but of course we can only think of it as it was when we left.

Jerusalem is cooler than Sarafand, and however hot the days are, there is always a fresh breeze to make them bearable. We also find the air is relaxing and I think it is rather like Torquay where we were nearly always so sleepy. I little dreamed when we were there, that I would be in Jerusalem now.

I met a lady a few days ago, who is the wife of the surgeon in charge of the English Mission Hospital here. She has invited me to tea with her whenever I can go so that will be nice to visit someone outside the army life.

Well, I am afraid there is no more I can tell you just now. It will be lovely to get your letters even if they are out of date.

Much love to Muriel and Geoff. God bless you all.

Best love to you both,

Vera

P.S. Note the English postage stamps. A new rule!

14.7.40

Dear Mother and Father

One of our specialists is leaving here tomorrow, for England as he has some heart trouble and is unable to stay here to work. He has very kindly offered to post a letter from me to you when he arrives in England, which he hoped will be in about fourteen days. I can be much more sure of my letter reaching you, in that way, so am writing now.

Have you received any of my letters since 11th June? I hope so. This is about the fifth since that date. We always feel so uncertain about their arrival in England.

I am still on night duty and we are very busy with an epidemic of malaria. At least it is not exactly an epidemic, but this is the season for malaria and we are flooded out with cases. It is very interesting to nurse and the experience of tropical diseases is very good out here.

As I told you in my last letter, I am working now in a fine hospital which, until recently, was the Italian Hospital, but we have now occupied it. The wards are very nice and spacious and we have a splendid view over the whole city from the flat roof of the building. Some of our Sisters are working in what was the

German Hospital but now we have made it British and the wives and children of soldiers are nursed there.

Since I came out here, I have been in three different hospitals and each one we have had to establish ourselves and bring each one up to date. First I was at Sarafand, then the German Hospital for a time, and now, the Italian. It is very good experience to have to improvise and gradually bring a hospital up to an efficient standard. I shall be able to run my own hospital when I come home!

We have received many thousands of evacuees from Egypt into Jerusalem, since Italy entered the war. They are living in various hostels in the city. The general feeling is that Jerusalem, being the Holy City, is the safest place in which to take refuge from aerial attack. Let us hope that is true!

I have recently been for a visit to the Dead Sea and Jericho. You know the saying 'Go to Jericho!' Well, I have been! I went for a bathe in the Dead Sea. It is the most amazing experience I have had since I came to this extraordinary country! You do not sink even if one is unable to swim, for the water is so heavy with salt and chemicals that you are held up indefinitely, and can float about without using any energy. I found myself bobbing about like a cork, and swimming is most difficult as your feet and arms just will not go under the water. It was so funny to see old ladies and tiny children all bobbing about on top of the water, well out of their depth. The Dead Sea water tastes dreadful, if you are unfortunate enough to swallow any. When we came out into the sun, a fine white powder formed on our costumes where the heat had dried them. It was a most bracing swim and although I had been on duty the night before, I felt very fresh and energetic after it.

The heat was terrific at the Dead Sea and Jericho. They are both 1,280 feet below sea level – the lowest place on earth. It was like being in a vast cauldron. There was not a breath of air, and the heat seemed to rise out of the ground. On the opposite side of the Dead Sea we could see the Mountains of Moab, which are on the edge of Trans Jordan. On the way to Jericho after our bathe we were able to see the River Jordan but could not get very near to it.

Jericho is a strange little town, full of tropical trees and wells of water. It is like an oasis on that dry empty plain. Bananas grow there, and also dates and mangoes. It is definitely tropical and I thought it a very romantic place, but I don't suppose the British troops stationed there think so.

We passed beneath the Mount of Temptation on our return journey. What a mountain. It is terrifying in its height and desolation. One can easily associate it with the devil! There is a monastery for monks who have attempted to break their vows, which is situated on a wide ledge half way up the Mount of Temptation. What an existence! They are doing a life sentence of complete isolation.

The road to Jericho is unique. Everything is dead, like the Dead Sea. It winds in and out among barren dry hills, where there is not a blade of grass. People say it is like Dante's *Inferno*, and it is quite true, for the heat is unbearable. This road is the most dangerous in Palestine for bandits, but lately it has been much safer. The only sign of life we met, were a herd of mountain goats and a convoy of camels with two Arabs. It was amazing to think that I was passing over the Wilderness.

I do hope you are all well and not having too many nerve shattering air raids. Do take care, all of you. How we all hope here that you will never have this awful, threatened invasion. Of course everything will be all right in the end. Dear old England, what is it like there now, I wonder. Are you being very strictly rationed now? I am sure you must be. We heard last night that you will not be having any more cream buns and cakes etc, until after we have finished off Hitler! What bitter news!

We are living quite ordinary lives here except for the ARP which is going strong. How I often wish I could share some of your discomforts. I seem to be having all the privileges, but then we did not join up to come here, and did expect to go to France.

Well, I do not think there is any more news just now. May this reach you safely. I hope you are not working too hard and take plenty of rest, with feet up on sofas after dinner. And no mowing · the lawn, if you have any patch of lawn left now. (You know who that is meant for!) My love to Muriel and Geoff, and of course to you both and Peter.

God bless you.
Your loving
Vera

24.7.40

Dear Mother and Father

I hope by now that you are receiving my letters, as I am sure you have also had to wait a long time for them, just as I have for yours. I have had one letter since the 11th June received about a week ago. It was sent by air, and took a month and five days to come! Thank you so much for it. I hope you received my cable sent on the following day. We were all wild with delight when that first mail arrived. English newspapers also came and were sold in a short time in the streets of Jerusalem. They were dated the 14th May – and some were a little more recent, but none had been published later than 27th May. All the news in them was, of course, like ancient history, but we were most grateful all the same to be able to read English papers, because anything from England is valuable!

I am so glad you sent me a cable. It was good to think that you were all well and I hope you received the cable from me in answer. I don't want you to cable too often as I know it is such an expense and you are having a very hard time at home. I will cable every few weeks as I feel sure you will be glad to have just a few words when letters are so scarce.

We heard a few days ago that some districts in England were being evacuated completely, for purposes of defence for those areas. I am wondering if you have had to move, as you told me some time ago that you were likely to do so.

You will have heard of the air raids on Haifa recently. The death tolls for both raids were rather heavy and there was a fair amount of damage done. Also we had a slight earthquake two nights ago, which was felt all over Palestine, but I am glad to say, I slept through it!

The heat continues to be intense, even in Jerusalem, which is said to be the coolest part of the country. We have cold showers as often as possible but even then, we can feel the perspiration oozing through our skins a few minutes afterwards. There is never a cloud in the blue sky and the heat is almost as oppressive during the night. In our two hospitals we are still coping with many cases of malaria and sandfly fever. Patients 'run' the highest temperatures possible out here. We have plenty of work, which is what I like.

I wrote to you about two days ago, and gave the letter to one of our specialists who was leaving for England owing to ill health. He was going to post the letter when he landed home. He went from here to Alexandria with many other patients who were not fit to stay here. In a few days we are expecting them all back again as it is not possible to send them to England owing to transport and convoy difficulties. It is so sad for them to go as far as Egypt, feeling so thrilled and excited at the prospect of returning, and then to have their hopes dashed. There may still be a vague chance of their going after all, but we doubt it. In that case my friend will not be able to post my letter in England and he may send it from Egypt or else bring it back to me, when I will post it by air immediately. You will most likely receive it after this letter.

I have started learning Arabic, and it is a most interesting language, but very difficult as the letters are not like our alphabet. I am afraid I shall be a very slow scholar.

We are still able to go to Jaffa sometimes for a bathe. It takes about one and a half hours by car from Jerusalem to Jaffa. The sea is so warm and refreshing in this heat, and one does not get any shock of entering cold water as you do when bathing round the English coast. The waves are usually very big and some people are often able to go 'surf-riding'. I am so sorry to hear that you are not having any holidays at all in England. It is to be expected when everyone is so busy helping to win the war, and you are all being very noble. I am sorry Muriel is having so little off duty. I feel dreadful, telling you how I spend my half-days, when you are having so little free time.

There are many thousands of Polish, Czech, and French soldiers here from Syria. They are such smart and efficient men and we are proud to have them, just as they are thankful to be here. We often see these troops marching through the streets singing their national songs. Many of the Polish men took part in the defence of Warsaw and have had terrible experiences.

Well, cheerio for the present, and I will write again very soon.
Heaps of love to all.
God bless you.
Your loving
Vera

With two Arab waiters on the steps leading to our mess in Jerusalem

Dear Mother and Father

Thank you so much for your cable. It was good to hear from you, as we are still not receiving letters. We are expecting a mail in now, but it is overdue. I do like to know that you are all well, and am glad you are receiving my letters.

We have settled into our new hospitals which are both very busy and full of patients. A few days ago we moved from our billets in the hotel, and are now living in our own Sisters' quarters. These consist of four houses standing together on the outskirts of the city. They are of Arab architecture – flat roofed and built of stone. The rooms are of quite good sizes with several windows each.

We are in a pleasant situation, on one side of the Kedron Valley, almost opposite the Garden of Gethsemane!

As we are some distance away from our work, we have our own bus to take us there and bring us back.

I am going away for two weeks' leave on the 18th of this month. We are due for this every six months and my turn has come. I am going with one other Sister to stay in a little seaside town about thirty-five miles from Haifa, and sixty-five miles from Jerusalem. It is called Nathanya. There is a lovely beach there, with golden sand and high cliffs. We shall stay at a small and very nice hotel, and I think we shall have a very pleasant rest. My address will be the same as any letters will be forwarded from here.

I feel so sorry for you at home – unable to have even a day off, while I can have two weeks. It makes me feel quite selfish. If only you could be here to enjoy a lovely holiday. How I should love to be spending my leave with you, as I did when we were stationed at Tidworth.

One of my patients, a Captain of the Essex Regiment, was talking to me about his work, and I found out that Connie's brother was quite probably working under him. As I have never met him I could not describe her brother, but this Captain said that he knew a young Private of the same name when he was in Khartoum. The Captain came from Colchester.

We have been in Palestine for nearly eight months now, and it seems so much longer. To think that the war has been in progress for nearly a year. May it soon be over! I cannot think what you must be feeling like in England, with those constant air raids while we have only had four raids on Haifa, as our share, so far. Palestine is collecting for a Fighter Aircraft Fund and already we have a large sum of money.

There seems to be so little news to tell you just now. I am afraid this is a short letter.

The heat is not quite so bad now, but we still have plenty of malaria and mosquitoes. The last drop of rain we had fell at the end of March! It will seem funny to see rain again, I have almost forgotten what it is like.

May this find you all well, I will try not to worry about you too much.

Writing again soon.

Very best love to you all

Vera

❦

5.9.40

Dear Mother and Father

I hope you are receiving my letters safely. How we love to have letters – they are worth their weight in gold. If you could only see us clamouring to see the infrequent piles of letters when they come in, all anxious to know if there is one for each of us. We are so cut off from England since those dreadful Italians came into the war, for it means that the Mediterranean must be left almost clear of shipping, and our letters must take the Cape route.

I am thinking of you so much these days. How hard it is to be standing by, just watching, and praying. We hear the same news every day, bombs, and more bombs on England. 'Damage done to houses and property. Some casualties – a few fatalities.' Some days we hear that 'casualties occurred in many districts, but in proportion to the severity of the raids, they were not numerous.' Dear old England! We never dreamed that such things could happen there. I keep hoping that you are taking every care, and I am sure you are. We can always be thankful for our wonderful Air Force, for it is giving one of the chief contributions to victory. What anxious times for you, the strain must be very trying.

I am wondering these last few days, if you have received two cables I sent during the last two weeks. I cannot help feeling worried about them and have been expecting a reply to say that you were all well. Even cables have been going astray so I may still receive an answer.

I went to a lovely service in St George's Cathedral here last Sunday. It was the Harvest Festival. The church was packed and there were many soldiers and officers there. Among the decorations were beautiful palm branches – so suitable for Jerusalem. I thought of you at home when you will soon be having your Harvest Festival at the end of this month. I was at Everleigh Parish Church for last Harvest!

As I sit here writing in my room, I can see the Garden of Gethsemane from my window! It looks so peaceful and holy, with the sun shining through the trees. It does not seem fair that I should be in this quiet place, while you are in all the danger, and it was I who 'joined up' to go into the danger – as I expected! There may be trouble out here, on a wider scale, and we are prepared for it. The report concerning the bombs on Jerusalem, which you heard, was not true. It was a piece of malicious German propaganda. They are in the habit of saying such things, and according to them, the country is in a state of revolution! Haifa is the one place which has been bombed – six times so far.

I have returned from my 'leave' for a week now, and settled down to work again. I feel much better for the change, and ready for the winter. The heat makes one feel very tired and in need of a holiday. Now the days are cooler – the temperature is not more than 84 degrees and being in Jerusalem, we have cooler breezes at the end of the day.

I have my own ward, a very nice one at the top of the hospital, with a grand view over the city. There are thirty patients – all medical cases – and mostly tropical diseases. It is good to be really busy, as I always am, as it keeps one's mind fully occupied for most of the day, and there is less time to be anxious.

I expect I should not tell you this, but two more hospital units have arrived here, with 140 Sisters. They are mostly from the north of England, and Scotland. They had a wonderful journey. They were two months coming, having come round the Cape, and visited India, before passing on through the Red Sea and Suez Canal to Palestine. Now they will open their own hospitals in this country.

We had another slight earthquake a few days ago. It was a short sharp one and was over before we had time to remark about it.

Well, my dears, I must stop now. May this find you all well, as I pray you are.

Cheerio for the present.

My love to Muriel and Geoff and Peter.

God take care of you.

Your loving

Vera

❧

8.9.40

Dear Mother and Father

Since writing my last letter two days ago, I have been very pleased to receive two more letters. One was from Muriel and the other from Mother. Both took between four and five weeks by air.

What lovely photos you sent in Muriel's letter. Thank you so much for them. I was thrilled with them, and passed them round for my friends to see, who also agreed that they were excellent. I am going to have them all enlarged. How sweet Peter looks in the photos. He is sitting as if he is quite used to posing for photographs. I love the way he has his ears cocked up – and as for that intelligent expression on his face – he is almost human! How nice to have photos of Mother. They are so good and she is just as sweet and young as ever. The photo of Mother with Peter is excellent.

I love the photos of Muriel and Geoff, and I am pleased to see them both looking well and cheerful. Geoff in the deckchair is such a natural picture, and he has that smile on his face which causes all the girls' hearts to flutter!

I have such a nice set of photos now and I will value them very much.

There are to be mass evacuations of women and children from this country to South Africa and India during this month and next. Only women who are nursing will be permitted to stay. This new order will affect a large proportion of the British population. The Jews and Arabs are not included, of course. Many people were evacuated from Egypt to us, and now will be re-evacuated. So the old war goes on, breaking up one home after another and scattering people to all parts of the Empire.

We have just heard in the news from London on the wireless that the raids have become very much more severe and a great mass attack on London took place last night. We listened in horrified silence to the accounts of the damage inflicted, fires started, and more terrible, civilian deaths numbering 360 and injuries to civilians many hundreds. Poor old East London has suffered very badly, and many districts where I worked, have been heavily bombed.

11.9.40

It is three days since I started this letter, and I must finish it today. The news is the same, all night raids on London with serious damage and casualties. We hear wonderful accounts of the people's courage and endurance and of how they are carrying on with their daily occupations. How like the Londoners! It seems incredible that such things are happening to London and to all England! One can hardly imagine those familiar streets, blocked with wreckage and lined with damaged buildings. I often wish I could wake up and find that all the incidents of the war were only a dream.

I expect you spend most of your time taking shelter from raids. We hear that many people go to bed in their shelters automatically. I hope you have a really good shelter, those in London seem to be very strong. How wonderful that the King and Queen should go round seeing the air-raid sufferers, and take shelter with them when the siren sounds!

You will probably have heard today of the big raid on Tel Aviv two days ago. There were 112 people killed and 150 injured. It is very sad and a brutal piece of work by the Italians. Tel Aviv is such a fine town, purely residential with no factories and no military objectives of any kind. We all know it well, and often went there for shopping when we were at Sarafand.

Yesterday I received a letter from Father, and it took nearly seven weeks to get here by sea route. That is not so long as usual. He tells me that he may be going abroad with some children sometime to one of the Dominions or USA. How interesting and what an experience it would be. I wonder if he will go now that the former mass evacuation scheme has been abandoned. Only small numbers are leaving, I believe. Somehow, I don't want him to go, and I hope he doesn't.

This letter seems to be full of air-raid talk and I must not dwell so much on it, but you know how hard it is not to discuss the subject which is uppermost in your mind.

I am sending back a 1/– stamp, but I expect you have been able to keep those which I have sent on my letters. I was sorry we had to stop using Palestine stamps as some of them are really pretty. We do not use cents and dollars as Father asked me but piastres and mils. 1 mil = 1/10 piastre; 18 piastres = about half a crown and so on. The mil pieces have holes through them, and knowing that a robber would not attack a woman, the Arabs string their mils round their wives necks, in order to keep them safe!

Well, I must stop now I'm afraid and get this posted.

I received your cable safely, after three weeks. It seemed a long time coming as they have always been so quick before. I was so glad to hear from you. I hope you don't mind me bothering you with cables sometimes, and I will try to remember what you said, 'Don't worry.'

And now cheerio for the present. Best love to all.

Tell Muriel I received her letter and am writing very soon.

God bless you all and keep you safe.

Your loving daughter

Vera

Dear Mother and Father

Your last letter dated the 4th August (from Mother) I received safely. I remember I thanked you for it in my last letter. I sent that by airmail, bearing a 2/6d stamp, which I hope Father will find useful.

I do hope you are all well, and managing to accustom yourselves to air raids. I think about you most of the day, and when the nights are very quiet here, I wonder how much noise you are having to listen to. From the accounts we hear on the radio and read in the papers, the din of AA guns and planes overhead is persistent for nearly all the twenty-four hours. Now that London is suffering so badly, are you having some respite from it? I wonder! How we wish, often, that we were not so far away. The men over here feel it dreadfully that they cannot be at home to look after their wives and families. Still we are told that this is a vital part of the Empire and must be defended by troops – which is true.

We are now receiving convoys of wounded men from Egypt. We expect a fresh batch about every week, so will be even busier than before. I am glad we have such a nice, comfortable hospital for them. They certainly deserve the very best of everything, after fighting in that intense heat of the desert.

I am now working in the operating theatre, which is what I like very much. The work is interesting and varied. It is strange to think we are nursing men wounded by the Italians, in a hospital previously built and used by the Italians.

We had a beautiful service in St George's Cathedral on the Day of National Prayer, two weeks ago. There was not an empty seat anywhere in the building. The High Commissioner for Palestine accompanied by his family, attended, as well as many soldiers and officers. We went in uniform, having come straight off duty to go. The Bishop of Jerusalem preached a very fine sermon. He is quite elderly and looks very clever.

Although Jerusalem has so many fine churches, I think our own English cathedral has a far more sincere atmosphere than any of them. It has an atmosphere of its own and as well as having a beautiful interior it is quite like any cathedral in England. So many of the older historical churches here are over-decorated.

I am enclosing two views of the outside of the Cathedral. I am sure you will agree that the view of the tower is very like Chelmsford Cathedral.

I am afraid this is only a short letter but there is not much news to tell you. Take care of yourselves and don't run any risks. Give my best love to Muriel and Geoffrey.

God bless you all and keep you safe.

Cheerio for now.

Your loving

Vera

❧

1.10.40

Dear Mother and Father

It was good to hear you were all well. I cannot help feeling very worried at times, especially when I hear of Essex being bombed. I am sure you take all precautions, and please don't run any risks. Can you imagine what it was like in peacetime now that you are always hearing the AA guns and sirens? I am wondering how you are managing with so little sleep, as I am sure that even your afternoon rest must be disturbed.

There is not much to write about, but my last letter was sent on the 20th September, so it is time I wrote again. I know you don't mind a short letter, as long as you hear from me.

I have sent off two parcels, one for Mother and the other for Muriel. They will probably arrive in time for Christmas! Mother's is for her birthday, and the other, a Christmas present for Muriel. I am sending some others too, in a few days' time. We are told they will be delivered free of duty, but if they are not, please let me know. Compulsory! I think most parcels arrive safely, so I do hope these do too.

I went down to the Garden of Gethsemane yesterday, as I had not been for some time. It is now more beautiful even than when I saw it some time ago, for it is full of tropical flowers, lavender, and lilac. I wish you could see it.

Afterwards I walked through St Stephen's Gate in the City Wall, and went through some of the most fascinating streets of the Old City, coming out through the Jaffa Gate. Everything is so colourful and so extraordinary in Old Jerusalem. Some of the streets are so narrow and twisting that people must walk in single file. Goats and donkeys mingle with the crowd and 'rub shoulders' with you as you pass. The little Arab children are so sweet with their black curls and dark eyes and brown skin. Of course they are all amazingly dirty!

The days are growing cooler now and we shall soon start the rainy season. We expect the first great deluge within a few weeks. The sky is still a lovely blue in colour and it is hard to believe that it will ever rain again. Jerusalem is noted for cold, bleak winters with bitter winds, so we shall go from one extreme to another. We will soon be putting aside our white summer uniforms, and wearing the grey, once again.

As I told you in my last letter, I am now working in the operating theatre, and gaining some useful experience.

It is ten months today since I left home after my last leave. It seems an eternity! I have also been mobilised for one year.

We feel like pioneers here now, for so many more Sisters have arrived from Britain, and for a long time we were the only reservists out here.

There will be a number of hospitals formed after a short time, staffed by all these new units.

Well, I have no more to tell you just now. Give my love to Muriel and Geoff and all the Heybridge people, including Connie, and of course, Peter.

Much love to you both. God bless you all.

Your loving

Vera

❧

Dear Mother and Father

Thank you so much for the cable received, to tell me that you were all well and my letters were arriving. I am always so glad to have word from you by cable, especially just now with all your raids.

You will see by my address that we are now not permitted to give the name of the place where we are stationed. We have not moved, but new regulations have forbidden us to continue giving our previous form of address.

The weather here now is very strange. We have intense heat again, after thinking it was all over. At night the sky is full of lightning, of the real tropical kind, and the clouds are so black that one would expect rain at any minute. But it has not come yet. We are using electric fans, especially after dark, when the blackout makes the atmosphere very heavy. It will be a relief when the rains start, and the air is cooler.

Among the Sisters who have recently arrived in this country, there is a girl who worked with all my friends in France.

Nearly all these new Sisters were in France or Norway, and have had terrible experiences, many of them only just escaping in time. They were on duty day and night during the fighting in Holland and Belgium. I was very glad to hear that all my friends arrived back in England safely.

The Fast of Ramadhan is now being kept in the Arab countries, especially in Jerusalem. The Arabs fast all day from 4 a.m., and at dusk they break their fast and eat all night. I think most of them must go on 'night duty' for the air is rent by the sounds of Moslem music and chanting. This Fast continues for a month. There is a minaret close to our Mess, and we see the Muezzin appear on his little balcony there, calling the faithful to prayers, hour after hour.

In today's paper, we read the Prime Minister's speech to the

House of Commons. It was fine – and so reassuring, but not over optimistic as I am afraid many of Mr Chamberlain's speeches appeared to be. How glad you must feel to have Churchill to 'lead the way'. We are all fervently hoping and praying that the danger of invasion will pass as the winter comes.

I think about you every night and early morning, wondering how severe the raids have been for you during the day and night.

I have had your photographs enlarged and framed. I love to see you all 'sitting' on my dressing table and you seem so real! They have all turned out so well, Geoff reclining in a deckchair, Muriel standing in the garden, Mother sitting with Peter in her lap, and Geoff and Mother standing in the garden with Peter. I also have one of Father taken some time ago, and another of him standing next to the church door. Even Peter seems so real that he might almost be about to spring out of the frame and smother me with wet kisses!

I hope you do not have such a bitter winter as the last. People have to spend so much time in shelters and will feel the cold more than ever. Still, I think last winter was exceptionally severe for you, so it may not be so bad this time.

Well, I am sorry to say there is no more news at present. My last letter was written on the 1st October, a week ago.

Hoping you are all well, cheerio for now.

God bless you all.

Ever your loving

Vera

୭

17.10.40

My Dear Muriel

Thank you so much for your nice long letter. It was posted on the 27th August and arrived on the 14th October. Nearly seven weeks by airmail! Still, as the Arabs say, 'Maleesh' (never mind).

You gave me so much news of interest, and, as usual your letter was most descriptive. I was thrilled by your story of how you can watch the air battles in progress. What an age we live in!

How wonderful to be able to watch our grand little fighter aircraft dashing through the air to intercept the enemy. We can only imagine such things by the news on the radio. I am so sorry to hear you have not been overlooked by the daily visitors, but can well believe it, especially as one of my friends here, whose home is near you, has heard in a letter that you have had bombs, as well as her home, (a large town with a castle, where you started your training). I know you take great care, and don't run any risks. Don't forget to take cover, even though the fight may be interesting!

I know how proud you must feel of our amazing RAF. One just cannot express in words what one thinks about the skill and bravery of the men.

I often think of the exciting times you are having, and compare your lives with mine, out here, in this now quiet country. At present it is a rather prosaic life, but maybe we shall have our 'turn' before long. (Re events in Balkans.) It is a strange war. I wonder how it will all end. I only hope that soon the air battles over England subside and you are given a measure of peace.

I gave a lecture to the nursing orderlies, a few days ago. I was asked to speak for one hour and did not see how I should manage it, but to my surprise I only just finished before the hour was over. It was a lecture on various nursing points, observation of the patient etc. What would Father say to that for a long sermon?

18.10.40

St Luke's Day. I went to church at 7 a.m. with two other Sisters and there were a number of people there. The service was in a sweet little chapel dedicated to St John of Jerusalem in the Cathedral. We are fortunate in having a daily celebration there, two on Saints days, and Evensong every day at 4.30 p.m., before blackout.

Jerusalem is going to be very cold in a month or two. Even now we are having 'chilly' evenings and are reminded of our early days here when we piled blankets on our beds, drew on our bedsocks and snuggled down with hot water bottles every night. Even then we often felt cold. What a contrast to the tropical nights in summer here, when we do not even cover ourselves with a sheet, as the heat is so intense.

I have read some interesting books lately. One was *Rebecca* by Daphne du Maurier. Also I have read *Haworth Parsonage* by Isabel Clarke. It is an excellent description of the lives of the Brontës. You would love it. Now I am reading *Insanity Fair* by Douglas Reed. It is an interesting book, all political and tells the story of Germany's rise to power since the last war. I expect you have read it.

We are able to tune in to the London radio station and it is so clear usually. It is grand to hear Big Ben as clear and firm as ever. We often listen to variety programmes, concerts, talks, and of course, all the news bulletins. It is wonderful that the 'reception' is so good.

Well, there does not seem to be much news just now. I will write more often to you in future, as you send me so many nice letters.

I was most upset to hear that the High Altar in dear old St Paul's Cathedral has been wrecked. Now a number of bombs have fallen near Canterbury Cathedral, and the wonderful building just escaped damage. How sad to think of our ancient and priceless treasures in danger of destruction by those devils. To them, nothing is sacred. We have today heard of the casualty list for September. It sounds dreadful, but in proportion to the population of the UK I suppose it is not great. You can't imagine how we feel for you all going through so much. It is no use trying to do anything, we are so far away, and can only just hope that very soon you will have weather which will make intense aerial warfare impossible.

Take care always. Cheerio for the present. My love to all.

Yours ever, with love

Vera

ॐ

22.10.40

Dear Mother and Father

It is over a week since I last wrote to you, but I have written to Muriel during that time, so I have not really missed writing my weekly letter.

I think I thanked you in my last letter for the cheery cable received. We are told that in England, the next of kin of members of HM Forces serving overseas, may send two cables a month at the rate of a penny per word. If you enquire about this, you will probably find it is correct. I hope so, as it must be expensive sending them at the usual rate.

I am receiving your letters, but many weeks pass between each one. The mails are very irregular, but we must expect that. I hope you are not being kept waiting long for mine.

I have not much news for you this time, so I am afraid this letter will be short.

I was pleased to have Muriel's long letter, written on the 29th August. It was nearly seven weeks coming, by airmail. It seems hard to believe that when we first arrived here our letters were only ten days to fourteen days on the way to their destinations. Still I am sure the good old Navy works hard to get our letters safely home. We have been given the latest dates for posting Christmas mail, so every effort is being made to get our parcels to 'Blighty' for 25th December.

We have had the honour of a visit by Mr Anthony Eden to Palestine, as you will know. He was very fully occupied I believe, or he would have inspected our hospital I am sure. A few of the Sisters met him, but not in this city. He was very cheery and had quite a conversation with them, after which he had his photograph taken. The Sisters were most thrilled. I should have loved to see him, but as he only spent two days here, there was not much chance. I have been introduced to Sir Philip Neame, the GOC for Palestine, however. He inspected our hospital. He won the VC in the last war. General Barker, who is now in England, held the same post when we arrived here.

Last night we listened in to the Prime Minister's speech to the French people. It was relayed via America. It is wonderful that we have such a clear reception from our wireless set. We listen to Big Ben, and might almost be standing on Westminster Bridge, it is so loud and distinct.

It must be growing very cold in England now. We are all hoping that fogs and bad visibility will lessen the severity of bombing attacks for you.

I am sorry that this is a short letter, but as long as it is a letter of some kind, I know you do not mind. My love to all, and especially to both of you.

God bless you. Cheerio for now.

Your loving

Vera

❧

Dear Mother and Father

Thank you so much for your cable received today. I expect it has taken some days to reach me, but cannot tell, as it was undated as usual. I have replied immediately, and I hope you receive my cable safely. I am always so glad when I have your cables, as it is comparatively recent news.

We are all very anxious about one of our Sisters who has left us to return home to England, owing to her ill health and other reasons. She sailed on the *Empress of Britain*, which as you know has been bombed and sunk. With this Sister, travelled two of our officers whom we also liked very much. As most passengers were rescued it is quite likely they are all safe, but what an ordeal! The Sister was older than most of us and served in the last war. She was glad to be going back, so we do hope she has arrived safely. What a tragedy to lose such a fine ship!

The war seems to be coming much nearer to us now that Greece has joined in. What a world of complications it is becoming. You saw it in the last war – one country after another taking up arms to defend their freedom. Still it will all be smoothed out one day, and may it never happen again.

I am enclosing a snap of two of our Arab servants and myself standing on the steps leading up to our Mess. Later I will send some snaps of myself at work in the operating theatre, which I hope will turn out well as they will be interesting for you to see. I am also sending two Egyptian stamps for Father, but he may already have them as they are not uncommon.

I am having a book sent to me every month from the Book

Club in London. Muriel belongs to it also I believe. The cost is only 2/6d per month (3/– for me, being abroad). The books are so good, and most of them would cost 7/6d normally. We need to have good books to read out here, as there is not much else to do in one's spare time. I shall have quite a big library when I return.

From the news, it seems that your air raids are not quite so severe or so many in number. I hope this is so. They surely cannot go on through the winter. The weather is much cooler here now, but the rains have not yet started. We are going to put away our white uniform soon, and wear grey again.

We still have plenty of work to do, and I am really loving the work in the operating theatre. Not having done much of it at KGH I am glad now of the chance of gaining fresh experience. It is really invaluable knowledge, and one becomes much more useful with theatre experience, especially in wartime.

Well, it seems that I have no more news at present. I hope you are receiving most, if not all, my letters.

My best love to all, especially both of you. Cheerio for now, and God take care of you.

Your loving
Vera

❧

10.11.40

Dear Mother and Father

I have just received Mother's letter, dated 28th August, and finished and sent off on 22nd September. I have since cabled to you, and as I also sent you a cable a week ago, you should receive them both any time now. The letter was over six weeks coming, as usual!

I am so sorry you have sent so many cables and not received answers from me. I have received several cables from you, and answered *each one* on the same day. All I can think is that I am not receiving all your cables, or else you are not receiving my answers. Also I always write every week by airmail, but I fear you do not receive every letter. I am sorry to say your letters arrive very infrequently, that is, about once a month or once in six weeks. We are all trying to be patient and not over-anxious for letters, knowing the difficulties, but I am afraid we often find it a great trial, having so little news from home. I know you write weekly, and are just as anxious for my letters. In future I will cable regularly, at least once a month, and I think the 1st of each month would be a good date to keep to. When you cable I will reply at once, in the usual way. I hope that in time these mail difficulties will improve, but up till the present, I think they have become more infrequent. We expect an airmail every weekend, but also must expect a disappointment when it does not arrive.

Does this little grumble sound very trivial to you, when there are so many more important matters hanging in the balance? I hope not. I think we are all becoming more reconciled to this isolation now, and I think that when letters do come, they give us greater joy because of the longer period of waiting.

If you only knew how I long to be with you, often, especially during these last two months. We try to imagine what you must be going through, but can only have some idea what it is like. We do not get all the news, you have told me a good deal in your letter which we did not hear each day on the radio we are told, the areas which have received the heaviest attacks, but it is hard to imagine just what those places must look like. I know the East End so well, I expect poor old Plaistow and that district have had a bad time. I am glad KGH is intact, and hope it always will be.

I think you are all grand to carry on so nobly. Your description of the soldiers' canteen shows how hard you are working for the troops, and I am sure it gives you great pleasure. They deserve the best of everything, and I have always thought that out here, and we try to do our best for them. Some of these boys have also lost their homes and relations, others do not know what has become of their families, owing to the big evacuations, and being so far away from home, it is a long time before they can get their new addresses. In spite of all this, one could not find a more cheery and humorous crowd of soldiers anywhere. They keep so hopeful and never stop singing and whistling.

It is certainly a good thing that you are kept busy with happy occupations, but don't overdo it and get too tired. I can't bear to think of you having so little sleep.

From the news during the last two days, it seems that your raids have been less severe, and I think for about a week the news has not been so startling. I hope this is true of Essex. I am glad you have a good shelter, and that even Peter knows he must get down there in 'double-quick' time!

We are now starting our second winter out here. The rains started with a terrific deluge about two weeks ago, but we have since had lovely sunny days. When the next rain comes, it will probably go on for a week without stopping! We are now obtaining a store of winter woollies, and have brought out our 'wellingtons' and macs, etc, ready for use. Jerusalem is said to be extremely cold and is noted for bitter winds, so we will all have to wrap up well, and pile the blankets on our beds at night. I hope your winter will not be so bitter as the last.

About a week ago, we had quite a number of men admitted to us, who had either been in contact with, or bitten by, a mad dog. As you know, rabies is very common in dogs and jackals here, so we have to take every precaution. The dog died, and the men were given anti-rabies serum immediately. They have a course of injections daily for some time, so have to remain in hospital under observation. Being in the best of health otherwise, they are full of energy and humour. Most of them occupy several small wards together and outside in the corridor, one man has written in large letters on a slate 'Beware of the Dogs'!

I am sending you several snaps which I hope you will receive safely, also two stamps. One snap shows an operation in progress. I am on the extreme right of the picture, but you could not tell who I am, as we are all masked.

Tomorrow being Armistice Day, I hope to go to a Service at 6.45 a.m., to be held in the British War Cemetery. This is situated on Mt Scopus, overlooking the city. This morning (Sunday) I went to the 10 a.m. service in the Cathedral. It was very well attended, as usual and the singing was fine. The choirboys have new cassocks, deep purple, and white ruffles and cuffs. I always enjoy the services there so much, and often imagine I am with you in church at home, for when we go to our 10 a.m. service, you are just starting Holy Communion at 8 a.m.

I do hope Father is not making himself too tired with so much work, but at the same time I am sure he enjoys it.

Would it be any trouble for you to send me some books, which would be very useful to me? They are four books called *Modern Professional Nursing*, and they are somewhere among Muriel's books, I believe. They may be too heavy to send all together, so it may be easier to send them singly. There is so much useful information in them, and I should like to lend them to our nursing orderlies. Please don't bother if there are any difficulties in sending parcels, and also there is no hurry for them.

I am keeping very well, so there is no need for you to worry about me.

Well, my dears, I must stop now and get this posted. May it reach you safely, and in quieter times, and may it find you all well. -

Writing again soon.

My love to all, and a kiss for Peter.

Take care, and God bless you always.

Your loving

Vera

ço

27.11.40

Dear Mother and Father

Thank you very much for the cable received safely. I received it on the 25th, and replied the following day, so I hope you will receive my answer safely. It was good to know that you were all well and I was especially pleased to hear that you have received the parcels from me, also letters.

We are told that a Christmas mail has arrived for us, but there are so many bags of it that there has not been time to sort it all yet. We are very thrilled of course and longing to have it.

I am always wondering how things are with you now. I listen carefully to the news from London, and it does seem sometimes, that you are having less trouble from the air. I do hope this is so. How I wish I knew just how much you have been through as I know you cannot tell me much. I think nearly all the Sisters receive cables from home, and we rejoice with each other that our families are safe.

There seems so little news to tell you just now. I am still working in the operating theatre, and liking it very much.

I received a very nice letter recently from Matron at KGH. She told me quite a lot of news about nurses at the hospital. I do hope KGH has escaped from damage. Today, I met a doctor who was there in 1936 when I was in my second year of training. He has been with our unit for some time, and I did not recognise him as the same man. Now I remember him very well, and we exchange reminiscences together.

I hope to send you a letter by someone who is going home in the future (can't say when). He is a patient of mine who has been very ill and is going home for a less strenuous job. I don't suppose he will be able to visit you, owing to the usual restrictions, but I will give him your address, so that he can try. There are such fine soldiers (and good patients) out here! I should like you to meet some of them, and hope you will, one day when they return. We have a Czech doctor working in the theatre as an ordinary British private. He had a large clinic in Prague and I believe, knows his work well. Now he has had his practice taken from him and had to leave his country. Later, he will be able to join the RAMC as a medical officer, and surgeon, and he is looking forward to it so much. He had been sent to the theatre to learn the 'running' of it, but especially to learn English, and the English names for instruments etc. We are quite enjoying teaching him, and he was so grateful to me today that he said he would show me all over Prague after the war!

30.11.40

St Andrew's Day. I went to church this morning at 7 a.m. to a lovely service in the Cathedral. I have been thinking of you all very much today. Do you remember how I have always loved that hymn, in which there is a verse, which says, 'As of old St Andrew heard it, by the Galilean Lake'. To think that I am so near to Galilee now!

Well, I must not write any more now, but get this posted. I wish I had more news to tell you, but the comparatively quiet life here and the strict censorship, leave little news to write.

My love to all and God bless you and keep you safe.

Your loving

Vera

ॐ

5.12.40

Dear All

This is to wish you a very happy and quiet Christmas, free from bombs etc! We are all writing one page home by special airmail, which, it is hoped, will reach you by Christmas. This is a special arrangement which has been made for HM Forces in the Middle East, and we are very grateful for the kind thought.

I am wondering if your Christmas will be anything like other years. I am afraid rationing etc, will make a great difference. We only wish we could give you some of our wonderful fruit out here, you have so few oranges and lemons.

On Christmas Eve I hope to go to Bethlehem! If the Carols and bells are broadcast, as in former years, you will be able to 'listen in', and think of me! It is wonderful to think that I can be in Bethlehem at Christmas. I wish you were going to be there too.

Do you know a boy whose surname is 'Vince'? He lives in Heybridge. He has just recovered from a mastoid operation but was in another military hospital near here, so I did not meet him. He told a Sister at this hospital, that he knew a Sister Jones whose Father was the vicar of his town. I wish I had been able to see him. He has quite recovered and has left the hospital now.

There is very little to tell you I am afraid, as I have just written to you a few days ago.

I shall be thinking of you all at Christmas and hoping you are all well and happy. Very best wishes to all and much love, especially to you.

Cheerio for now.

Your loving

Vera

Dear Mother and Father

I have written to you quite recently when I sent an airmail letter by special Christmas post. I hope you will receive it by Christmas. I always write every week and hope you are receiving my letters often. I am afraid yours still arrive very irregularly but they give me great joy when they do come. I have also sent several cables in the last few weeks. I sent one yesterday to Mother so let me know if you have received it safely and in good time.

Christmas is drawing very near, and we are making preparations and hope to give the patients a happy time. Yesterday we stirred the Christmas pudding and it smelt very good. The shops are looking very bright and decorative with Christmas trees, tinsel, paper lanterns and crackers, etc. There seems to be plenty of everything out here like pre-war days in England. How I wish it was the same in your part of the world now!

We are getting magazines and papers from England, showing pictures of air-raid damage. How terrible it all is! We expected to see such pictures when they arrived, but they were even more of a shock to us than we had anticipated. I wish I knew how much Maldon and Heybridge have suffered. A picture of ruins in one street in London very much resemble a part of Ilford High Road. We are not told the names of places damaged, of course. Several of our staff have had their homes destroyed.

Palestine is beginning to look less dried up and barren now that the rains have started. The Mount of Olives has patches of green all over it, where new grass is appearing. The trees no longer droop in the heat and the rain has brought out new buds on the olive trees. In our garden fresh green grass has made a lawn as if by magic! There are narcissi and jonquils appearing and we shall have daffodils too, later on. It will be wonderful to see the hills covered with the scarlet 'lily of the field' again. I think this country is blessed with spring flowers twice in twelve months, as we had lovely flowers in February and March and even April and they have come again in December before winter has really started. I wish you could see some of the beautiful sunsets and sunrises we have in Jerusalem. The sky is full of the most exquisite colours, and with many domes, minarets and towers outlined against it, it is a sight we will never forget.

I know you will be pleased to hear that I have once more made a chapel for our hospital. Up till the present, services were held in an ordinary lecture room and then only about every other week. I was very glad when I was asked by the Chaplain and Matron to be responsible for arranging a chapel and for telling the patients when services would take place, etc. I had an altar made by the hospital carpenter, and as I had altar frontals and white altar cloths, which we used in our last hospital, I was able to make it look really lovely. Although it is Advent, we had flowers last Sunday, red and white carnations, as the patients love to see flowers. At 7 a.m., we had a number of convalescent patients for Holy Communion. Several walked with crutches – they are casualties from the Western Desert. At Christmas I am going to make the chapel as nice as I can, with plenty of flowers. Later on we hope to have a new chapel built, but for the present I think we shall manage very well.

On my birthday I am giving a small party to some of my best friends. In my next letter I will tell you how we enjoyed it.

There seems to be very little to tell you just now. When you receive this it will be 1941!

I do hope you are all well. It would be wonderful to see you all again, even if it was only for Christmas.

My best love to all.

Your loving

Vera

ço

20.12.40

Dear Mother and Father

Thank you very much for two nice letters received today. Earlier in the month we were able to send a one-page letter by special airmail and have since been told that it has arrived safely in England. I hope this is so, as I did hope you would receive my letter by Christmas.

I always reply to each cable you send, so you would have an answer each time.

I am so glad and relieved when I hear that you are all well. I know the strain must be awful and do not know how you keep so calm. You know how we feel about it, being out here in comparative safety, when we had joined up to 'go to the war' as we thought. Instead of that, we have gone away from the war and you are the ones who are holding the Front lines! Will we ever be able to take a really active part, or are you going to receive the whole force of the war all the time? Now we have begun our 'Blitzkrieg' in the desert and are doing wonderfully well, but that does not stop the wholesale murder in England. As you say the troops feel it badly that their families are in more danger than themselves. It is the same out here. We have been 'standing by' for so long now for things that never happen, while all the fighting is on the Home Front!

I am very interested in your description of the soldiers' canteen. How they must appreciate it. It is so like you to want to give them a good time and plenty to eat. You must be famous in the neighbourhood, and if I know anything about soldiers, they will never forget Heybridge and will talk about their good times there wherever they go. I can just see you cutting up sandwiches etc, and presiding over the club each evening.

How dreadful to think of the little Isolation Hospital being attacked! It is all among fields, and a long way from the town, so there is no excuse for it. It seems like a bad dream to think of Chadwell Heath so badly damaged, and poor old Plaistow, it never was very beautiful, so what it must be like now, I cannot imagine. How is KGH? I scarcely dare ask!

I gave a nice little party on my birthday. Ten of my friends came and we had quite a merry time, with all the usual Christmas atmosphere as well as a large cake, nuts and sweets and crackers, etc.

I went to a very nice dance given by a unit stationed near here, a short time ago, and enjoyed it very much. There were soldiers from all over the Empire there. Among them were two New Zealanders, one from Taranaki, and the other from Wanganui. They were very jolly and most interested to hear that I had been to their country. That was the first time they had been able to go to a dance in the Middle East. One man knew Bulls very well, also Raetihi. What a small world!

They certainly seemed to enjoy their evening, and I am glad they did, for they were leaving here again the next day for the Western Desert where there is no time for such relaxation.

I went for a visit to Ain Karim, a few days ago. This is a small village about ten miles from here, situated among the hills. It is the birthplace of St John the Baptist, and of course is a very ancient village, as well as being very pretty and peaceful. We climbed very high up a steep hill and sat on a rock near the top from which we had a perfect view of the village and the country around, for many miles. It was a glorious day, especially for December. We were very high up, and could look down upon other hills, brown and bare, except where the ground had been made into terraces which were cultivated and green with fruit and cypress trees. One could not imagine anything more tranquil. It was so quiet that we could hear the sound of chanting in Arabic coming from the houses lower down the hillside. (Can you think of any peace at all with the guns and sirens going day and night!)

Well, this year will soon be over. When we think what a lot has happened during it, surely there has never been such a year. What will 1941 bring I wonder! The end of the war? Wouldn't it be wonderful!

Well, my dears, there is no more to write just now so I will end here. I do hope you will have a quiet and happy Christmas. I will write again very soon, and tell you about my Christmas in the Holy Land.

God bless you all. Much love to you both and all.

Your loving

Vera

෨

My Dear Mother and Father

Here is my first letter of 1941. It will be too late to wish you a happy New Year when you receive this, but I do say this to you, may you all be kept safe and well all the year, and may we all be together again before next New Year's Day.

In my last letter I thanked you for two letters, one from Muriel and one from Mother. On the 28th December, I received three cables from you, two for Christmas and one for my birthday. Thank you so much. They gave me great pleasure. I hope you received my cable in time for Christmas, and also the one for Mother's birthday.

I thought about you all so often during Christmas. We were all so relieved to hear that the 'Blitzkrieg' was suspended for two days or so. I hope then that you had some peace and rest.

We had a memorable and happy Christmas here. All the patients were very cheery and enjoyed a good dinner, etc. The wards were all gaily decorated and in each, there was a big Christmas tree covered with gifts, tinsel, and electric candles. Even one small room, where there was a very ill patient, had its own 'baby' tree. This patient a lad of twenty-one, has been very ill, but by Christmas he was much better and able to enjoy the sight of a homelike Christmas tree especially bought for him. The flowers from the chapel were also presented to him, much to his delight.

On Christmas Eve, I had hoped to go to Bethlehem to the Carol service there, but much to my disappointment I had had a bad cold and temperature, so as it was a very cold night I had to give up the thought of it. I went to bed early instead, and felt much better on Christmas Day when I went to our own service at 7 a.m. for the patients It was a very nice service, and well attended. During the morning we were able to hear a service broadcast from St George's Cathedral, as we were too busy to go there to church. It sounded very nice and the patients enjoyed the singing of carols. I was able to hear the carols broadcast from Bethlehem on Christmas Eve, although I was unable to go, and I hoped you had been able to listen in also.

After the patients' dinner on Christmas Day, I had two hours off duty, so, with another Sister I took a convalescent patient to Bethlehem. He had been wounded in Egypt and is now walking about on crutches. We had a very pleasant drive to Bethlehem, it was a beautiful day, and the country round here is always fresh and verdant looking at this time of the year. There were many pilgrims visiting Bethlehem, among them were hundreds of soldiers. We went into the Church of the Nativity. What were you doing at midday on Christmas Day? At that time, 3 p.m. here, I was down in the very place of which everyone is thinking at Christmas, the stable where Christ was born. I thought of you at that time, as I went down the narrow, winding steps and thought how little I realised that I should be able to go to such a place, on such a day!

Our patient was very thrilled to think that he had been able to see Bethlehem, as he will probably never have such an opportunity again, after returning to his unit.

As we came out of the church, which, as I told you before, is the oldest in the Christian world, the Bells of Bethlehem suddenly pealed forth! You may have heard them 'on the air' – if not, I hope you will one day. They are simply beautiful, and words cannot describe the sound of them, as you hear them, standing in the streets of Bethlehem.

On our return journey – which by the way is only four miles, we had a splendid view over the hills to the Dead Sea, while nearer, we could see a plain on which it is believed the 'shepherds abided, keeping watch over their flocks by night'.

You may have listened in to a short broadcast on Christmas afternoon at about 4 p.m. (1 p.m. for you). It was an Empire broadcast by men of all colonies and allied countries out here. The English soldier who spoke and wished everyone a happy Christmas, is a friend of mine, as he is in our unit. We were so pleased to hear that he had broadcast. When we returned to the hospital the gifts from the Christmas tree were distributed and tea and Christmas cake served. There was a happy atmosphere and plenty of noise, of course. Some of the convalescents even had a game of football with a large grapefruit in the corridor!

Altogether it was a happy time for all, but we thought a lot about you all at home, and everyone kept saying 'I wonder what they are doing in Blighty' or 'I hope they are having some sort of Christmas at home' etc etc. On New Year's Eve I went to a Watch Night service in the Scottish Church of St Andrew, here. It was such a nice service, and very well attended, by the troops especially. As midnight struck, bells sounded all over the city, and as we came out of church, we all helped to pull the bell-rope in the porch, and so ring in the year. For you, it was still then 1940. It did seem strange to think of that. What a year it has been! We have heard many rumours of a big Christmas mail coming, but so far, very little has materialised. We are having bitterly cold weather here. It is as cold now as it has been hot. It has rained a good deal, but the rains have not really begun in earnest yet. I have a new raincoat – a very good one, as well as being warm to wear, so it will keep me dry. I do hope you will have a milder winter this time, and not get bad colds etc. I dread the thought of those I flu epidemics which England has, as they will be dreadful, combined with air raids. Never mind, perhaps the flu will not be so widespread as we imagine and let us hope the air raids will decrease.

I hope you are all keeping well and not finding the food shortage too bad. I am enclosing three stamps which you may not already have. Please give my love to all. I will write again soon. God bless you all and take care of you.

Your loving
Vera

☙

Dear Mother and Father

Thank you so much for the nice parcel which arrived safely two days ago. I am so pleased with the silk undies, also the very acceptable handkerchiefs with my name embroidered on them and the chocolates are very nice, too. The parcel was in very good condition and had been almost three months coming. It is such a pleasure to receive a letter, so you can imagine the excitement a parcel causes. We all see the contents of each other's parcels, for they have come so far, and the presents have been bought in England! My mail seems to arrive all at once. Yesterday I received, as well as Muriel's letter, a letter from Rose Tredgett, and one from Mrs Murchison. They were all very interesting and all so cheerful. What a wonderful spirit is prevalent in England! Mrs M seems very well and full of energy as usual. All her family are well. She sent me a very nice leather writing case for a Christmas present. It is over a year ago that I went in to visit her, all unsuspecting, and found you both waiting there to see me. What a pleasure that was! One day I will walk in and give you a surprise instead! I believe St Philip's, Plaistow, has been partly destroyed, at any rate, it is quite unsafe. KGH has had several narrow escapes. I am very pleased to hear that Sister Beet has written to you. I thought she would, and I know she would go and see you if possible. She is quite old, and worked out here and in France all through the last war. This time she was called up and came to Palestine with us, but her health was not good and she seemed tired out, so was sent home on compassionate grounds. We all liked her so much, and were very sorry to lose her. She went from here on the *Empress of Britain*, but very fortunately, she was transferred to another boat at a South African port. Otherwise, she would have been on the *Empress of Britain* when she was sunk. For some time we thought she had been lost during the disaster, and it was not until weeks later that we heard she was safe in England. I spoke about it to you in a letter, at that time. What do you think about our success in the Western Desert? We are all as thrilled as if we ourselves had driven the Italians back, and captured all their important bases! It reminds one of the days when the Germans were pushing across France with such rapidity. We are moving just as fast now. Yesterday Bardia fell, and we moved on across the desert to Tobruk. Our patients follow the news closely. Nearly all of them are war casualties from this present offensive. They have great stories to tell, of course. I could not repeat them in a letter, as they concern the various regiments, names I must not mention. We have been much busier lately, owing to convoys arriving. I am sending you a magazine which is published weekly for the members of HM Forces out here. It is the Christmas number, and has some pictures of Bethlehem in it.

I am afraid there is not much news to tell you now. I will write again in a week's time. I do hope you are all well and not having quite so many air raids. We are always relieved to hear 'bad weather and poor visibility kept Nazi planes away from Britain last night,' as is not infrequently reported on the wireless. If only they would leave you alone altogether!

Well, cheerio for now. God bless you all and keep you safe. My love to you both and all.

Your loving
Vera

တ

17.1.41

My Dear Mother and Father

Thank you very much for the cable received recently. I sent one to you on the 8th January, so you probably received it at the same time as yours arrived. On the 9th, I received a very nice letter from Father which was most welcome, and so cheery. I was very glad to hear that you are, (or were then,) having quieter days and nights and managing to sleep more. I hope this is still so. The news certainly seems more reassuring by the papers and wireless. Thank you very much for paying my State Registration fee, the receipt for which, you sent me. It was due on the 31st December, and if not paid, my name would have been removed from the Register! It would have needed explanations and excuses to get it put back again, so I am very glad you saved me the trouble.

I was glad to hear that you do take some rest from your good work, and sit down to relax for as long as possible each day. Now listen to me! You are both under orders from me, compelling you to rest with your two pairs of feet up, for two hours each day! As long as Adolf leaves you unmolested you are to obey this order. Of course, if the siren goes during this resting period, I know you will have to take shelter, but otherwise you are to relax. I was very pleased to hear about you both sitting down and listening to the music on the wireless, but that must not be a rare event. You do so much for other people and use up so much energy, that you will wear yourselves out if you do not settle down for a 'nap' or a quiet read at some time during the day. Now don't take advantage of my absence! You know what I would do if I was with you, and I would be quite strong enough to tie you both down on sofas!

I am sending you a copy of our weekly picture paper for the Middle East, each week, as soon as I have read it. You will find it very interesting as it concerns this part of the world chiefly. I hope you will receive all the copies safely.

I was looking at a copy of the *Nursing Times* (November number), a few days ago, and to my dismay I saw a picture of the children's Ward at King George Hospital, with a bomb crater in front of it! There were several people looking through the ward windows, among them being Sister Brunt and several nurses whom I knew. It stated in the *Nursing Times*, that the children were all safe, but had narrow escapes. I also had a letter from Mary Insley, who trained with me, and she told me that the hospital has been hit several times, without causing much damage. I am afraid I felt most depressed at that news, but realised how much more seriously other hospitals have suffered!

Last night I met an officer from New Zealand, whose home is in Gisborne. We had a very interesting conversation. The Cook Hospital in Gisborne has been much enlarged and Gisborne has grown a lot. I heard also that Napier is a fine city now, and a great improvement on the old city. The marine parade is the finest in New Zealand, and the port is quite new and up to date. Westshore, which was such a fine bathing place, is quite dry and the land is being reclaimed for farming!

Well, I am afraid this is not going to be a long letter, but there is not much happening that I can tell you.

I hope you are all well, and taking care of yourselves. I am writing to Muriel. Please give her, Geoff and everyone, my love.

God bless you all, and take care of you.

Very best love from your loving

Vera

ᔌ

28.1.41

Dear Mother and Father

I have not received a letter from you recently, but am not worried, as I know they are often delayed. My last letter to you was posted on the 18th.

I am afraid there is not much news to tell you this time, as life is uneventful just now. This is my day off for the month. (How I wish I could hop onto an Eastern National bus and come home!) I am sitting in my room just now, and keeping warm by a nice oil stove. Outside the wind has risen to a gale, and it is combined with a sandstorm. The hills surrounding us are obliterated, and even the great dome of the Mosque of Omar can only just be seen from my window, although it is only a short distance away.

A week or so ago, we were aroused from our sleep at 1 a.m., by the 'Banshee wailing' that you know so well. I thought it was part of my dream at first, but when I realised it was reality, I had some idea of what you are all standing up to at home. The 'visiting cards' were dropped some distance away in open country. The same thing happened a few nights ago at 9.30 p.m. but this time the visitors left no traces behind them. These are the first 'alerts' we have had for several months.

I am sure you are all feeling pleased about our successes in the Middle East. We are so thrilled to know that we are advancing on all Fronts, and especially that we have taken so much of Libya. We are still kept busy with our sick and wounded, although the convoys are not large. All the men are in high spirits, with excellent morale. One man gave me a brass ashtray, which had been presented to him by an

Italian officer who was most friendly towards him, and who said that he, like all other soldiers he knew, was not interested in the war, and only had to fight because Mussolini wished it. Many of our men have had the same experiences when meeting Italian prisoners.

I have left the operating theatre for a time as I have finished my course of three months, and am now back on a busy surgical ward of fifty beds. The orderlies in the theatre were a merry crowd, always full of fun, and I was sorry when I stopped working with them. A few days after I was moved, I received an amusing document, which I am enclosing for you to see. It is full of nonsense of course, but just typical of their cheery outlook on life. (I have erased the name of a certain city as a precaution.)

I do hope you are all keeping well, and having a quieter time now. In the newspaper today, we see that London has not had any raids for a week! If only it would last.

If you should have any more photos of yourselves, do send them to me, as I cannot have too many you know. I have you all smiling at me in my room, including Peter.

I have just finished seven years' nursing! What a long time it seems since I went to Brighton. We are now having our inoculations of TAB (anti-typhoid vaccine). The first injections we had at Tidworth, you remember. We have to have it each year, that is every twelve months. The effect is not quite so severe the second time fortunately, but we are allowed to take a day off after it to get over the headache and shivering etc, which follows the injection. I have not yet had mine. The cases of typhoid which we have had here, have nearly all been mild with quick recovery, due to the vaccine they had had, so the injections are well worth having.

How is the canteen going? I often think of you serving out sandwiches and hot drinks to the men. I know just how much they are appreciating it!

Well, my dears, I must stop now. Please forgive this short letter, but I have not very much to write about. I know you do not mind as long as a letter comes.

My love to all at home, especially both of you. Will write again soon.

Your loving
Vera

My Dear Mother and Father

It is a long time since I heard from you, but a week ago I received your cable telling me that you also had not had a letter from me for some time and were worried. I sent a cable back the same day to reassure you. Don't worry about me ever, I am very well and not in any danger, as you are. I write every week, without fail so you should receive the letters in time. It gives me such joy to hear from you, but the letters do seem to take such a long time to come! I know you write regularly also.

I am hoping to go on holiday again for two weeks on the 1st March. By the time you receive this, I shall probably be back here again! I am going to Cairo this time, and of course I am very excited at the prospect. Fancy seeing the pyramids and sphinx! We go by train, and travel down in the daytime, and return at night time. The train journey takes about twelve hours and I believe is very tedious and dusty, but I expect quite interesting. I shall pass very near to places we saw when coming through the Suez Canal from New Zealand.

I will write to you very often while I am in Cairo, and tell you about the places I am seeing. The letters do not take so long to reach you from there we are told. I am going to stay in a very nice pension where several of our staff have spent their holidays. It is in the best part of the city, close to the Nile, with lovely walks and gardens nearby, and within a few minutes tram-ride of the centre of the city. Cairo is said to have the best tram service in the world, so I am wondering what the trams will be like. It should certainly be a very pleasant change, and very interesting, especially as people travel from all parts of the world to see Cairo. What wonderful places I am seeing since I came out here. How I wish you were all here with me!

I have recently met an old friend who was at KGH with me. She has come out with her unit, and is stationed somewhere near Cairo. You do not know her. She did not train with me, she is a good deal older, and used to come to Ilford whenever there was a Sister needed for relief work during holidays. She is very nice and knows all my friends at KGH of course. She came up here on 'leave', thrilled at being able to see the Holy City and could hardly believe it when she met me here. We have had long talks and when she goes back to her hospital, I am going to see her when on 'leave'.

I have told you before about Ain Karim, the village where St John the Baptist was born. I went there again a few days ago with some friends, and it was so beautiful now that the hills are greener, and fruit trees are covered with blossoms, and wild flowers grow everywhere. We climbed a hill and sat on some stones to admire the scenery. It was one of those cool sunny days which we have between days of tropical downpours of rain, and the very day for such a visit to Ain Karim. As we came down the hill we picked flowers, anemones, lilies-of-the-field, and cyclamen, which grow everywhere in this country.

Today I went for a walk up the Mount of Olives. At this time of the year the grass is so green and fresh, that one would never believe that in a few months the Mount of Olives will be brown and dry again. It was a very pleasant walk, and when we reached the top we had a perfect view of the Jordan Valley and the Dead Sea beyond us. It was just like a painting, almost too amazing to be real. The Dead Sea is so blue and shining, and the Mountains of Moab on the other side are quite a purple colour. Unless you see such views, it is hard to imagine such contrasts of colour.

We are still kept busy here. What do you all think about our advances on Libya? Our men are so excited and the patients we have in from the desert have great stories to tell, and they are full of good humour and confidence. We have a great collection of races in my ward, Britons, Australians, New Zealanders, Czechs, Poles, Turks, Greeks, Frenchmen, Arabs, Jews and Egyptians! I wish I was a linguist. We have fun trying to make the men understand us. Sometimes an Egyptian will be able to tell a Frenchman what a Sister is saying, but then when you ask him to translate his answer into English, he does not know enough English to tell you it. The Turks may be able to converse with the Arabs, but only the Greeks can talk to the Greeks. I have never heard such a strange medley of languages. It is all very interesting. I know enough Arabic now to make myself understood to some of my foreign patients.

Well, it is eleven o'clock, and I must be off to bed. I wonder if you are sleeping better now and not being disturbed so often. I do hope so. The news is certainly not so startling concerning raids. You will be pleased to hear that our chapel is still being well attended and we have very nice services every week.

My love to all. God bless you both.

Your loving

Vera

ꝏ

17.2.41

My Dear Muriel

I am writing this letter while sitting near the window in my room. The sun is pouring in and it is a glorious afternoon. We have had some beautiful weather lately, although it is winter. The nights are very cold, but on most days the sky is blue and the birds are singing as though it were mid-summer. We have not had nearly enough rain, (for this country) and people are getting quite anxious about the ground being so dry. However, there has been enough rain to make the grass green at last, and the Mount of Olives, so near to us, is a joy to look upon. It seems as if the Almighty has granted specially green grass to the Mount of Olives as a recompense for the long dry months when not a green blade can be found upon its slopes! I have been for several walks up there recently and I still say to myself, 'Can it be true that I am really here?' Many people have become used to Jerusalem, and do not feel the same thrill about being here, but to me it will always be a source of wonder!

In my last letter home I told Mother and Father that I am shortly going on 'leave' to Cairo for two weeks. That will be wonderful and an opportunity to see a place which I never thought I should have a chance to visit. I do wish you were going with me, we could have such fun. What a long time it seems since we all went to Torquay together – like another life. I wonder how long it will be before life is like that again. I seem to have lived in this country for years. I am very glad Father did not go abroad with evacuee children as he contemplated. You remember that I wrote some time ago when I first heard about the idea, and I said that I did hope he would change his mind. I had a very strong feeling that something would happen to the ship, as it did. In fact the presentiment was so strong that I nearly cabled you, but decided that you might think it silly of me. You can imagine my feelings when the *City of Benares* was sunk. Not long afterwards your letter came to say that Father had decided not to go after all. It is strange how these things work out!

How is Peter these days? Is he still as energetic as ever, or is his old age creeping on? I often think about the walks we used to take him for, and how he loved them. I have a brown and white china dog, so like Peter, and he sits on my table in my room. He has one ear cocked up, and the other down, and he has a white streak running crookedly between his eyes, believe it or not his eyes look quite soulful although they are china, and he has a very small tail curled round his little china bottom. I first saw him sitting in a shop and could not resist buying him for 22 piastres (4/6d). To me he represents Peter, and is the next best thing to having the real one here with me. I almost expect him to come jumping off the table when I enter the room, to cover me with wet kisses!

I have been doing theatre work for about five months, and am now back on a ward again. I am on call for the theatre cases every other night, however, and sleep in a room which has an extension to the telephone so that I can be called up when necessary. I have only been on call a few nights so far, but have been out twice, once at 10 p.m. for an appendix op., returning to bed at midnight. The second time for an emergency op. on a bad gunshot wound which happened to the man in Jericho. He came into hospital at 10 p.m. and I was just stepping into bed at 11 p.m. when ting-a-ling went the phone and I said to myself 'no bed for you my child just yet.' I dressed and was called for by an ambulance and taken back to the hospital. We started the operation at midnight and finished at 2.15 a.m. I left the theatre at 2.55 a.m. arriving back just after 3 a.m. I do not mind being on call as it is interesting and good experience. We are given time to make up our lost sleep.

I hear you have had a short holiday and spent some of it at Westcliff. I expect it has changed a good deal. I wish you could all have some of the peace and sunshine out here. It would do you so much good.

I have a friend here, who is an Australian trained nurse. She was in London when war was declared and joined up. She went to France and then soon after the Dunkirk evacuation was sent out here. We have a lot in common and get on very well together. Some time ago she nursed a very nice sergeant who was very ill and they have since fallen in love and are being married on 3rd March. I am to be her bridesmaid but will be in uniform of course. They are going to live in Jerusalem but he may have to return to the Front in which case she will take up nursing again but not in the army as it is not allowed after marriage. They are a very nice pair and I shall miss my friend very much when she leaves but hope to see her quite often.

I hear from Iris Ridler that Sister Wood, my friend at KGH, has gone to India, as an army Sister. She is even further a field than I am now. KGH has had quite a nasty knocking about, a bomb fell between Dagenham and Barking wards, and one in front of the children's ward, I have heard. Sister Brunt had a narrow escape, and Matron was away at the time, or she might have been killed, as she had been sharing a small ward as a bedroom with Sister Brunt, and this room was wrecked and Sister Brunt flung out of bed by the impact. They are not using the top half of the Nurses' Home, only the ground floor, and the nurses are sleeping on their respective wards, in the Sisters' sitting rooms there, so as to be on call for emergencies. Poor things! They must have very little rest. What changes have taken place at KGH. We never dreamed in peacetime that the well-ordered routine of the daily work there, could change so dramatically.

I hope Mother and Father are both resting whenever possible and not overworking. I know you will be firm with them and keep up the good work of making them relax. I am sure they are both giving out too much energy to their many good works. And you too, don't you go overdoing it!

I hope you are not having so many raids now. Our news out here seems to indicate that the bombers are not working so hard as in the past. I hope this is true. I am so glad to know that you have no real food shortage, as we have sometimes heard rumours to the contrary.

Well, I am afraid I must stop now. I will write more often in future. Hope you are keeping well. My love to all.

Cheerio for now, and much love from

Vera

P.S. Have just finished reading *Gone with the Wind*. Have never read it before. Thought it a marvellous book.

ട

23.2.41

My Dear Mother and Father

I have recently received three nice letters from you – one from Mother written on the 13th December, accompanied by a most welcome and amusing letter from Geoffrey, and another letter from Mother received a few days later, and written on the 18th December. Your letters all take over two months by airmail now! What a life! We never thought in peacetime that such a thing could be possible. How I love your letters – they give me the greatest happiness of all out here and it would be dreadful not to have them. Even though they seem to go all round the world before reaching me, I often feel as if I have just had a talk to you after reading them, and the news does not seem old to me. The letter written on the 13th December arrived on the 13th February and the one written on the 18th arrived on the 20th February.

I am so glad to hear that you have received the Bible safely, and like it so much. That news gave me much pleasure. I hope Father has received his parcel also, and that you (Mother) have received the second parcel sent on a later date. I am glad Geoffrey has his cheque.

You asked about the food we have here. It is very good and we have nice meals, well served, and good time to have them in. (Bad grammar.) There is plenty of food here, we do not have to go short of anything. As for the climate, it suits me very well. I hardy ever have a cold or cough, as I used to in England, and I am sure I am looking very well indeed, and have plenty of energy.

I often feel that I have shirked something when I read in your letters of all the dangerous days and nights you are having. I certainly never expected to leave the bombs and sirens for you to put up with. It is really a foolish idea to have, but I often wonder why I have escaped it all, and whether I shall ever see any of the war at all. That is the general feeling of all the Sisters here, and the troops used to feel the same about it, until the fighting in the desert commenced.

I met an Australian soldier here who had visited your part of Essex while doing service in England. Fancy an 'Aussie' going there and I have left it to come out here. He gave me some news about the town, details of raids etc which you could not say in your letters!

I am so glad to hear more news of your soldiers' canteen and the good work you are doing. It is amazing how you feel that anything you do for the soldiers is so worthwhile. I know just how much they are appreciating you, and I don't wonder they feel the urge to go to church. They do so hate to be forced to attend services, but when it is done by their own free will, how spontaneously they take part! While in hospital here they are given the choice of whether they attend church or not, and it is part of my work to go round and ask each one individually whether he wishes to attend. Many of them are surprised that they are allowed any choice in the matter, and I believe they are encouraged to go because it is voluntary. What a different atmosphere it makes when you know that the men are there because they wish to be, and not because the army wishes it! I think the custom of compulsory church parade definitely wrong, and the men often tell me how rebellious it makes them feel when they are marched to church whether they wish it or not. The padre here agrees with me, and the men like him all the better for it. He is a great worker for the troops and not only takes their services and preaches well, but also takes them to visit the Old City, and has them to tea with him, a few at a time, when they are convalescent.

Our chapel is still as nice as ever, and we have really lovely services there. Every week we have a Holy Communion service (7 a.m.) and an evening service at 5 p.m. I am adding to the chapel furnishings and love to keep the linen freshly ironed, and also find pleasure in arranging the flowers. You would like our services, they are so homely and sincere, like those you have at home, and that is what the men appreciate.

24.2.41

I have just received a very nice long letter from Muriel. Thank her very much, please. I am so glad Father's present has arrived and that he likes it so much. How terrible to think that St Thomas' Hospital is in such a state. We have several St Thomas' Hospital nurses here, and they are very sad about it. I was sorry to hear about the other damage to places, including Muriel's old office. So glad she has left it. I am sending Muriel a book called *Haworth Parsonage* as she mentions that she has not read it.

I was invited to a concert at the Palestine Broadcasting Company a few days ago, and it was very good as well as being an interesting experience. We have a nice broadcasting house here, and some good programmes. We were told that when a red light showed in the hall we must not talk or scrape our chairs on the floor etc, but must not be afraid to cough or breathe! There was a huge microphone in the middle of the hall and the artistes stood near it to sing or talk. It was a military concert and all the members of the band and other performers were soldiers. There was one person who was a civilian, and he was a Jewish pianist who played most beautifully. I have never heard Mendelssohn's Spring Song played as he played it. I could not describe how it sounded!

I am sending a parcel for Muriel and Father for their birthdays, but it will be late in arriving I am afraid.

I hope to leave here for Cairo on the 4th March and return on the 17th. I am so looking forward to going. I will write often from there as I shall have plenty of time and much to write about.

We are suffering from a severe shortage of heavy rain just now. There have not been the torrential downpours of rain lasting for days as Palestine has had in past years. The crops are suffering badly and we are expecting an even hotter summer than the last one.

Well, my dears I must stop now. I do hope you are all well and happy and sleeping better. DON'T FORGET TO REST.

God bless you always.

Best love from your loving

Vera

ဖာ

13.3.41

My Dear Mother and Father

I have not received a letter from you recently, but as I am now away on leave, I expect there may be one waiting for me when I return. I sent you a cable a few days ago, which I hope you will receive safely.

I am staying in Cairo for ten days, and having a really restful and interesting time. I left Jerusalem with two other Sisters on the 6th March, and we came by train, which took us over fifteen hours. It was a dusty and hot journey, mostly across the Sinai desert. Some parts of it were very interesting, however. We went for miles along by the Mediterranean. I saw the Suez Canal for the second time in my life when we crossed over it by ferry, and then changed to another train on the Egyptian side.

We reached Cairo at 1 a.m. and were glad to go to bed. My two friends went to a hotel right in the centre of the city, but I had been advised to go to a smaller place, a pension in a quieter district. I am very glad I came here, as it is much nicer than the hotels, quieter, cheaper, and more homely. It is the very place you would appreciate. There are only about ten people here, mostly officers and their wives. The rooms are very comfortable, mine is high up at the top of the building and there is a lovely view over the city to the Nile.

I was surprised at the size of Cairo, especially after Jerusalem which is quite small in comparison. It reminds me very much of London, as there are wide streets, huge buildings, and really fine shops. The trams are excellent and one can travel for miles very cheaply.

There are some very nice residential districts. The part where I am staying is quite like Regents Park, and there are parks and tree-lined streets all round here. We are close to the Nile, and I have had some pleasant walks on the banks of the river where there are lovely gardens.

Although I am not with any other Sister here, I have not been at all lonely. In fact, I have enjoyed the change, in being away from so many uniforms. I have enjoyed wandering round the shops, and seeing all the wonderful curios of Egypt displayed there. I have a friend whom I knew at Ilford (I have mentioned her in a previous letter I believe), and she is working here, so I am able to see her.

I have also had a great surprise since I came here. One day I received a phone call, and could not imagine who it would be, but when I answered it, who should be speaking to me, but Nurse Insley who was at KGH with me! You know her, or have heard me speak of her. She is in the army, and has recently arrived from home for service in the Middle East. I was simply dumbfounded and of course most excited, for I had no idea she had left England. We met as soon as possible and had so much to say to each other. Since then we have been out seeing the sights together and have had some very happy times. You can imagine my pleasure also at hearing that Sister Wood was also here. You know her of course, I worked with her for so long and we were such good friends. We have also met, and of course talked for hours! It is so good to meet old friends after such a long time, and I feel quite an 'old-timer' out here, now that so many new people have arrived.

Sister Wood thinks I have not altered at all since she last saw me, and she says I look healthier, which you will be pleased to know.

The weather is glorious here now, and I think I have come at the best time of the year.

I have seen the pyramids and sphinx and we rode round them on camels. I went with a party of Sisters who were staying in Cairo. The pyramids are incredibly large, it is like gazing up the face of a mountain when you stand at the foot of one of them. I did not know that the outer surface of a pyramid was not smooth but could be climbed. Dozens of soldiers were climbing up the side of the great pyramid, the largest one of all, and they looked just like ants going up an anthill. The view from the top is said to be wonderful, but we did not climb up to see. It looked a dizzy kind of expedition.

It was very interesting seeing the sphinx, and the expression on her face, which is described as 'inscrutable'. It was a wonderful piece of work by the ancient Egyptians, for the whole thing is solid stone.

A few days ago, I went with another party – three other Sisters, to Sakkara, about twenty miles from here. This is the oldest part of Egypt, where the most ancient pyramids stand, and where all the priceless jewels and coins etc, were discovered. We rode donkeys this time and found that we had to ride a short distance into the desert. We saw the strangest and most wonderful things, carvings of the ancient Egyptians at their work, statues of kings which were 4,000–5,000 years old, and vast temples with pillars of alabaster. We were even shown several mummies! Most of them, however, have been taken to the Museum. There was one complete village which has been unearthed. We also visited Memphis, believed to be the oldest city discovered, and here we saw a gigantic reclining statue of King Nemesis II, the ruler of Egypt at that time, probably 2,000 years BC!

We have been able to see something of the countryside of Egypt while down here, and I do not think it is nearly as pleasant as Palestine. It is very flat and dry, although some parts, such as the Nile Valley, are quite fertile. Still, I will appreciate the hills again when I go back.

There is a beautiful cathedral here, All Saints. It is of modern architecture, and has a great tower which is quite one of the sights of Cairo. I went to church there twice on Sundays, and it was a pleasure to see a church so well filled, especially with members of the Services.

I really have had a very nice time here, and it has been a complete change from the military atmosphere. I go back in two days' time. I have been so fortunate in being able to see such famous places since I came out here. I often wonder why I should have all these opportunities when there is a war on, and we joined up, expecting only to face bombings and constant hard work. It is the same old question over again, a thing we are always discussing among ourselves, why you at home are having to stand in the Front line, and we are nearly always sitting on the fence!

I am sending a parcel for Father's and Muriel's birthdays but it will be late in arriving I am afraid.

I do hope you are all well, and not having too many raids. The news in the papers of England being bombed, especially the South East coast, gives me a good deal of anxiety, but I feel sure you will take care, and be taken care of.

My love to all, God bless you always.

Best love to you both

Vera

༄

On a visit to Cairo

༄

My Dear Mother and Father

I have just received a cable from you saying that you are all well, and have not been receiving my letters recently. I was so glad to hear that you were well, but most sorry that my letters are still being delayed. It is a great shame because I write by airmail every week and you should receive most of the letters. If ever you are worried, you can enquire about me at the War Office. Several of the Sisters have heard from there that their parents have enquired, after not having received letters for some time. Do not worry though, I will send you cables more often, to fill in the gaps between the letters.

I sent a cable on the 7th March, while in Cairo, and hope you have received it by now.

Well, I am now back from my 'leave' and at work again. I did so enjoy my stay in Cairo, it was quite an education in itself, seeing the life in Egypt after Palestine. I saw every place of interest, and have described them all in a previous letter (stamped about six times with the head of King Farouk!). Cairo is so much bigger and dirtier than Jerusalem. On one day we had an awful sandstorm which was like a pea-soup fog, and nearly choked and blinded us. That is a thing we never have in Jerusalem, as the city is too high up in the hills.

I was glad to return to Palestine really, as it is so much more beautiful and cleaner. It was good to see the green fields and hills again after the complete flatness of Egypt. We have recently had a severe drought, when it should have been raining, and people were anxious about the dry cracking ground and the spoiling of the crops, so one day was set apart for prayers for rain, and Moslems, Christians and Jews, each in their own way, joined in intercessions for the long delayed rains. In two days we were being drenched through with really tropical downpours, and the rain continued for nearly a fortnight! One could almost see the new grass coming up, flowers appeared and the trees lost their dusty appearance. Now there is great thanksgiving everywhere.

I am now on night duty and have charge of two medical wards, each with thirty-six beds. We are kept quite busy with dysentery now, and the malaria season will start soon. It is very cold at night, I am sitting down by an oil stove and am wearing my overcoat. It is 2.30 a.m. I have just been wondering what you are doing now, 11.30 p.m. in England. Are you safe in bed, or are you taking shelter from night-raiders? The news has given us great anxiety lately, especially news of the heavy fire raid on London and district a few nights ago. It is so good to have cables from you saying you are well. I do hope you are sleeping better, or is it silly even to suggest it, you may be spending night after night in the shelter unable to sleep. If only I knew just how you all are, and how much you are going through!

Well, I am afraid there is little news just now, so please forgive this short letter.

Give my love to all.

God bless you always and take care of you.

Ever your loving

Vera

ؚ

2.4.41

My Dear Mother and Father

I have recently received Muriel's letter of 19th January, which I told you had arrived, in my last letter. I have not heard from you since except for a cable, which I answered.

There is not much news just now I am afraid. I am still on night duty, so do not go out so much, and therefore life is rather uneventful.

I have several boys from our own county regiment, as patients here, but none of them is actually from Maldon, although they all know it well. It would be so nice to meet one who lives near us, and I expect I will one day.

I am reading a good book called *Bewildering Cares* by Winifred Peek. It was published last year, and is all about the life of a clergyman's wife. It is true to life, too, and I am sure it would interest you both very much.

Do you have much free time these days, or are you going hard at it all day? Do obey my orders, and rest as much as possible!

I am so glad to hear that Geoffrey has such a good job now. I hope he is liking it and has settled down well. Muriel says he has a motorbike now. I hope he will be careful on it and not 'speed' too much.

I am so sorry this is such a scanty kind of letter. There is just nothing to tell you. I feel I must keep up my regular correspondence, however, so that you do not have to wait too long for my letters. After all, as long as a letter arrives to let you know that all is well with me, that is the most important thing, I think, and I am sure you agree.

Are you having a quieter time now, or are the bombers still giving you anxiety? We really hear so little news here, at least, concerning raids on England, we only hear which region (such as South West or South East England) has been attacked, and hardly ever know which towns have suffered most.

I hope I shall write a more interesting letter next week, but I have no more to write about just now.

Much love to all, and especially both of you.

God bless you always, and keep you safe.

Ever you loving

Vera

∽

8.4.41

My Dear Mother and Father

I am writing, as you see, on our new, cheap-rate, airmail letter-card. Postage rate is only the equivalent to 3d! It is a fine idea, and much appreciated by the troops. I hope you receive this safely.

I have not heard from you for a long time, and my last letter was from Muriel. We are told that the mails sent on certain dates have been lost through enemy action, so I am afraid some of our letters to each other have been lost on the way. Do not worry if you are not hearing from me so often. I will send cables more frequently, and some, or most of my letters will arrive in time, even though they may be taking longer to arrive. I always write every week.

I sent a cable a few days ago to wish you a happy Easter, also birthday greetings for the 15th and 22nd April.

This is Holy Week. I am wondering what you are doing, and what you think about me being here at such a time! On Palm Sunday all the churches were filled with the most beautiful green palm branches. St George's Cathedral was especially impressive and I went to a lovely service there in the morning. Many people attended pilgrimages to Bethany and the Mount of Olives, but being on night duty I had to be in bed at that time – 3 p.m., so was unable to go. It was such a lovely day, and I could well imagine that joyful day almost 2,000 years ago, when palms were laid in the streets of Jerusalem and the people cried, 'Hosanna in the Highest'!

I could not help noticing the donkeys, heavily laden as usual, toiling up the hillsides, and I thought that on one day, at least, in the Holy Land, a donkey was honourably treated, and carried the Messiah through the Golden Gates, treading upon palms!

It will be wonderful spending Easter in the Holy City. Being on night duty, I shall be able to go out during the day, as this is such a special occasion and rules are relaxed. On Maundy Thursday I hope to go to the Garden of Gethsemane to a service at 6 p.m. That should be beautiful.

The war is spreading further afield than ever, now that Yugoslavia has been drawn into the conflict. Are you still having an anxious time – being bombed often? I only hope the latest Balkan developments will postpone or prevent the invasion of Britain. That is what we, out here, dread more than anything else, and it is a relief to us that an offensive has begun on another Front.

Well, I have nearly finished this page, so must stop I'm afraid.

My best love to all, especially both of you. Don't worry and keep smiling as I'm sure you do!

God bless you always.

Your loving

Vera

13.4.41
(Easter Day)

My Dear Mother and Father

I have just received your very nice and welcome letter dated 10th February, so it has taken just over two months to come by air. This airmail service is only for part of the way and the letters travel some distance by sea, so it is not surprising that some are lost.

We are quite used to hearing of the terrible raids on the larger towns in England now. Coventry, Birmingham and Bristol etc, have suffered very much lately we fear. At first the news of such destruction caused great anxiety and sorrow here, but now we seem to accept it with more calmness, but no less sorrow. I think one can get used to so much, in time. I feel so sorry for the soldiers who have moved about a good deal, and consequently have not received their letters for months. They are so worried about their people at home.

I have had a wonderful Easter here. It is my first in the Holy City, as the last was spent in Sarafand. On Maundy Thursday, I visited the Garden of Gethsemane, which as you know, we can see from our Mess. There was a service there at 6 p.m. attended by a very large and cosmopolitan congregation. It was held in the Church of All Nations and many nations were certainly represented at that service. As I sat in that church with its exquisite mosaic roof and wonderful life-size paintings of the Betrayal and the scenes in the Garden of Gethsemane, I had to keep telling myself that I was really there, in that very place where Christ Himself had prayed so long ago! Could I ever have dreamed a few years ago, that I should be there on such a day, and that it would be a war which would send me to the Holy City?

On Good Friday morning I went to the Via Dolorosa, to all the Stations of the Cross, in a large pilgrimage of Sisters and other members of HM Forces. It was so impressive, and such an experience as I will never forget. I cannot tell you how I felt, as we walked up and up the winding stone-flagged street, following that same Way of Sorrows which led to Calvary on the first Good Friday! How well we can now understand the burden of the Cross, carried in the midday heat, up that long stony road, and how easy it is to see Christ falling again and again from exhaustion!

Later I went on to St George's Cathedral to part of the three-hour service, and then to bed, for I am still on night duty.

On Easter Sunday, we had very nice services here in our chapel for the patients. The first was at 6.30 a.m., after which I went on to St George's to a service at 8 a.m., which was very well attended. The church was so beautifully decorated with white flowers – lilies and daisies and ferns. At 10 a.m., I went again to the service which was broadcast, and it was so well attended that there was not an empty seat anywhere. The Bishop preached a fine sermon. Never have the Easter hymns sounded so beautiful, after such a Good Friday, of such realism!

I thought of you often during Easter, wondering what you were doing and whether Easter was being celebrated in anything like the usual way. I am sure it cannot have been nearly the same, for we heard that people carried on with the work, especially in factories, but the churches were well attended – so the significance of Easter was not forgotten. We know that you are short of certain foods and the shortage has become more acute lately. That has added to our anxiety about you all at home.

What do you think of the latest turn of the war? Life is certainly becoming much more active for us now, and we are much busier. I have four wards in my charge on night duty, two medical, one surgical and one for nerve cases. I have plenty to do, and fortunately am sleeping well during the day. How often during the night I think of you leaving your beds for the shelter, at the sound of the siren.

Well, I do not think there is much more to tell you just now. Don't ever worry about me. I am very well and looking fine.

God bless you all and keep you safe.

My love to all, especially both of you.

Your loving

Vera

28.5.41

My Dear Mother and Father

I have recently received a nice long letter from Muriel written on 14th March, and one from Father written on 27th March. Both took over two months to come. I am using these airmail letter-cards and airgraph letters as we hear they do not take nearly so long to reach you.

I am very well and have not much news to tell you. We are having very hot weather, with plenty of flies and mosquitoes. I am working very hard, as I am now on the tropical diseases ward, where we have all cases of dysentery, malaria and sandfly fever, as well as other types of tropical fevers. This being the season for such diseases, we are kept very busy. I find I do not have so much time to worry about other matters, when I have to concentrate so much time and thought on the patients.

I have you all constantly in my mind, however, and do hope you are not going through too much and trust the air raids are not very bad over your district. Sometimes we hear that enemy air activity has diminished greatly, and we feel relieved for a while, but then become anxious again when news comes of more large scale attacks on Britain.

Each time I write to you, the war has come nearer to us. Just now we are all anxiously awaiting the end of the Battle of Crete. How sad to think of the New Zealanders being there and taking part in such intense fighting. They are showing wonderful heroism and doing well, we hear. I wonder if we know any of the men.

Syria, our 'next-door neighbour' is now enemy occupied territory! There is fighting going on all round our little corner of the globe, but this country is quiet and calm, so do not believe any rumours of internal disturbances here!

I have had letters from Rosie, Liz Hood and Mr Rand, (an ex patient) recently. Mr Rand is doing fire-spotting duties between 1 a.m. and 4 a.m. every morning! He is 72.

I hope you receive this before Geoff's birthday so that you can give him all my best wishes for his 21st. I am sending him an airgraph letter, and a present, which will be late.

Do take care of yourselves and don't work so hard!

Please remember how I used to 'bully' you for doing too much, and not resting!

God bless you all and take care of you. Will write again soon.

Ever your loving

Vera

ஒ

9.6.41

My Dear Mother and Father

I have recently sent you a cable in reply to yours, and today I sent an airgraph form, both of which we believe reach England quite quickly. Let me know how long they take.

I have not had a letter for some time, but expect the mails are delayed somewhere. The airmail letter-cards and airgraph letters are a great blessing to us here, for they are quicker and cheaper than letters. We hear that 80,000 airgraph letters reached home recently in nine days.

I am very well and very busy. Tell Muriel I wish she could be here to speak French to some of my patients for me! We have quite a number of the Free French Forces and they did not bother much about English when they were at school!

You know what my French is like. There are a number of black men also, from 'somewhere in Africa'!

We keep hard at it all day, and feel we are doing something useful. It is an amazing life in the army, and I shall have such things to tell you when I come home!

Now don't worry about me, because things are happening near here, (Syria). We are quite all right and I don't want you to think we are at all disturbed. I often think about you all, in fact you are always in my mind, no matter what I am doing, or where I am. If I could only see you, even for a short time, it would be wonderful!

The sun is always shining here, and will do so for another five months without rain. I wish you could see the incredibly blue sky and the lovely moonlit nights we have. How often I have wished you could see some of the loveliness of this country too!

We are always fighting the fly menace here. I have never seen so many flies before, except perhaps in Cairo, where there are swarms of them. We have achieved a complete absence of flies in our wards, by putting fly-proof netting in front of all windows and hanging a double thickness of netting over the doorways. All patients possess fly-swatters *in case* a fly penetrates our defences, and we go round the ward with a spray periodically to make the air unpleasant for such invaders!

Talking seriously of invaders, we have heard more, recently, of the possible invasion of Britain. May it never happen. It makes me feel very worried to think of such an awful thing, although we all feel sure the enemy will suffer very heavy losses, and will never take our island. The thought of you being so near the coast and in another kind of danger other than air raids gives me a cold shiver down my back.

Well, this seems a short letter and I never seem to have much to write about these days.

Now remember – you are to rest as much as possible! Secondly, don't worry about me.

My love to all.

God bless you darlings.

Your loving

Vera

∾

25.6.41

My Dear Mother and Father

Thank you so much for Mother's letter written on Good Friday and received on the 20th June! I have just sent you an airgraph letter.

How glad I was to hear from you again, as it was some time

since I had had any word from you and you know all the things one thinks and fears! I cannot help worrying about you all, but just lately, though I do not like to 'talk too soon', the bombing of Britain has been somewhat lessened, and now that Russia is taking Germany's attention so much, I do so hope it will give you as long a period of peace as is possible.

What do you think about this new phase of the war? It will certainly have a very important effect on the course of the war. So we now have Russia as our ally! What an amazing war.

I have received two letters which have been saved from the sea! One was from Matron, KGH, and the other from Iris. They were sent in January and were blotched with sea water, and the envelopes were unstuck I was able to read them all right, but of course the news was very old.

The Prime Minister's speech was relayed to us on Sunday night and we all thought it excellent. It was very clear. We sat on our beds rubbing our mosquito bites and killing the brutes that inflicted them, while listening to the speech!

We have a very good wireless set and can hear dear old Big Ben striking as loudly as if we were standing on Westminster Bridge!

I feel very anxious about your rationing, and do hope you really are not 'feeling the pinch'. I think you are all very good about everything, and I am very proud of you.

I should like to see Geoff in his uniform.

Please excuse this funny paper, the ink seems to have come through from the other side.

No more room – so must stop. Fondest love to you all. Writing an airmail letter soon.

Ever your loving
Vera

ﾏ

29.6.41

My Dear Mother and Father
I have just received Father's letter dated 6th May, and it was

most welcome. The letter arrived in a very battered state and some of it had been torn away, but actually only a few words were missing and I could read it quite well.

I was so glad to hear you were all well and have been receiving most of my letters. Are you also receiving the airgraph letters and airmail letter-cards which are said to take less than a fortnight to reach you? Have you written me any of the airmail postcards which some people have received here in less than a month. We are certainly having our correspondence troubles dealt with effectively!

Out here we are working hard and having little spare time on duty. I cannot tell you much, but the new war-Front north of us has made a big difference to our hospital. We have prisoners of war (Vichy) among our patients, for the first time.

I am still specialising in tropical diseases and have bought myself a new and most interesting book, dealing with them. Studying is still a never-ending source of pleasure and interest to me, and one can never learn everything in this job.

By the way, do not bother to send those books entitled *Modern Professional Nursing*. I asked you for them some time ago but realise how easily they could be lost on the way.

We are having endless days of heat and brilliant sunshine with clear blue skies and lovely sunsets. I am sitting in my room now, and from my window can look over to the Mount of Olives beyond the Kedron Valley. Everything looks so peaceful. It seems unfair of me to tell you about all the lovely things I am seeing, but how often I long to be in dear old England with you! I do hope that one day, you will be able to see all the places I have seen.

Are you having fewer raids now? I do hope so, and by the news it often seems as if this might be so. The war on the Eastern Front will probably give you a respite at home. I am so glad you do not have to spend night after night sheltering from bombs. Do you all sleep well, and does Mother still lie awake, worrying, until dawn? I do so hope not! I often wonder about such things – and I wonder if you all have enough food.

Our little hospital chapel is still going on well, and I enjoy being in charge of it. The padre calls me the 'church warden'.

There is one Sister here who is hoping to go home on

'compassionate grounds'. Her sister in England, has lost her husband in the war, and as a result has become mentally affected. It is very sad, especially as these two sisters were alone in England, having gone there from New Zealand, some years ago. This Sister is hoping to transfer home as soon as possible so that she can be with her sister. If this happens, she says she will come and see you, as she will be visiting Essex. I should love her to be able to do that, as I have told her a lot about you, and she will be able to tell you how well I am looking!

I am glad you were able to have a visit to Macclesfield. I think the cable you sent from there was quite definitely the one which I never received, as you sent me another one later stating you had cabled on 29th April. I always answer all the cables the same day, or next day after receiving them. Did you receive my last one, sent at about the beginning of this month?

Well, my dears, I think there is no more news just now. Remember, don't worry about me at all, and take care of yourselves. My love to all.

God bless you always.

Ever your loving

Vera

☙

7.7.41

My Dear Mother and Father

I have not had a letter from you lately, since the one received (in a battle-scarred state) from Father! I told you how it looked as if Peter had tried to devour it, but I know he had not, bless him. I think I will save it, to show you after the war.

Well, we are working very hard, and all feel really tired these days. We have more patients than we have ever had, and we are always admitting and discharging and transferring them – in true wartime style!

I cannot remember working harder, even in my training days, and that is saying a lot! It is however, a worthwhile job and I shall always feel happy – nursing the troops! Their sense of humour is unequalled and they are so grateful, and anxious to be well again so that they can 'go back'.

There is really very little news for me to give you, as I do not do very much in my off-duty times. Most of us relax and rest our feet. I am in the very best of health so you need not worry about me. Remember 'Saturday's child works hard for a living'. That's me, and I thrive on it.

I do hope you too are all well. We all hope you are having quieter times lately, and believe that is the case.

How I shall love to see you all again. However much longer will 'duration' be? I little knew – when I 'signed on the dotted line!' It will be two years, soon, since the beginning.

Please excuse such a short letter, but I know you only want to know that all is well with me, so will not mind.

Best love to all. God bless you and take care of you.

Ever your loving
Vera

✤

15.7.41

My Dear Mother and Father

I have not heard from you for a while, but I know a letter will arrive in time, so go on waiting patiently.

I wrote to you last a week ago, when I sent a letter-card, like this, and an airgraph letter. I am shortly sending you a parcel.

I do hope you are all well, and having some peace. At the moment we believe you are, but do not dare to hope it will go on for a long time, as by the time you receive this, life may be very noisy and dangerous for you again. These spells of quietness (comparative quietness I should say) over England, give us much relief, and we feel so glad to know you are not living in shelters and having no rest, day and night.

You will be pleased to know I am still in fine health and full of energy. We are working as hard as ever. You would be amazed if you could see the size of our hospital!

We are feeling very satisfied about our conquest of Syria.

Lt General Sir H Maitland Wilson who commanded our Forces is very much liked and admired. He inspected our hospital and we were able to meet him.

We are afraid one of our Sisters who married out here over a year ago, is already a war widow. Her husband is missing, and believed killed. It is sad, for she is such a nice girl and quite young. We think she will go home if she does not receive news in a few months' time.

I wish I had more news to tell you, but life is really quite uneventful when one is off duty, even though we never stop for a moment on duty. The days seem to fly by – I can hardly believe it will soon be August. We shall have Christmas again in no time and then we shall have been here two whole years!

Well, my darlings I will have to stop as I am nearing the end of the paper. My love to Muriel and Geoff and Peter. Please don't work too hard, and rest whenever you can.

God bless you always.

Fondest love from your loving

Vera

ఞ

6.8.41

My Dear Mother and Father

Yesterday I received some magazines from Muriel which have been quite a time coming. Please thank her very much for them. I am writing to her today.

It was so nice to receive English magazines, and I was pleased to have the two copies of the *Church Times*. If you could send them to me often, I should be very glad, as such papers are not obtainable out here. I am sending some books to you today.

It is a burning hot day today. This heat seems to go on and on. At present we are having much trouble with water. The supply is frequently cut off, and we have to put aside supplies in buckets and baths and use it sparingly. All our drinking water must be boiled.

I wonder if you are having hot weather, being August. I have had some good snaps taken of myself recently, and one, in particular I am sending to you, in a day or two when I write an airmail letter. I cannot send it with this as you know.

I went to a moonlight picnic recently with three others of our staff, and we went up to the Mount of Olives and had a wonderful view of the Jordan Valley on one side of us, and Jerusalem on the other. It was quite a cool evening and so pleasant after a hot day's work.

I do hope you are having more peace at home now. Are you resting as much as possible? Please don't work too hard. If only I could be there to *make* you lie down, as I did in the good old days!

I am afraid this is a short letter, but I will write again in a day or so. My best love to all, and take care always.

God bless you, dears.

Your loving

Vera

❧

15.8.41

My Dear Mother and Father

Thank you so much for Mother's long and welcome letter written on 23rd June, and received on 8th August. How I love your letters! We all say the same about news from home – we feel so much happier and ready for any amount of work after receiving just one letter or postcard.

I have also had a postcard from Mother which I acknowledged in an airgraph form sent recently. That was only a month coming and gave me even more recent news, so I should be very glad to have more of those cards from you.

Once again I must tell you not to worry at all, as I have never been in better health, though working harder than ever before. It is so like you to think so little of your own troubles when it is you who have all the hardships. I cannot help being anxious about your rationing and I do hope and pray it will not become even more severe and that you will keep in good health in spite of it.

I am so glad Geoff had such nice presents for his birthday. I hope you will receive the cheque I sent him. If not (that is if the letter in which it was sent does not arrive) I will send another. I was interested to hear about him being in the Home Guard, and should love a photo of him in uniform. I am so pleased to have Muriel's photo and have it in a nice frame beside your other photos in my room.

I heard the Queen's speech to the women of America on the wireless and it was very clear and sounded as if she was in the room with us, although it was from London. What a good speech, and how beautiful her voice sounded. I am so glad she made a special mention about the nursing profession. We all feel so proud of our fellow nurses at home!

I think you are doing wonderful things in connection with the church. Fancy making £7 at the garden party at such a time. It seems sad about the garden party at Bishopscourt, having to take your own tea. It is still very hot and oppressive here, and will be for the next two months at least. We are having much trouble with our water supply and are rationed quite severely where water is concerned.

I will write an airmail letter soon. Please always take care and REST!

God bless you my darlings.

My best love to all.

Ever your loving

Vera

25.8.41

My Dear Mother and Father

I have just sent you an airgraph letter which I hope will reach you soon. I have recently written an airmail letter-card in which I thanked you for Mother's letter received after about two months by airmail.

I am writing by ordinary airmail because I wanted to send you a snap of myself recently taken. I am also sending some other snaps later, as they are not yet developed.

How are you all at home? You are constantly in my thoughts, and I try to imagine, sometimes what you are doing at certain hours of the day. Today is Sunday, and while walking to church at 6 p.m., I thought, at home they are probably having tea or else, I hope, having an afternoon nap. Now it is 9.30 p.m., and I am writing this in my room, and beating off the mosquitoes with my free hand. It is cooler lately, but we are expecting more heat next month and during October before the rains come.

I went for a lovely walk a few days ago, up the Mount of Olives. We followed a stony track past the Garden of Gethsemane and the lovely Russian Church of St Mary Magdalene, right to the top, where we sat down for a rest and admired the panorama of the city below.

Later we walked through the grounds of a Russian convent, situated near the traditional site of the Ascension. From here we could see for miles right across the Wilderness to the blue stretch of the Dead Sea, looking like a sparkling sheet of glass. The sun was setting and all the hills around became tinted with pink and purple shades. The sky, too was full of soft colours, as the deep blue faded into pink before the darkness came. It is just like that here, brilliant sunshine, a sunset perhaps lovelier than anywhere else, then darkness.

I don't think I have ever seen such an amazing view as that of the Jordan Valley and Dead Sea from the Mount of Olives. We could see Bethany some distance below, and far in the distance, Bethlehem. It was a very peaceful scene, though a lonely and barren one, for now the hills are dry and without one blade of grass, and some of the hills seem to have appeared there by a volcanic eruption of the earth, as they are of such strange formations.

I also visited the Pool of Bethesda recently. This is a wonderful place, and one has to descend some very worn stone steps to reach the Pool. There is water there still, and it is believed to have for its source, a deep reservoir beneath the foundations of the city. The Crusaders preserved the Pool of Bethesda, and built a fine church over it. The pillars and arches are still there, though most of the original building has been destroyed. One might almost be standing in the small side aisle of an ancient church, except that the floor is deep in water.

The Church of St Anne, also built by the Crusaders, stands in the same part of the city, and is intact. It is a lovely place, so full of a holy atmosphere, and very dignified. Strangely enough this church was offered to the Church of England, as our Cathedral, many years ago, and we declined the offer! I can't think why. Now it belongs to the Greek Catholic Church.

There is so much to see here, that I always feel I can go somewhere different whenever I go for a walk. It would take a very long time to tell you about all the historic places. I only wish you could see them too. I feel almost selfish, telling you about all these things I am able to see while you have no such chances.

I am enclosing another snap I have just received, which shows me out for a picnic with three friends. We are sitting in a plantation of fine trees which I am sure you will agree, looks very pleasant with the sun shining through the trees. It was a pleasant change from the busy daily work. The photo is not as clear as it might be, but I am sure you can pick me out!

Well, there does not seem to be any more news at present. Do always take every care, as I know you do. I hope you will receive my parcels safely, sent several weeks ago. Best love to Geoff and Muriel. Did you receive a cable sent about the 2nd June?

Goodbye for now, darlings, and God bless you.

Ever your loving

Vera

༄

2.9.41

My Dear Mother and Father

Although it is some little time since I heard from you, and I have little news to give you, I am writing this airmail letter-card today. I expect when I have sent it, I will receive a letter from you, and then will have more to write about in answer to it.

I am very well and still busy. My friend Mary Insley (one-time at KGH with me) is coming here on leave soon, so it will be very pleasant seeing her again, and showing her the sights of the city.

It is still very hot here. I suppose you are having cooler weather. The earth looks white with dryness in the brilliant sunlight, and the few flowers we can get, look lovely for a few hours, then droop and die in the heat. When I think of the bitter winters we have, I don't know which extreme I prefer.

I am always thinking about you all and wondering just how you are. I do hope it is true that you are not having so many raids now, as we gather from the news in the papers, and on the radio. Perhaps they will not be as bad this winter as last, owing to the heavy German losses on the Eastern Front. We all hope so fervently, for we could all stand up to anything better than the anxiety about your people at home going through all those constant air raids.

I am sending you an enlargement of a photo which I have already sent in a letter. I think you will like it, and be glad to have it. I shall have such a wonderful collection of photographs to show you when I come home. I have some wonderful views which would probably not be passed in a letter, so they must be saved until that *Day of Days* when I see you again!

I am sending on some *Auckland Weeklies* which I had given to me, but I am afraid they will be very out of date when they arrive.

Well, my dears, I must stop now, as there is no more room on the paper.

Very best love to all. God bless you.

Your loving

Vera

&

9.9.41

My Dear Muriel

I don't know what you must be thinking of me for keeping you waiting so long for a letter. You have written several to me and they were all such long, interesting ones. It is not that I am not thinking of you, as you will understand.

You will have read all my letters home and heard plenty of news from me. I have sent you a Christmas card which I hope arrives safely.

We are not quite so busy as we have been during the past months. I now have a nice ward of my own, a medical ward of thirty-four beds – some patients are nerve cases. I have plenty of interest in it, and keep quite busy.

We are nearing the end of the hot months now, and are even feeling quite cold in the evenings. You cannot imagine how dead everything in the countryside looks. The hills are white and tiring to look upon. By white, I mean that the grass has shrivelled up and the earth beneath is devoid of moisture and has a chalky appearance. Someone wrote an article about this country for the local paper a few days ago, and I am going to enclose it with this letter for you to see. It is very much to the point and shows how homesick the writer must be. In spite of it all, however, I am sure she cannot have seen Palestine in spring time, with the new green shoots of grass covering the earth, the trees bursting into bud, and best of all, the scarlet, mauve, and yellow flowers making beautiful patches of colour in the fields I am sure she has not seen Galilee in spring time, and the white daisies growing on the hillsides round the lake. Don't we all long for England with long twilights 'quiet as a nun, breathless with adoration', green fields, fat cows, cosy fireside evenings with our dearest people about us. But all those longings will not blind us to the beauties of other countries!

I am still receiving books from Foyles Book Club and lately I have had a book called *Lovers Meeting*, by Lady Eleanor Smith. It is very good, very unusual, and fascinating. It deals with the theory of reincarnation and tells about two lovers who are living in 1812, and because of a magic spell, find themselves in 1934. Later, after three years they return by the same spell to 1812, and compare the life with that of the 20th century. After a few weeks the man becomes tired of 1812, and wants to live again in 1934, but the girl is happy enough in the 19th century. However, she is in love and would not stay in 1812 alone, but at the last moment she is stopped and held back by a jealous suitor, and the poor fiancé returns alone. He goes back thinking his sweetheart had given way to the temptation of remaining in a life she preferred, and he is of course very upset. It has a dramatic ending and is really an amazing, if fantastic book. It probably sounds a lot of nonsense to you, but I could not stop reading once I started it. Have you read it? If not I hope you will be able to. I will send it to you if you would like it.

I am enclosing an enlargement of a photo I sent home some time ago, as I think you may like it.

I was interested to hear about Geoffrey joining the RAF, as a despatch rider. We are all doing our stuff from Father down! We never realised three years ago, what kind of work we were to be engaged in, and we certainly did not think we should be in the midst of a war!

I think 'that man' is getting a hot time on the Eastern Front don't you? What a strange war! Not so very long ago we were planning to help the Finns against the Soviets, and now we are helping the Soviets against the Finns and Germans, Russia is doing much to help our war effort and giving us a breathing space, at the same time weakening Germany greatly.

By the way another book which I have enjoyed very much is *A Prophet at Home* by Douglas Reed, author of *Insanity Fair*. Have you read either of these books? They are both excellent, and just your taste. I enjoyed every word of them, as they express my sentiments exactly. The author must be a very shrewd and clever man as he sums up our faults and mistakes as well as the good we have done and are doing. *A Prophet at Home*, was commenced before the war, and finished in February, 1941. I wish many people could read it.

I do hope you are having a quieter time now – regarding bombing. I have just had a long letter from Mother in which she says you went three weeks without a raid – then had one in the night. That certainly sounds more hopeful than a year ago when the Blitz started. Everyone out here in the Forces complains of the great anxiety about their homes. Some of the troops, in fact, many of them have not heard from home for months, in fact over a year in some cases! I feel so sorry for them and fear that their homes have been destroyed. There are men suffering nervous breakdowns as a result of worry, they are all so brave and hardly ever complain but keep their troubles to themselves. I never knew such patient people. They always manage to find something to joke about!

Well, I am afraid if I write much more this will be overweight. I promise not to keep you waiting so long for a letter next time.

Thank you so much for your photo, which I have in a pretty blue frame in my room. I like it very much.

Cheerio for now – God bless you.

Fondest love and good wishes

Vera

My Dear Mother and Father

Thank you so much for five airgraphs already received, each taking from three weeks to a month to come. They are all clearly written and very neat. I have also had a very nice long letter from Mother, giving me much news.

You say in your letter that there is a great deal in the papers about correspondence to and from the Middle East. I am glad to say that your letters come more regularly now, and I should *never* think you were not bothering about me if I did not hear for a long time. This is what is happening in many cases, however. There are many soldiers who are most worried about their homes as they have not heard from them for months. Others have written week by week, and then receive letters from wives and sweethearts or parents, as the case may be, to say that they are distracted with worry as no news has been received for so long. It is a great problem, particularly as so much mental strain is being caused to people out here. We see it!

I am very well indeed. I have some new kind of news for you. For some time I have been thinking of applying for a move, as I have now been almost two years in this unit, and it is good to have a change after that length of time. The Principal Matron, the head of the Army Nursing Services in the Middle East, made her usual twice-yearly visit here a few weeks ago. She is a very charming person and was full of praise for the hospital. I asked for an interview with her to discuss my transfer elsewhere. Our own Matron was present at the interview, which proved to be very

133

pleasant and satisfactory. You will be pleased to hear that she told the Principal Matron that I was one of her best Sisters and had an excellent record. The Principal Matron then asked me if I would like to be sent to a hospital ship, and as this kind of work is just what I should like, and have wanted to do since I was called up, I said, yes. Our own Matron then said that I should be most suitable, and she highly recommended me! I have discovered that it means a great deal if one is recommended for a hospital ship as this is not like an ordinary hospital, as you can imagine, and Sisters are selected according to their past reports. After writing down all about me in her notebook, the Principal Matron then said that I would hear from her later.

I do not know how soon this will be. Sometimes we are only given three hours' notice to go, so I am now all prepared to leave in that time. I may not be sent for some weeks or even two months. It depends on the vacancy occurring. If there are no vacancies, I may just go to another hospital, but do not think this very likely.

I do hope you will not mind me making this change. Please write soon and tell me what you think.

As soon as I hear something definite, I will send an airgraph to you. After that I will send my new address, but in the meantime you can go on writing to me at the same address, and letters will be forwarded.

All this may not happen for some time, however.

I do hope you have enjoyed your holiday at Torquay, and feel better for it. I shall be so pleased to hear all about it. It was very wise of you to have a holiday as I am quite sure you needed it.

Well, my dears, I must stop now, I am afraid. Take care of yourselves. My love to all.

God bless you.

Ever your loving

Vera

19.10.41

My Dear Mother and Father

Thank you so much for a card and an airgraph sent on 23rd September, and 27th September. I have answered by airgraph today.

I am so sorry it is a month since you have heard from me, and do hope that by now you have had my letters and airgraphs. Never think I have forgotten to write, or am writing less frequently as I will always write very often. I write at least once a week, sometimes more often, so you should receive the letters in time.

I have also had an airgraph from Geoff, which pleased me very much. I am so glad he received his cheque safely. I have sent off three parcels of provisions which we have been encouraged to send home, and which I hope will arrive intact, and not the worse for wear. Father said in a letter that you did not need them and have regular rations, but you may find the things useful, all the same. I am so glad you seem to be faring better than we are led to believe!

I have also sent a parcel of Christmas gifts and I do hope this arrives safely. In my last airmail letter-card sent about the 3rd October, I told you about my expected move. So far I have not heard any more from Headquarters. My best friend, a very nice New Zealand girl, Grace, who joined up in England and is in this unit, is also expecting the same kind of transfer and has not heard further. We are hoping we shall be sent to the same ship together. I hope you received my last airmail letter, if not you will wonder what I mean by this. I am expecting a transfer elsewhere, most likely to a hospital ship. If this letter arrives, and not the last one, let me know straight away, and I will write again immediately.

I should have started two weeks leave on the 15th of this month, but it was cancelled, in order that I should be here if sent for at short notice.

I have only one uncertainty about it – the rest is all pleasure. I am afraid you will be sorry I am making this change, and wish I was staying here. Please do not feel worried about my wanting to work on a hospital ship. If you should think there is danger attached, I can safely assure you that there are many hospital ships in operation out here – always at work, and always unharmed. The patients who come to us speak very highly of them and say how comfortable they were, while at sea. I have also come in contact with Sisters from hospital ships, who have loved the life and were sorry to be moved back to a general hospital. It will be a new and interesting experience, both from a nursing point of view, and from the point of view of seeing new places and new people. Please let me know what you think, when you next write.

I think this unit will not remain here long, as it is due for a move.

It is becoming very cold here now, especially at night. The rains started a few days ago. It was an unusual sound for me to awake in the night and hear the rain swishing down and beating against the walls. The first rain for seven months! How the earth must welcome it!

I have plenty of warm clothes, and a new winter uniform coat, very smart and military looking.

Well, must stop, darlings. Cheerio. My love to all.

God bless you always.

Your ever loving

Vera

෯

28.10.41

Dear Mother and Father

It is a short time since I heard from you, but I expect a letter will arrive when I have posted this, and then I will write another in answer to it.

I wrote an airgraph, and an airmail letter-card about six or seven days ago, and hope you have received them.

I am now on night duty again. It is eight months since I was last on. Tonight is my second night. I have three surgical wards. We are not very busy just now and do not have so many convoys. We think it is a lull before the storm, as we expect to be much busier when the winter months come, and with them, probably more fighting!

I have not yet heard any more about my transfer. I think I should hear some kind of news regarding it, before very long. Of course, there may not be any vacancies on a hospital ship for a time, and I may be here for quite a while yet. In any case, I will let you know, as soon as I hear more about it.

Did you receive my cable sent on 8th October, in answer to yours? I have received a book from Muriel, which she had told me she was sending. Please thank her for it. I am writing to her.

I expect you are missing Geoff now that he has been 'called up'. I often think of him, and wonder how he is getting on. I am sure it will be good for him, and he will like it.

There is such a pretty little kitten sitting on a chair next to me. The patients have given her a very amusing and appropriate name, 'Marmalade'. She is just that colour.

The film *Gone with the Wind* has just come here. I expect it is a thing of the past in London, I hope to go and see it when I have my night off duty.

It is getting very cold here now. I have taken up knitting in earnest, and am making myself some woollen things for the winter. Clothes are so very expensive here and the prices seem to be still going up. I am sure you must be finding the cost of living very high indeed.

Someone lent me some copies of a Southend newspaper recently and I found them very interesting especially as there were some items of interest in them. There were pictures of the ruins of a yacht club 'somewhere on the coast', and I am wondering if it was BoC, as there was a large club there. We do a lot of guessing about air-raid damage in Great Britain. So much is left to our imagination when we only see the pictures of ruins.

I am afraid I have not much news just now, as life seems very quiet.

I am in the best of health, and do hope you are too.

I will write again very soon. Don't worry if my letters are delayed, there are always some on the way.

Best love to you both, and all.

God bless you, dears.

Your ever loving

Vera

ഌ

My Dear Mother and Father

I have just sent you an airgraph letter. I also sent an airgraph and an airmail letter-card a week ago. We have not had any letters lately – the reason being that a large number have been lost at sea.

I am very well, so you have no need to worry. I am still on night duty. There has been no further news for me about my expected transfer. I think that what is to be – will be, and if I am meant to be sent on a hospital ship, I shall go, in due course. I very much want to go, and will be greatly disappointed if I do not have the opportunity. However, one must just wait and see in this army life, as we rarely receive orders in advance, and don't know what is in store for us until a few hours before we are due to move on.

In any case, if I do not have the transfer I expect, I shall not be remaining here, as the time has come for us all (this hospital) to move on from our present position. I can tell you no more, I am afraid, and have probably said too much already. We do not know our destination of course. When it is known, and we are able to write more, I will tell you all I can without causing the letter to be waylaid!

Are you receiving my letters safely now? When you last wrote you said it was some time since you had heard from me, and I sent you a cable immediately. I write most regularly, and send many airgraphs.

I do hope and pray you are having a more peaceful time now. We do not hear much about raids over England just now. The Eastern Front campaign must be drawing German air strength away from Britain. How thankful we are for that!

Well, I think my letter must end here as I have no more news. Life is very quiet on night duty, and one seems to live in a different world!

I am going to see the film *Gone with the Wind* tomorrow, and am looking forward to it very much. I shall be able to get up early and go to the afternoon performance.

Fondest love to you both and all.

God bless you always.

Your loving

Vera

My Dear Mother and Father

I have recently received an airgraph from Mother. It took just over a month to come. I was very glad to hear from you, as we had been without letters for a while.

I was very interested to hear about Geoff being in the RAF, 'somewhere in Yorkshire'. I am very glad to hear he is liking it and feel sure it will be a fine life for him. He will make some good friends.

Your airgraph, which you were afraid might not be distinct, was as clear as any I have seen. All your airgraphs have been easily readable, and you manage to write so much on them.

I have still heard nothing more about my transfer to a hospital ship. One needs much patience in the army as the moves are often very slow in taking place. However, I will be prepared to wait a long time if necessary, and if no such chance comes my way, I will know that I was not meant for such a change. I will be very pleased, of course, if I am able to go.

I spoke in my last letter about a move for us all from here. This is about to take place, and there is great activity and excitement amongst us. Well, I have spent one Christmas in the real place, but this coming one will find us in another land. As usual we have been told very little, and can only imagine our destination. If I can give you any clue in my next letter, I will certainly do so.

I am so looking forward to receiving your photograph. I hope you received a postcard-size one of myself, sent in a letter to Muriel, I think.

I am sending a cheque to Mother in an airmail letter within the next day or so. I will also send a newspaper cutting – about the Bishop of Chelmsford. It interested me very much. I hope you will receive my Christmas parcels safely.

Well, my dears, it is 2.30 a.m. (I am on night duty) and I have some jobs to do, so must stop. Will write again very soon.

Fondest love to you all.

God bless you always.

Your loving

Vera

ꙮ

My Dear Mother and Father

I have just received an airgraph from Muriel and it was only three weeks coming. Also I had one from Mother, which I mentioned in my last letter. That took a month to come.

There is not much news to tell you, but you will remember that in my last letter I spoke of a change of scenery for us all. Well, we expect to see new places very soon, on our way to an unknown destination!

A hospital from 'down under' has taken our place, and we are all ready for whatever is allotted to us. It is strange to be going on our way after almost two years among the Holy places. I would like, as you will realise, to say much more, in much plainer language, but you know how careful I must be. I will keep on writing to you regularly, wherever I am, but must warn you in advance, that you may not receive my letters so often, and I will certainly not have yours for a time! It will all straighten out, of course when we settle, but there is bound to be some postal disorganisation.

There is, as you can believe, a great deal of speculation regarding all this. There is nothing I can tell you, but will try to give you a clue at a later date.

I am keeping very well so don't worry. I am so pleased to hear that Geoff likes his new life.

Is it true that you broadcast to me in a Forces programme relayed from Swansea on 14th October? I did not hear it myself as the radio in our Mess had been packed, and I was not on duty where I could have heard it. If it was you, I shall be terribly disappointed as it would have been more than wonderful to hear one of your voices again. A number of patients and Sisters 'listened in' and are convinced that the message was for me. I went to Broadcasting House here in the hope that they could tell me when I may hear it again, but they could not, as the programme was from England. Perhaps it was not you after all, but what a *pity* if it was.

Must stop now. Fondest love to all and God bless you always.

Cheerio for now.

Ever your loving

Vera

෴

19.11.41

My Dear Mother and Father

Thank you very much for an airmail letter from Mother, dated 8th September, and just received today. Of course I have had a number of airgraphs and letter-cards since then which tell me much later news, but it is very nice to have a longer letter in which you are able to write more fully.

I am sending this by airmail and using ordinary paper, in order to enclose a cheque for Mother, for her birthday, also a newspaper cutting. I have sent a parcel containing something for each one of you for Christmas and also a parcel of food, which I only hope arrives safely. I am sending off a small parcel, or packet, with a small gift for the 18th December, also, but this will arrive sometime next year, I am afraid. It is a brooch, made in this country, and has a turquoise stone set in the centre. This is a real turquoise and had just arrived from Persia, (or Iran) when I got it. It is Mother's birthday stone, and mine too. If it does not arrive safely I will have another one sent.

To think that I shall be twenty-five next month, and when I last saw you I was only twenty-three. That was 1st December 1939. What a long time it seems.

In my last two letters, I told you about our forthcoming move from here. We are all ready to leave for other places but have no idea where we are going. My trunk is packed and roped up, and has new numbers and letters painted on it. (All very mysterious letters and numbers which gives us no clue at all!) I have not been told anything more about my expected transfer to a hospital ship, and feel very disappointed. Matron, however, is sure I shall have that move sometime, if not in the near future, as my application was accepted and my name is awaiting a vacancy. A Sister has just come to us from a hospital ship and has been on it for a year. She was very happy and loved the life, and has travelled to many places and countries, even to NZ, where a special train was put at the disposal of the ship's staff so that they could travel all over the North Island!

You will have received an airmail letter-card by the time this arrives, in which I have warned you to expect a delay in my letters arriving to you, owing to this move. However, it may not be for long, and you will not need to worry if this delay does occur, as you will realise the reason. We may not go very far away, but there are also rumours that we may travel some distance. Rumours! More rumours! I never realised how many rumours one hears in army life when any change is taking place. How and where they originate we can never discover, but someone always seems to have heard something 'on very good authority' and the speed with which the rumour spreads is amazing!

I recently visited Solomon's Quarries here, a wonderful gigantic cave which lies beneath the Old City. It is cut out of thousands of tons of solid rock and has existed for centuries. It is a special meeting place for the Masons and I expect Father has heard of it. The stone used for the construction of some of the most beautiful and the most ancient buildings in the city, comes from this vast quarry. When the Masons hold their meetings there, all outsiders are excluded, and we could see the hooks in the stone walls where lamps are hung during these gatherings. It is a weird place, and becomes more so, as you walk on and go down deeper into the earth, and one must step carefully as there are deep pits, the bottoms of which are scarcely visible. At one place we were told we were 300 feet below the Mosque of Omar, which is a huge building in the Old City, and which is built from stones taken from the quarries. I bought a souvenir made of stone and marked with the symbols of the Masons, and will keep it and give it to Father when I come home.

You say in your letter, that you want to hear about my engagement. Well, you dear 'matchmaking' pair, there is nothing to tell you about that. One must wait for the right person you know, and he does not seem to be in the Middle East.

I was interested to hear about your visit to London. How different it must be! I really cannot imagine St Paul's standing alone, with all those old streets wiped out I should think you were reminded of Napier, after the earthquake, except that most of London's debris would have been cleared away when you went there. Don't go up there too often, will you, as I should not at all like you to be caught in a 'Blitz'. I recently met a New Zealand soldier who was in my ward, and he was from Napier, and was there at the time of the quake! We had an interesting talk about it.

I am looking forward to having your photos. It will be the next best thing to seeing you. I am so glad you have received two parcels. Let me know if the contents were in fairly good condition please. I shall be sending more, in spite of your saying that your rations are sufficient.

Well, my dears I must stop now and go to bed. Also I have written enough for airmail. It is quite cold tonight, and the wind is howling round the house, and rattling the doors and windows. It is such a change after the boiling heat.

Would you please send me Geoff's address.

Fondest love to all including Peter. I hope that Muriel received my letter.

God bless you always.

Ever your loving

Vera

ॐ

26.11.41

My Dear Mother and Father

I have replied to your last letters, and had no more since, as mails are coming slowly just now. However, I shall probably have another airgraph from you soon, as they are coming through quite quickly.

We are still 'sitting on the fence', waiting to jump off to a place unknown. We think this is one of the best-kept secrets of the war! You will, I hope have received my last letters in which I told you about our expected change from our present situation in this part of the world. We are all quite ready and prepared to go at any time. We may find ourselves going further away from home than before, but after all, the further east we go, the nearer we are to home, really, if you think of it in that way!

I have written before, to tell you that my letters to you may be delayed, as yours will be to me, but please do not worry, as it may not be for long.

It is getting much colder here now, and we gather round coal fires in the evenings and find it very cosy, with the wind blowing round the house. As we are very high up here, it is quite the coldest part of the country.

I wonder what kind of Christmas you will have this year. There must be many things you will be unable to get. I only hope you are left free from raids, so that you can have a peaceful Christmas, as it should be.

I have sent off a small parcel for Mother, which I hope arrives safely.

How is Geoff? Would you please send me his new address.

I hope Muriel received my last letter safely.

Well, I am so sorry that there is so little news to tell you and I hope there will be more next time.

My love to Muriel and both of you, also Peter.

Cheerio for now.

Your loving

Vera

❧

My Dear Mother and Father

It is quite a while since I heard from you, but our letters are not arriving as they should, so I feel sure they are on the way.

We are now in another place, this being the first stopping place of our journey which I mentioned previously. Of course I cannot give you any details at all, and shall not be able to tell you anything for a long time. However, I will keep writing every week or more often, and send you airgraphs frequently, so that you do not go without letters.

By the time you receive this, we should be settled somewhere, but we have only a vague idea where!

I am keeping well. I do hope you are too. We are having a lot of rain now and the earth is looking fresh and green. We are only a short distance from fields of orange groves where the trees are laden with golden fruit. We are able to pick oranges whenever we feel like it. How I wish you could have them. We hear you have very little fruit, and oranges are almost impossible to get. It seems wrong that we should have far more than we can ever eat, and you have *none* at all!

Well, there is no more news to tell you, I am afraid, as there is so much that I must not mention. I shall be thinking of you often at Christmas – wondering what you are doing and how you are. Where shall we be, I wonder!

Don't worry – my letters will continue to be sent, and if there is any delay, you will understand that it is because we are not stationary.

My best love to all and God bless you always.

Ever your loving

Vera

ঙ

My Dear Mother and Father

I have just written you an airmail letter-card, and an airgraph letter, and I said in them that I had not received any letters for some time. Before the letters were ever posted, a Christmas mail arrived and there were two letters for me, one from Mother and the other from Father! The former was dated 16th September, and the latter 18th September. What a joy it gave me! I was especially thankful to hear from you now, as there may be no more mail for us before we embark on our new adventure.

I told you as discreetly as possible, about our future change of scenery. At present we are experiencing quite a pleasant change from a civilised life, eating army rations (loads of bully beef, which I like) and sleeping temporarily in a hospital ward which has been out of use for some time. We have a lot of fun, living such a community life, and we find plenty of humour in it. We have been compelled to leave half our luggage behind us, it was quite a wrench, but we shall get used to it. I have quite enough luggage to take – plenty of clothes etc.

I am so glad to hear you are all well. It is a relief to know that. I am glad you received one, if not two, parcels and found the things in fairly good condition. I do hope the tea and sugar and also a third parcel of food arrive safely. There is a parcel for Christmas also on the way. You should never have attempted to send me a parcel for Christmas, it is quite wrong to think of such a thing and I would never have expected it. You are too unselfish and generous, but I hate to think of you using your coupons and spending money on me when you need so much. I am so looking forward to receiving your photo. I have postcard size ones of you, and have them round me wherever I am.

My love to Peter, and tell him to keep up the good work of making you lie down after dinner!

Well, my darlings, there is no more room I fear. God bless you. My love to Muriel and all.

Writing again in a day or two.

Fondest love

Vera

In transit, going to a place unknown

∾

2 Reserve J/766
QAIMNSR
No 60 General Hospital
In the Field
13.12.41

My Dear Mother and Father

Please note my new but only temporary address. It will probably give you some idea that a change has taken place, but that is the most I can tell you. There is so much I would like to write to you. You will think I have given you a vague kind of address, but that is all I can say, and it will be understood by the postal authorities. I don't know how long this letter will take to reach you – but I hope not much longer than usual.

You will most likely remember how I spent my first Christmas away from England – 1939. Well, I am spending my time now in the same kind of way, and shall be doing so this Christmas. Later I hope to be able to write a better letter, instead of one full of hints, hoping you will come to the right conclusions.

I am afraid it will be some time before I receive your letters, but we are all resigning ourselves to the fact that we must wait for mails for a time. You should not have quite so much delay in my letters coming to you.

Don't worry about me, at all, as we are being well looked after. I think about you all very often, and hope you are well, and not being bombed. I shall be thinking of you on Mother's birthday, and at Christmas. On Tuesday I will be a quarter of a century old – yet still the youngest Sister here!

Well, my dears, I am afraid there is no more that I can say now. I have written many letters and airgraphs, lately, to keep you supplied and will continue to write often.

My love to all, and God bless you.

Your loving

Vera

క్ర

16.12.41

My Dear Mother and Father

Here I am writing to you on my twenty-fifth birthday, and wouldn't you like to know where I am!

All I can say is that I have been in this part of the world before, when we were on our way home in 1931, I am still on the move.

It is a pity I cannot write more fully, but we all understand the consequences of such indiscretion and are being very careful in our correspondence. I hope to say more in my future letters.

You will be pleased to hear that I have had a very happy birthday. Several of my friends gave me presents, although it must have been difficult to obtain them under the circumstances. Another one had a cake made, and iced, with greetings written on top. This was a complete surprise when it arrived at teatime, and it was much enjoyed by all. I am sure I am getting much too old to have so much spoiling on a birthday, but it was very nice and reminded me of home!

I shall be thinking of Mother on Thursday, her birthday, and hope she has a happy day too.

I wonder if you are receiving my letters regularly. You should do, as I have written every three or four days lately. I am afraid I shall have to wait for yours for a time.

Well, my dears, here I must stop. Don't worry as I am in the best of health and should be settled again before the New Year.

Writing again soon.

Best love to Muriel and all.

Your loving

Vera

∾

2 Reserve J/766
QAIMNSR
No 60 General Hospital
Base Depot
c/o GPO
Bombay
30.12.41

My Dear Mother and Father

Here at last I am able to give you a definite address, although we are told it is only for the time being. If you write here next time and for all your future letters, until you have a new address from me, the letters will reach me safely.

We are most surprised that we are able to mention where we are, but as this is a peacetime military station, and we are just passing through, it is quite in order to discuss our whereabouts.

How I wish you were here with me to see this really fine city! We arrived on Christmas Eve. We had expected to be at sea for

Christmas and we certainly did *not* expect to come to India as we were bound for a place north-west of this country. (I cannot tell you where.) The land of magic carpets and fluffy cats! All that was changed at the last minute, however, and Christmas at sea was out of the question for us.

We had a pleasant and uneventful journey as well as a very hot one! I wrote to you twice on the way, and posted the letters at two ports of call. I hope you received them safely. Also I cabled to you on 18th December. On 27th December, I cabled again to tell you my new address. I shall be very glad if you would cable me to let me know how you are, as I do not expect to have letters for a long time. That will be our best means of communication for a time.

It is wonderful to think I am being given the opportunity of seeing even one small part of India. How I have travelled since the beginning of the war, and how much more travelling I may still have before me! I am not able to tell you any more about our future, and in any case it is still uncertain.

We do not know whether we shall remain in this country or not.

We are billeted here and are not working at present. We have therefore had time to see the city and have found it very interesting. At this time of the year it is the winter season, but how hot it is. What must the summer be like? Unfortunately we have left our tropical kit in the Middle East – why, we do not know, but the army moves in a mysterious way, and one can never know why some things happen. It is being sent on to us, however, so we hope we shall not have to wear winter uniform for too long.

There is a beautiful Cathedral here, St Thomas's, and I was able to go there on Christmas Day, and to several services since. I thought of you so much and wondered what you were doing on Christmas Day. You little realised that I was in Bombay did you?

I do hope you are all keeping well and happy. To think that I am now another 4,000 odd miles further from home!

How the war is spreading now that the Far East is involved! It must have been upsetting for the people at home at Christmas time. Everywhere else we seem to be making good headway and it would have been a cheerier Christmas but for the war in the Far East.

Well, my dears, there is no more I can say just now. I will go on writing every few days, and give you more news when possible.

Don't worry about me – I am in the best of health.

Fondest love to you both and Muriel.

Cheerio for now.

Ever your loving

Vera

෴

The gateway of India

෴

2 Reserve J/766
QAIMNSR
No 60 British General Hospital
c/o Army Post Office
Base Depot
Bombay
7.1.42

Dear Mother and Father

Please take note of my new temporary address. As you see, I am still in Bombay, and we must call ourselves 'British General Hospital', as there is a 60th Indian Hospital, which has been confused with us.

I wrote to you on the 30th December, so hope you receive the letter. On the 27th December, I sent you a cable to let know I have arrived safely, and am well. When you write back to this address we shall undoubtedly be elsewhere, but the letters will be forwarded.

As to our future destination we know nothing at all! It is all a mystery whether we shall move further east, or go to our former destination, west, or whether we shall stay somewhere in India. We hope to remain as a complete unit, but there is always a chance, unfortunately, of our being separated, and going in small detachments to join other units. How uncertain is army life!

We have been here now for two weeks and have had quite a pleasant time seeing the city. We are staying at the Taj Mahal Hotel, a huge place overlooking the Bay. It is the best hotel in Bombay, (it has nearly 600 bedrooms), and we have been very comfortable. There are a large number of Army, Navy and Air Force men staying here so we have made many friends. As you can imagine the Navy and Merchant Navy are well represented, this being an important port.

This is winter, but it is quite hot enough for an English mid summer. I have a lovely view from my window of the blue sea dotted with the white sails of fishing boats, and all along beside the sea there are tall green palm trees. We have wonderful sunsets here, but I do not think they are as lovely as those we saw in Palestine.

It seems a long time since we were working, it was in fact 3rd December, when we started off on our journey. Except for looking after a few sick people in the ship's hospital we have been idle since that date. However, we shall be ready to start again as soon as we can, we all agree about that. In case you do not receive my last letter I will tell you again here that we came on the same ship which brought us through the Mediterranean at Christmas 1939! It was a great coincidence, and we were very glad to see the dear old ship again, and had our second happy trip on her without any exciting events at all. I cannot tell you about our route but you will be able to guess the way we came easily enough.

We have strange contrasts in this kind of life. Sometimes we are living in real camp fashion sleeping between blankets under canvas, and eating off tin plates and drinking out of tin mugs. For washing we collect water out of a camp boiler in the middle of a field. All this was part of our journey here, when we stayed for several nights at desert hospitals while awaiting transport. It is all good experience and we found plenty of humour all the time. Now we are staying in this luxury hotel, just for a change, but where we shall go next is yet to be seen.

Well, there is very little more I can say just now. I will write again soon and hope to be able to tell you something more definite next time.

Did you 'see the New Year in'? I went for a swim on New Year's Eve – in the afternoon! In the evening some Naval officers took several of us to a dance which we enjoyed very much.

Are you receiving my letters safely? I wrote to you many times before we moved on, in order that you should have a number of letters coming to you. We are no longer able to write airgraphs or airmail letter-cards I am afraid, while we are in this country.

Cheerio for now and God bless you.

Love to Muriel and Geoff, and both of you.

Your loving

Vera

❧

My Dear Mother and Father

I have just received your cable in answer to mine, sent on 27th December. I was delighted and much relieved to hear from you. Now it will not be so bad, having no letters, for I have had word from you and know you are well. We are all settling down to a long period of being without letters, so most of us have sent cables. My friends were glad my cable had been answered, and even felt some satisfaction in reading it although it did not concern them, but it was something from England, which means a lot to us!

I will send you another cable soon, and when my address is changed I will cable that also.

We are still here in Bombay at the moment but do not know how long this will continue. We shall only have very short notice as usual, when we go. It is now a month since we arrived here, and we are tired of waiting about and wish we could go soon. Most people think we shall go to our original destination, the place for which we were intended when we left the Middle East. However, nothing is definite and we may find ourselves on the way to somewhere quite different!

What do you think about the war in the Far East? It does look grim at the moment. It is important to India as the war is now so much closer to this country. What a turmoil the world is in!

It is pleasantly warm here now with cool breezes at night, but the hot weather and monsoons will come soon. I have been swimming very often. Fancy swimming now, when you are sitting around fires and hearing the wind and the rain beating against the house. We have not had any winter really as it was only just beginning in Jerusalem when we left.

We have found Bombay a very interesting city. It is very thickly populated and there are many poverty-stricken people and beggars. As a contrast there is evidence of great wealth. The houses of the rich are like palaces, and there are many of these but the slum areas are appalling. There are lovely parks and gardens and a fine marine parade bordered with palm trees. The bay is very picturesque for there are many pretty little islands dotted over it. It is always interesting to watch the many different kinds of ships entering and leaving the harbour.

We all hope we shall be on one of those outward bound ships soon, as this waiting about is very tedious.

I hope you are all keeping well and are still more or less free from raids. We read of bombs being dropped on south-east coastal areas at times, and I hope they have not been near you.

I will write again soon, until then cheerio and God bless you.

Your loving

Vera

ॐ

29.1.42

My Dear Mother and Father

I have written to you to tell you that Phyllis Carr is returning home and hopes to visit you. I am giving her this letter, and one for Muriel also, so that she can deliver them herself.

I am thrilled to think that she can see you and give you all the latest news from me. She will be able to tell you how well I am, and what a pleasant time we had together since meeting in Bombay. How I envy her, seeing you! Fancy going home to dear old England, the best place on earth, in spite of all that has been said about the lure of the East!

She has been on a hospital ship for a year, and was then very ill and lost a good deal of weight. She is now going home to meet her fiancé, who is an officer in the Merchant Service. Her contract with the army has been broken, so she would have had to pay her own fare somehow, had she not obtained a post as nurse to a child in return for a free passage. I am thankful she was able to take the chance, as she will be able to sail soon and she will have a pleasant occupation on the journey.

I am still here waiting with the rest of my unit, and wondering when we are to move on. We have been here for five weeks, and it seems much longer. Phyllis will tell you how we managed to come to Bombay and where we should really have landed. We may still go there, but on the other hand we may be moving in another direction. Time will tell. At present we are weary of doing nothing and feel we could be doing much useful work somewhere. Our life in the Middle East seems very far away.

The weather is warm now, a little too warm at times. There is never a cloud in the sky and the sun shines all day and every day. Yet people here are talking about 'this nice cold spell'. The heat will begin soon and the monsoons will descend upon Bombay, and then, we are told, the climate is awful. However, we hope to be far away from here by then.

I was so pleased to have your cable in answer to mine, giving you my temporary address. Were you surprised to hear I was no longer in Palestine, or had you received one of my letters telling you that I was expecting to move on? I have written every week since coming here and have sent you a postcard, and a number of magazines which I think you will find interesting. I do not expect to receive any letters from you for a long time to come, as mails are always disordered when a unit moves.

I do hope you are not being bombed so much now. We do not hear much about it if you are, unless it is that the war on other Fronts has crowded the reports on raids out of the papers. Do you find the rationing of food and clothes very severe? I have met a number of people here, who have been in England until a few months ago, and they have told me a good deal about conditions there. I do feel so sorry for you all, having a limited number of coupons for clothes, and such foods as butter, sugar, tea, etc being so limited.

I am sending two pairs of stockings – for Mother and Muriel. Phyllis will bring them for you. I wish I could send more, but her luggage is limited. However, I am going to send more by post, and trust there will not be duty to pay.

Well, my dears, here I must stop. I hope this will find you all well and I hope it will reach you in about two months' time.

Best love to Muriel and Geoff, and to you both.

Ever your loving

Vera

❧

29.1.42

My Dear Muriel

I am sending this letter by Phyllis Carr who is going to see you when she arrives home. I envy her very much going home so soon, after one year out here, but she has been very ill and it is just as well she is not remaining in a hot country.

I am sending you an ivory necklace for your birthday, and I hope Phyllis will be able to give it to you before 22nd April. It is a souvenir of Bombay. There are many beautiful things I would like to send you, but they would be difficult for Phyl to carry, and bring into the country.

We have been here in Bombay for five weeks, waiting impatiently to move on to a new place, wherever it may be! At first we enjoyed the change, and found a new city very exciting. We met many people, and time seemed to pass quickly. That was for the first week, but since then we have become weary of waiting and we long to do some work. Phyl will tell you where we were expecting to go, but that may be all changed now owing to the war in the Far East. I don't think we will be kept idle much longer and when we start work, it probably *will* be work!

I know you have always wanted to see India. I wish you could be with me to see Bombay. I don't know whether my visit to this country will take me any further than Bombay. From my window in the hotel, I have a lovely view of tall palm trees fringing the wide sweep of the bay. The water is nearly always dotted with little white sails of fishing boats. It is a very large port, here, and we find it interesting to watch the many ships coming into harbour. Bombay as you know is called 'The Gateway of India' and I think that describes it well!

I will write to you again very soon. I do hope you are keeping well.

Cheerio for the present.
Much love from
Vera

❦

Dear Mother and Father

The airgraph system has just been started here, so I am sending one, and hope it will reach you sooner.

As you see by the address, we are still here, but do expect a change shortly. As soon as we settle in our new place, I will cable you my new address. I hope you are receiving letters from me, as I should not like you to be without mail, as we are here. We miss our letters very much, but believe there are many waiting for us, when we reach our destination.

It is very hot here but we are told this is cool as compared with the heat later on!

Hope you are all well. I have written to thank you for the cable. Best love to you both, and all.

Your loving
Vera

❧

3.3.42

My Dear Mother and Father

I have just received the most welcome pile of letters and parcels I have ever had. We have been without letters since November, and all our Christmas mail was held up at a certain port, owing to our unit moving. Now this wonderful mail has arrived here for us – all our Christmas parcels, cards, letters, etc. It seems that little has been lost, I am very fortunate for I have seven airgraphs, one cable, one postcard, three Christmas cards, two letters, and two parcels, from you. Also I had letters from friends in Ilford.

I wish you could have seen my pleasure when this great mail was handed to me. I spent such a happy absorbing two hours reading, unwrapping and comparing notes with my friends who were also happily tearing open envelopes and cutting string round parcels. How we talked and laughed and showed each other photos, presents, etc. We can talk of nothing else now, and we carry our letters about and read them over and over, it is such a joy to have news after three months.

Thank you so much for the lovely parcels. I was delighted with the books and they are new publications which will be interesting. I was so glad to have the magazines, and parish magazines which are a link with home. I am writing to Muriel to thank her, but please thank her also now. I love the green blotter and attractive notebook from Geoff. They will both be most useful. I will write to him and send the letter to you for forwarding.

It is very sweet and generous of you to send such lovely parcels. I really don't know how to thank you, for they have given me such pleasure. Books are such a blessing, especially in these times, and I appreciate them more than anything else as gifts.

It was so good to have seven airgraphs together. I put them in their correct order, from 11th November to 25th December, and then it made an interesting budget to read. The airgraphs are such a blessing to the Forces out here. What an invention! I have two letters (from Muriel) dated 3rd October and 6th November. They are both long and interesting, and I will answer them. The cable was sent at the beginning of December, wishing me a happy birthday, Christmas and New Year. I am so glad you received my cable sent at that time. Thank you also for the Christmas cards.

I hope you are receiving my mail safely, also my cables. I sent one on arrival here. Later I received one from you asking me to cable my new address, but as it was still the same, I cabled back by a full rate cable to tell you. I would like to know if this is quicker than the EFM cables. Today I sent you another cable to tell you that I have received my Christmas mail. I have written numerous postcards and airgraphs, also several letters since coming here.

You will be wondering what is to happen to us, and why we are waiting here in Bombay for so long. Well, we were destined for one of those countries we have recently occupied, north west of here. We were at sea when a wireless message told us to proceed here instead. On our arrival on Christmas Eve, we disembarked and the ship left shortly for the Far East.

We have since heard that we were to have left soon afterwards for Singapore, but as ships were scarce, time passed and there was no transport for us. The war in Malaya became more grave and when Singapore was threatened our projected move was cancelled. Now with Singapore and the Malay Peninsula in Japanese hands, and Rangoon and Jarva prepared for a blitz, we are still here waiting and wondering just where we will go to!

There is a possibility that we shall remain in this country, but in which part we shall have our hospital, we do not know. We may still go to our original destination. In any case we only hope and pray we shall be back at work soon, for we are impatient about this inactivity and feel it is just too bad in wartime when there is so much to be done everywhere. I feel quite sure I shall not think about 'leave' again for a very long time, when we are back in harness.

Fortunately I have been able to do some work during the past week. I have been on night duty at the military hospital here and have one patient in my care. She is one of our own Sisters and a friend of mine, who has had a major operation and been very ill. The hospital is very short of staff and very busy, and as we have no work to do ourselves, three of us have been nursing this Sister in the military families hospital. Two are on day duty and I am on night duty. I jumped at the opportunity of a job, and Matron said she was giving me work because she knew I would be much happier doing something for my salary! Also I had asked her to give me some temporary duty at this hospital on a previous occasion, so when my friend became ill she remembered my request. Now the others quite envy me having something to do to pass the time away.

This hospital exists in peacetime, (not like our own, which packs itself up and wanders over the face of the earth, and was never heard of before the war). It is situated in lovely grounds which go right down to the rocky shore of the bay. In the section where I work the rooms are small, some single-bedded, others with three or four beds. There is a wide verandah all round the building. In front of this is a small garden, and then the sea. At night it is so quiet, except for the waves washing up over the rocks. Tonight there is a full moon, and the bay is shining like silver, and the garden is like fairyland!

I am able to watch the dawn breaking every morning, and it is an indescribable sight. The colours in the sky are exquisite.

I am still living in the hotel, while working here, and we are taken backwards and forwards by ambulance.

I have told you about St Thomas's Cathedral in a previous letter. It is a lovely church, and I have been regularly there since we came. The chaplain, Canon McPherson, has got to know us, and I went with another Sister to breakfast with him after church on Sunday. He has been in India for thirty years! He is a very interesting person and we did so enjoy having a meal in a private house, after living a community life for so long. The Bishop of Bombay is also very nice, and very old. Recently the Bishop of Colombo visited Bombay, and we heard him preach in the Cathedral.

My transfer to a hospital ship has never materialised, owing to our unit moving. Individual transfers are automatically cancelled in such cases. However, I hope some day I shall have another chance, as I should like such a move very much.

I am so glad to hear Geoff has settled down in his new life and seems happy. I was interested to hear he is in Ireland. That will be an experience for him. Thank Muriel very much for his photo received safely. I am so glad to have it and I think it is very good. How smart he must look in uniform. You will look forward very much to his 'leave'.

I am very sorry that your clothes rationing is such a problem. You are so good about it too and complain so little in your letters. I have sent two pairs of stockings home with Phyllis and would have been glad to send more, but she had very little room in her luggage. I hope to send more by post, but I do hope you do not have to pay duty on such things. Would you please let me know. Send a cable if you like or an airgraph and ask me to send them, as I will be only too glad to help in that way. Also if there is anything else, *please* let me know and I will send it. There is no shortage here.

Your photo has not arrived yet and I do so hope it comes, as I want it very much. There is more mail to come to us, so it may be here with the next batch.

I am so sorry Peter has been ill. I do hope he is quite better now. He is such a darling – you must have been worried about him. I did not know dogs could have rheumatic fever. He must have been very ill.

One of your airgraphs was written on my birthday. On that day we were in the Red Sea! Someone had a cake made for me, to my great surprise Wasn't that a kind thought? I wondered what you were doing. On Mother's birthday, we were still in the Red Sea. On second thoughts I may as well tell you we were in Aden, and risk what the censor thinks! It was very hot there. That was my second visit, and I remembered we saw it in 1931. I sent you a cable from there. Did it arrive?

I am glad to hear it was not you who broadcast a message, as I thought. I did not hear it, but many patients did and told me they were sure it was for me. I went to Broadcasting House the next day for details, but was told that no details were available as the message was from London, relayed by Cairo. I did really think I had missed you, so now am glad to know you did not speak in vain! I hope one day I *shall* hear you on the radio.

I expect next time I write I shall be able to tell you where we expect to settle down. Since starting this letter I have heard it is very likely we shall remain in India after all! We are so anxious to start work somewhere, so hope the end of this hotel existence is in sight. I will send you a cable when we move.

Well, my dears, I must stop now or this will not be able to go by airmail.

Take care of yourselves and rest all you can. Give my love to all. I will write another letter soon.

Fondest love to you both.

Your loving

Vera

4.3.42

P.S. The photograph has just arrived. It is beautiful, and you haven't changed a bit. I shall treasure it dearly and am getting a nice frame for it. I have shown it to my friends and they all admire it and say what sweet parents I have! I heartily agree, needless to say. It couldn't be a better photo. How it makes me wish I could see you again! It was very well packed and not even creased after the long journey. Many thanks. I feel I shall carry it about and show it to everyone in Bombay!

My Dear Mother and Father

I hope you are receiving my letters safely as I am writing often. I have not heard from you lately but do not worry as I know our letters are being delayed and will arrive eventually.

As you see, we are still here and still hoping we shall go soon. There is much that we have found out lately, regarding what might have been! When we arrived here, our equipment had not come with us as it was all on another ship. We were to have been attached to a certain division as there is always one hospital to a division. This division moved on to Singapore, and we should have followed but our complete hospital equipment had been landed at another port by a misunderstanding, so without that we could not embark again. Therefore we are still here and our ill-fated division was trapped in Singapore! It is only recently we have discovered how very nearly we went to Malaya, and how much we have missed. We have all been very shocked to hear that sixteen Sisters have been killed, many more injured, and a number are prisoners of war in Singapore. Today a party of Sisters has arrived here, having been torpedoed and rescued after their evacuation from Malaya. The more tragic stories we hear about Singapore the more tragic and disastrous it all seems. To this country it has been an awful blow, just as the fall of Rangoon has been also. There must be a vast amount of work to be done in the hospitals left behind. We often think about those Sisters there and wonder if they will be allowed to work and live in the same way as before.

Now that we have definitely lost our division, it seems that the unit will be divided up and we will all go different ways. There is no division here which is without a hospital, so there is not one to which we can be attached. It will be a sad thing if our hospital is broken up as we have been a unit since the beginning of the war. However, I feel that as long as we find work soon, I don't mind where it is, for there must be plenty to do. It seems shameful that we have been kept idle for so long after always being so busy in the Middle East. One can never really know why some things happen in the army.

It has been whispered that there is a chance that we may return home. That is too wonderful to be contemplated, however, and we are trying not to think about it as we do not think there is any hope of such a thing happening. There is a lot to be done out here, and there will be many more big events taking place, so we do not think for one minute that we will be sent back. It will be a great day when we do see dear old England again, but I feel it will not be for some time yet, even though we have been out here nearly two and a half years.

We have a new outdoor uniform now and it is much cooler and more practical. We have been wearing white tricoline with long sleeves and a grey and scarlet cape. It was very unsuitable, although the material was thin enough. Now we have white drill dresses with short sleeves, and grey and scarlet epaulettes and two 'pips' on each shoulder; white topees in the day and white felt hats in the evening, white shoes and stockings. Our working uniform is the same, also being white drill. It is very sensible material for a hot climate and looks most fresh and smart when well washed and starched. We are now all ready for work in the hottest of climates and have put our winter uniforms away for probably a long time to come.

It is becoming hotter every day and the temperature is rising steadily. At night it is stifling and the blackout is making the heat much less bearable, as the black painted windows must be kept closed until after lights are out, so there is very little air.

By the time you receive this, we shall be having the monsoon season and will know what a really humid climate is like.

Since beginning this letter today, I have received a cable from you to say that you had received a second Bombay letter from me and also the brooch. I went out straight away to cable back to tell you I am well and I sent you Easter and birthday wishes. Thank you so much for the cable, it is very welcome and I do know now that you are all well.

There is much excitement here concerning the visit of Sir Stafford Cripps, who has just arrived to discuss the question of

Home Rule for India. I wonder what will come of it! It seems a strange time for such a demand to be made, with the enemy on the doorstep!

I have sent Muriel a book which I hope she receives safely. It is very good and I am sure you would both enjoy reading it also.

If there is anything at all that I can send, do please let me know. I do want to send whatever you need most. I will continue to send parcels of tea, sugar, etc, and there is one on the way now. Write and tell me about anything else, because I can get it here, and there are no rationing worries for us.

I hope Geoff is going on well and is still happy. I wonder if he has been home on leave yet?

I have much enjoyed reading the magazines and books you sent me. It was good to have the magazines and *Auckland Weeklies*, also the *Church Times*, (thirteen copies of which I received). I had not seen any of them and found them all very interesting. I thought it was so thoughtful of you to send them, and I have passed the magazines on to my friends to read. I gave the *Church Times* to an army padre, when I had read them, and he was very grateful. Thank you again for everything you sent. It was a lovely parcel.

I am writing to Geoff and will address the letter to you so that you can send it on to him.

I am glad you are enjoying the cinema as it must be a pleasant relaxation for you. I go quite often too, and we have some quite recent films here, not like Jerusalem where the films seemed to arrive long after the rest of the world had forgotten them! The cinemas are air-conditioned, and so, beautifully cool and a contrast to the atmosphere outside.

Well, my dears, there does not seem to be any more to write just now, so I will say cheerio for now. I wonder if this letter will be blue-pencilled as I may have said too much. Anyway I hope it arrives safely.

Fondest love to all and God bless you. Take care of yourselves and don't work too hard, and *don't* forget to rest!

Will write again soon.

Your loving

Vera

My Dear Muriel

Many thanks for your two nice long letters which arrived on 1st March. They were dated 3rd October, and 6th November, so have been a long time coming, and were held up on the way, owing to our move. I had a wonderful mail, and it all arrived in a pile. Thank you ever so much for the two books and all the copies of the *Church Times*. I am most grateful and am very pleased with the books. Dorothy Sayer's book is very interesting and I had been wanting a copy, strangely enough. *England is a Village* is a very fine book also and my friends have also wanted to read it, and have all enjoyed it immensely. I do not like to think of you spending your money on me, as it is so difficult to obtain most things in England, and I do not want you to go without things in order to send me presents. It was very sweet of you, and the Christmas parcels gave me great pleasure.

I have sent you a copy of Douglas Reed's latest book *A Prophet at Home*. I hope it arrives safely, and that you have not already got it. I am sure you will enjoy it for it is very absorbing, and exposes a great deal of our mistakes and failures. If you have read any of his other books you will appreciate it more. He is a man who knows his subject, for he was foreign correspondent for the *Times* in Berlin for seven years and he was able to watch Germany's rise to power. This book was written at the end of 1940 and the beginning of 1941. There is only one point which I know to be untrue. You may disagree with something else, but this I know is wrong. He knows nothing about Australians and we do out here! You had better form your own conclusions from that, for I should not say too much in a letter! (See Chapter VI.)

Please let me know if there is anything I can get you here, as we are not rationed at all. I am sending some stockings as soon as possible. At the moment there is some difficulty about posting them, and the authorities are being awkward, but I think we shall be able to send them. If there is something else you need, please don't hesitate to let me know, as I do want to get something you need.

I know you will have heard all my news in my letters and

airgraphs home. We are still here as you see by my address and are very anxious to work again. I feel really guilty about telling you that we have been idle here for over three months. We cannot do anything about it of course, but we feel useless objects just now. After being so active in the Middle East it is very painful to us to have to waste time here in idleness. We have really had a wonderful escape, however, as we were all set to go to Singapore, but our equipment was not here, being still in transit from the Middle East, so our departure had to be delayed. Soon afterwards Singapore fell. Later it was arranged for us to go to Rangoon, and we do not know why the move failed to materialise, but before we started off, Rangoon fell also! Now we do not know where we shall go. It is thought we shall be sent as reinforcements to various hospitals throughout this country, where we are most needed. On the other hand we may be required to go to another theatre of war, if there is a push somewhere near.

I have done some temporary night duty at the military hospital here, and found it a welcome change, and enjoyed it. The hospital is beautifully situated right on the edge of the bay, so there is a lovely view. Also it is surrounded by pretty gardens full of tropical plants and trees. In the moonlight the scene was very romantic and Eastern and typical of the words of *On Wings of Song* which we used to sing.

The war is moving very quickly in this direction and people here are beginning to realise it. Bombs were dropped on India for the first time yesterday. So much has happened this year, and we have had some severe shocks regarding Malaya and Burma. Are you free of raids just now? I do hope so, as we never hear of damage to Britain except on rare occasions.

It is going to be terribly hot here, and people say it will be a hotter summer than usual. Even now we have to be careful not to go out without a hat or topee, as the sun is so powerful and one gets awful headaches after going any distance with an uncovered head. We have white topees with a strip of the QAIMNSR, ribbon on one side, and white drill dresses for outdoor wear. It is very cool and fresh. The nights are also unpleasantly warm. Palestine had a dry heat, which is . more bearable than this dampness. It will be interesting to experience the monsoon season, which comes very soon, but we hope we shall be working by then so will probably not be here.

I have been swimming often. There is a large open-air sea water pool here and it is most pleasant. There are lovely lawns and gardens all round it, where we can sit and have tea after a swim.

You say in your second letter that you would like to know why I wore a medal in one of the photos I sent, and none of the other girls wore the same thing. Well, it just happened that my friends omitted to put theirs on, so it looked as if I was the only one privileged to wear it. The truth is, I was the only one who was 'properly dressed' as the army saying goes! We had one or two snaps taken of groups of the Sisters while on the way here. I will send you some as soon as they are developed, as they should be quite good.

I thought of you at Easter, although you would not have been doing the same things at the same times as I was, as we are five hours ahead of you. I went to the Three Hours Service on Good Friday, and to church at 8.30 a.m. on Easter Day. There were hundreds of people there and it was a beautiful service, and the choir sang very well indeed. It is a lovely cathedral, and very old, having been dedicated in 1750.

The book *One Foot in Heaven* which Mother and Father sent me and which I have so much enjoyed reading has been filmed, and is coming here next week. I am so looking forward to seeing it. I expect you have seen it.

What a delightful and human story. It so reminded me in many ways of us when we were all at home as children, for some of the incidents in the book are very similar. The family was always poor, the parson was always aiming at some ideal, always working hard, and always pacifying tiresome parishioners; the Mother was sweet, placid hardworking for the church and her home, and always helping Father with some problem; and the children were devoted to their parents, always crept about the house on Saturdays, and looked upon their Father as one who always had 'one foot in Heaven!'

I am enclosing two snaps which I thought you would like. One is of a typical hill in Palestine, wild, rocky and dry. The other is of a Bedouin and his camel. I am acquiring a great assortment of snaps and putting them into an album so I hope to be able to exhibit them to you one day.

I agree with your remarks about Russia. We have been filled

with wrong propaganda for years and have never been allowed to see any good in the Soviet. Now she is saving us, and helping to beat the common enemy. There is, in my opinion, a great deal which is sound common sense in her policy, and government system. I do think that the decline of religion there, was not so final and complete as we thought, and I am sure the spiritual lives of the people are by no means suppressed now, and religion is about to be revived. Do not think I am a red-hot Communist but I must say my ideas of some things have been changed since this war. I think we shall, and must, have a completely different system in Britain in years to come, and will learn by our mistakes of the past. If we allow ourselves to go on in the same way, it is inevitable that we shall have to fight another war after a period of twenty years or so!

Well, I had better not write any more or this will be too heavy for airmail. I am writing a lot of letters lately as I have plenty of free time, so can keep my correspondence up to date. I will not keep you waiting so long for a letter next time. I hope you will receive the airgraph I sent you for your birthday.

Well, cheerio for now, and all best wishes.

Much love from

Vera

ॐ

A Bedouin on his camel

A rocky hill in Palestine

Bombay
India
21.4.42

My Dear Mother and Father

Many thanks for a cable received on 18th April. I have just sent you a cable in reply. So glad you have received many letters. It is good to know, as I am writing every few days and sending cables often. I am intending from now on to send a cable at least once in ten days so that you are not kept waiting for news. I also send airgraphs frequently.

Still here, still waiting for orders, and still wondering *why*! I am longing for some really strenuous work to do and there must be plenty of work to be done in many places. I hope you are all well. I am very fit. We have all had inoculations against cholera.

I have sent off a parcel of tea and sugar etc. Hope it arrives safely. I also sent butter, and would be glad to know if it is okay.

Cheerio. God bless you.

Much love

Vera

ॐ

Bombay
India
14.5.42

My Dear Mother and Father

The last time I heard from you was an airgraph from Father, written on 13th March and received on 9th May. I wrote you an airmail postcard on that day. The airgraph had been halfway round the world, and nearly back again! Many thanks for it. I am writing you an airmail letter soon, as it is time I sent another, the last having been written on 27th April, but there is so little news to tell you that I am going to wait a few days more when I think I should have more to write about. All our Sisters are being sent to various parts of the country. My turn has not yet come, but it may be any day, and we have short notice when we do have orders. I will write as soon as I go to my new station, and send a cable.

Much love to all.

God bless you

Vera

❧

Bombay
India
19.5.42

My Dear Mother and Father

I sent you an airgraph a few days ago. I have not heard from you lately but we expect a mail in soon.

I am very well and do hope you are too. I can now tell you that we are starting our hospital again in a very short time, and we are going inland to a place on the plains, six hours' journey from here. We are all so glad to be moving soon, and will be so pleased to be back at work. It will be interesting to see more of India too.

I will write more about it in my next letter which I shall be sending soon.

Much love to all. God bless you.

Your loving

Vera

❧

Bombay
India
15.6.42

My Dear Mother and Father

My unit has gone to Ahmednagar which is a camp about 200 miles inland from here, and they have started the hospital and are very busy. I am looking forward to joining them, but just now as you will have heard, I am a patient myself and am still in Bombay. I hope my last airmail letter reached you, but in case it is lost I will tell you again that I came into hospital on Whit-

Saturday, having been feeling rather ill for a few days, and I have been here ever since. It is now just over three weeks. I know I did quite the wisest thing in reporting sick when I did, as Ahmednagar where I should have gone, is a wild kind of place, miles from anywhere, and it would not have been so easy to have medical care there, when the hospital had only just arrived and was in the process of formation. As it is I am in a very comfortable hospital and in good hands, you will be pleased to know.

I am having the operation the day after tomorrow, Wednesday, 17th June. I will send you a cable and an airgraph as soon as I am feeling better and then you will not feel so worried. The only thing I feel anxious about is that you will be worrying and wishing you could be here, but I do hope you will try not to worry.

Three of my friends from the unit are working here temporarily so I am not quite without my friends. They are very good to me, and have been to see me and bring me books etc. Also I have had letters from those in Ahmednagar.

I had not heard from you for weeks when your cable and letter came. I was so pleased to have so much news. Please don't worry about the Japanese being so near, although they now have all Burma. I cannot say much about our preparations, but you can be well assured that great changes are taking place in this country and preparations are tremendous!

I am so glad Geoff has been on leave and it is good to hear that he is happy and proud of his Service.

You all seem to be working as hard as ever. How I should love to see the spring flowers, and daffodils in the churchyard. The flowers here wither and die so quickly in the heat.

The monsoon season has begun. We had a terrific storm with the worst lightning I have ever seen, the other night, and then suddenly the heavens seemed to open, and what rain came down! I cannot describe how torrential it was. We are on the edge of the bay, and with the waves dashing against the rocks, and thunder rolling overhead, and the rain beating down, we could not hear ourselves speak! In the morning the trees were so green, and little buds were springing up on all the bushes and shrubs. The birds were singing joyfully and nature seemed to have taken on a new lease of life. It is very hot when the sun comes out after the rain, and steam rises off the ground making the atmosphere very damp.

Well, my dears I hope this reaches you safely, and I will write again soon. I am glad the airgraphs are arriving regularly. Once more let me tell you not to worry about me. By the time this arrives I should be on sick leave, or maybe I shall be back with my unit.

My love to Muriel.

God bless you always.

Ever your loving

Vera

❧

P/208528
QAIMNSR
No 60 British General Hospital
Ahmednagar
India
23.6.42

Dear Mother and Father

I have just sent you an airgraph and so this may arrive at the same time. I hope you received my cable sent on the 19th June telling you that I had had my operation on the 17th. It is such a relief to know that it is over and the cause of all my trouble removed. I am writing you an airmail letter to tell you all about it. I am very fit now and comfortable. Everyone has been extremely kind and I could not have been better cared for anywhere else. They tell me the surgeon performed a very clever and careful operation. He is very pleased with me.

Much love to all

Vera

❧

My Dear Mother and Father

I have recently sent you a number of airgraphs, letters etc to tell you that I am in hospital.

A few days ago, on the 19th June, I sent you a cable telling you that I had had my operation and was much better. Now you will be pleased to hear that I am making excellent progress and feeling very well. The appendix was in a very bad condition and contained quite a large stone. The surgeon was very relieved to find the cause of the pain. I have been wonderfully cared for, and had the very best attention. I was lucky to have such a clever surgeon.

There is no need to worry. I am writing again soon. God bless you.

Love
Vera

ဢ

Ahmednagar
India
30.6.42

My Dear Mother and Father

I have sent you a number of airgraphs and letters recently, also a cable to tell you that I have had an operation, and my appendix removed. I expect I shall have a reply from you soon.

You will be pleased to hear that I am very much better now, and it is two weeks since the operation. I am up and walking about, and shall be leaving hospital in a few days' time. I am having about a month's sick leave which I shall spend in Bombay staying in a very nice Sisters' hostel, where I shall be very comfortable. Then I will go on to Ahmednagar. All my mail will be re-addressed from there to me in Bombay.

I feel better than I have been for a long time and have a healthy appetite.

Writing again soon.
Much love. God bless you.
Your loving
Vera

❧

Ahmednagar
India
4.7.42

My Dear Mother and Father

I was discharged from hospital yesterday and started my month's sick leave today. I was in hospital for six weeks altogether – four weeks being spent under observation, and two weeks recovering from my operation. I pleased everyone by making a good recovery and now feel very well and look it too. I now have a whole month in which to rest and get really strong and ready for work again. The army looks after us when we are ill, and is liberal with giving sick leave, and if a Sister is not absolutely fit at the end of her leave, the period is extended until she is. However, I know I shall be in the best of health at the end of my month, for I feel so well already and have a good appetite.

I had a very nice room to myself for the first few days, in fact, for the first week, and then I shared a room with another sick Sister, who had arthritis following dysentery. I enjoyed her company very much. Our room was upstairs and opened onto a verandah which overlooked the bay, so we could lie and look at the sea and watch the ships coming into harbour. When we started to get up (she was also convalescent) we could sit on the verandah and enjoy the sea breezes. This Sister was Matron of a Salvation army mission hospital, and at the end of five years, her first term of service, she joined the army and was sent to a military hospital in Lucknow. She was ill soon afterwards, and while on leave in Bombay developed arthritis, so had to be admitted to Calaba Hospital. She had many visitors, nearly all members of the Salvation Army and so I met them and liked them all very much. They used to come and talk to me often and were very cheery and full of life.

The monsoon season is now in full swing. The rains started on 13th June and were heralded in by a violent storm. Since then it has rained every day and sometimes nearly all day! I have never seen such rain, even in Palestine. The sky is heavy and low with grey clouds and the wind howls dismally. Sometimes we have quite a hurricane. The sea is very rough and dirty. If the temperature was low one would quite enjoy this weather and gather round fires as we do at home. But not so! It is as hot as Hades, the humidity at times is awful. After a deluge of rain, the sun comes out, and steam rises everywhere so that you feel as if a hot wet blanket had been wrapped round you. We cannot go out without taking a mackintosh and umbrella for there is no knowing when the next torrent is coming down.

I am staying now at a very nice hostel for nursing Sisters which has just been opened. It is right on the seafront, or Marine Drive as it is called. It is very comfortable, with all new furniture, pleasant bedrooms and sitting rooms, and very good food. There is only one other Sister here, and we get on very well together. More Sisters are expected soon. It is going to be very popular, as it is near the town and pleasantly situated, also not at all expensive. It is a change from a hotel, and much more restful. At the end of my month, I have to report to the hospital and if they are satisfied with me, I shall return to my unit.

I am sure that you will not feel at all worried about me any more when you receive my cable and especially when you receive this letter.

How serious the news is just now. The situation in Libya is very worrying. We always feel a great interest in the Western Desert as we were so close at one time and had dealings with so many men who had been there. I do hope we can push back the Germans soon.

Much love to all. God bless you.
Your loving
Vera

☙

My Dear Mother and Father

On 31st July, I sent you another parcel of food stuffs, and will be sending another off soon. I do hope you will receive the parcel safely. I think you have had them up to the present.

I left Bombay on 1st August, and came here to Ahmednagar, to join my unit. The journey took ten hours and I arrived at midnight, and was met at the little wayside station and taken by ambulance to the hospital which is seven miles out in the country, from the station. The journey seemed endless, but it is not really long at all for India. Sometimes one has to travel for days and nights without a break. The scenery on the way was very pretty and I found it interesting to be seeing India for the first time.

One of my friends was waiting up for me when I arrived at the Sisters' quarters. It was very nice to see her again, and it was also nice to see my other friends the next day. It was pleasant to realise that I had been missed and that people were genuinely pleased to see me back. Matron was very kind. I was not on duty on 2nd August, so spent the day settling in to my room. We are living in bungalows, about five or seven Sisters in each, so we have quite a home-like atmosphere in our houses. In each bungalow there is a sitting room furnished with armchairs and tables. The gardens are very pleasant, full of trees (which you know I like), shrubs and flowers. We have become keen on gardening and have planted tomatoes and lettuces etc. At night we sleep out on the verandah, and like it much better than being indoors. There is an Indian native watchman on guard for each house, and he sits at the gate with a lamp, and wanders round in the night to look for trespassers. There have been strange people trying to break in to the houses so we have a guard for safety. There are millions of mosquitoes as well as other nasty insects flying about, so we never sleep without our mosquito nets.

The country round here looks lovely just now, so green and fresh after the heavy monsoon rains. Later it will dry up and there will be dust and intense heat, but this is the best time of the year, and reminds us of home. Often I feel I am back in Essex, for there are green fields, haystacks, streams, (which are just cracked earth and quite dried up before the rain), and cows and bullocks are grazing in the fields. It is flat country all round the camp, but not far away we can see hills. The roads are good, and ideal for cycling. As the Sisters' Mess is some way from the hospital, we either cycle on and off duty, or go by an army lorry. I have just hired a bicycle and enjoy riding it.

The nearest village, which is Ahmednagar, is seven miles away, and consists of a bazaar, a bank, and a few houses. We can buy quite a lot of things there, but mostly it is better to wait until one of the Sisters has two or three days' leave, after night duty, and is going into Bombay, and then she is given shopping lists from most of us.

This is a very ancient place, and has a great history dating back to several centuries ago. There is a huge fort here, with a vast stone wall, which reminds us of Windsor Castle, it is so imposing. There have been battles fought here in the past, and we are trying to find out all about the history of the fort. The camp in which we are living is very large and becoming more important. The hospital is being built out of army barracks, and all the wards are barrack rooms which hold fifty beds. We are making them very pleasant and up to date, with new ceilings, the walls painted a cream colour, fans installed and other fittings essential in a hospital. It is an amazing transformation when you compare a newly decorated ward with one that has not yet been altered.

I started work again on 3rd August, and have a new ward of fifty beds. Just now we are not very busy as we have not yet completed the building of the operating theatre, and so cannot take in acute surgical cases. These have to go to another hospital not far away, until we are ready.

There is very little for the troops to do here in their free time, so sport has become the main pastime. There was a big football match the other day, played between the teams of two famous Scottish regiments. I went to it, and really enjoyed it very much. It is the first time I have felt enthusiasm for football, but this was an exciting game, and almost the entire garrison turned out to watch it. Before the match began, the pipers came on the field and entertained us to some good old Scottish tunes. I have also developed a great liking for the bagpipes, especially as we hear them so much round here.

We have a nice little chapel and have furnished it quite well. I had some new altar cloths made in Bombay, also a Bible marker in green petersham material with IHS embroidered on it in gold. We are also having new green curtains made for the wall behind the altar. Just now I am busy covering the hassocks with some material which I was able to buy in the bazaar. Quite a lot of the chapel things, which we had in the Middle East, were lost in transit among them being an olive-wood cross and candlesticks which were very good.

It is very peaceful here after the noise of Bombay, and the air is much fresher. I feel sure I am going to like this place very much. We expect to have plenty of work to do when the hospital is completed. This is the fourth hospital we have opened in the East, one in Sarafand, two in Jerusalem, and now this one. It is all good experience.

The political situation is very serious in this country, just now, but we are glad that the Government has at last taken a firm stand, and many arrests have been made.

Please tell Muriel I am writing to her soon. I sent Geoff some cigarettes while in Bombay and sent them to his old address in Blackpool.

I would be very glad if you would let me know of anything at all that you need. I know stockings are very valuable, and much appreciated, but would you have to pay heavy duty on them? Let me know this, and if you would like them I will get some straight away, and send off a parcel to you. There is so little I can do to help you, and I want to do what I can.

Are you still having bad air raids? How weary you must be of them!

It will soon be three years since the war began, three years since I joined the army, and before long it will also be three years since I last saw you. Oh dear, what a long time, and how I miss you! It would be lovely to come home, but it would be even better to come home when England was at peace again. We must see this through first, and it does not look like ending yet!

I will write again very soon. For the present, cheerio, and God bless you all.

With best love.

Ever your loving

Vera

☙

Ahmednagar
India
23.8.42

My Dear Muriel

Many thanks for your airgraph, written on the 15th July, and received on the 19th August. Also thank you so much for your long letter sent on 12th June and received on the 19th August also.

As you see by my address I am now in Ahmednagar, the place we used to know only by name, and which we heard so much about! We are settled in and have a large hospital almost completed. It consists mainly of disused barrack rooms, which we have transformed by painting them cream colour inside, putting in new ceilings and electric fans, and making them just like wards in a modern hospital. It is really a work of art and we are proud of our wards now that we are working in them and have patients, who needless to say appreciate the cheerful wards very much after ordinary barrack rooms.

I have a surgical ward of thirty beds and am quite busy. The operating theatre has just been built and is very up to date also, as is the x-ray department, so we feel we have achieved a great deal in a short time.

The hospital is quite scattered, there are many wards and they are separated from each other by quite large stretches of ground. · When visiting another ward or a department or the Matron's office we find it far better to cycle, or we should wear out our shoe leather in no time. We nearly all ride bicycles, most of us have hired them for a small fee monthly. I have one and find it very pleasant to be able to ride on and off duty instead of going on an army lorry. The Mess is some way from the hospital.

Just now Ahmednagar is quite beautiful, for the rains have hardly finished and the grass is fresh and as green as in England, and the trees are lovely. It is all open country round here. There is no town where we are, only a village with a bazaar, and a station. We cycle in to the bazaar sometimes, but cannot buy very much there.

The mosquitoes here are worse than anywhere we have been. They are everywhere in their millions, swarms and swarms of them! We always sleep with our mosquito nets well tucked in all round our beds or the nasty little devils would find a crack somewhere, and get in. At night they sing in a loud high pitched tone, and the poor night Sisters sit with sheets draped round them when on duty, to prevent their legs from being eaten up! They suffer most from bites.

There are many other crawling, hopping and jumping things which startle us! There are brown beetles which fly and buzz like wasps; there are black beetles in scores of thousands, sandflies, centipedes, snakes, (which I have not yet met, thank goodness), and lots of strange creatures which flutter round our rooms and which do not seem to have any names. Last, but not least, there are *SCORPIONS*! I am scared stiff of them, and the other evening one came to visit me, to my horror. I was sitting on my bed, having just removed my shoes, when I heard something fall from the fan, and there a few feet from me was this awful brown scorpion, all ready to make a dash for my bare feet if I tried to kill it. I made a dash first, and in two leaps I was out of the room to summon the help of my friends in killing it. Having seen one before in Palestine there was no mistaking it. We soon killed it, and I have not seen any more since.

It is such a pleasant change to be away from the town and the air is so much fresher here than in Bombay, although we are not near the sea. Also it is peaceful after the noise of Bombay. I like it very much and do not find it at all isolated.

I am very glad to hear that you enjoyed *A Prophet at Home* your comments were most interesting. I think his last chapter was fine, in which he says how sure he is that Britain will 'decline to fall'. It is a great book, by a great writer, who has the courage of his convictions. Did you know that Ribbentrop demanded of the British Government that Reed should be recalled from Germany? That was at the time when he was writing *Disgrace Abounding*, in which his revelations are astounding. (That rhymes!) As Dorothy Thompson said 'to the everlasting disgrace of *The Times*', Douglas Reed was withdrawn, but he resigned, finished his book, while still on the Continent, and then returned home to write *A Prophet at Home*. I wonder if he will write another book soon, and I wonder what his feelings are, about the war today. So much has happened since he finished the book.

Please let me know if there is anything special you want and I will send whatever you need. It is so much easier to buy things in India than it is for you.

Yesterday I received four copies of the *Church Times* for which I thank you very much. They are always interesting and it is good of you to get them for me.

Well, I must say cheerio now, and promise to write again soon. God bless you.

With much love

Vera

৽

Ahmednagar
India
23.8.42

My Dear Mother and Father

Thank you so much for the cable received yesterday. I was very glad to hear you were all well and that you had received my letters and parcel. I have arranged with a shop in Bombay for a parcel of tea, sugar, butter etc, to be sent at least every two weeks, so you should receive them often in future. If there is any kind of food you would like sent in addition, please let me know. Also please let me know soon if you would have to pay duty or give up coupons for such things as stockings and other silk materials as I want to send you a parcel of stockings. Do tell me of anything else you need.

I received a nice long letter from Muriel a few days ago, and am writing today. Also I had an airgraph from her.

I am very well again, and feel better than I have ever been! I am now back at work and liking it very much.

Cheerio. God bless you.

Your loving

Vera

୭

Ahmednagar
India
30.8.42

My Dear Mother and Father

I have not heard from you for a time, but our letters are much delayed so I do not worry. I have sent you airgraphs, an airmail letter and postcard recently. I have also written to Muriel.

I am very well now, and looking better than I have ever been, everyone says so. It is very nice to be back on duty and feeling so well.

I do hope you are all well too. I am sure some of your letters are being held up, as we are getting very small mails just now. It is mostly due to the troubles here (internal strife!).

I have arranged for a sum of money to be sent direct to Father by cable, as you may not get it if it is sent through my account at home, or at least not for some time, and I do want to send you something to help as often as possible.

I was very pleased to receive your cable telling me you were all well and getting my letters. I am glad to know that. I am writing an airmail letter also.

Much love to you both, and all.

Ever your loving

Vera

୭

Ahmednagar
India
2.9.42

My Dear Mother and Father

I have received Muriel's letter today dated 24th June, much to my pleasure as it was some time since I had had a letter. You see how long they take, as much as nine weeks by *airmail*! I have written to Muriel a few days ago but am writing again in answer to the letter. I also wrote you a long airmail letter a few days ago, as well as a postcard and also sent a cable.

I am now very well, so don't worry about me any more as I am feeling so entirely different I have settled down to work here, and it is good to be back in harness. It is raining nearly all the time as it is nearly the end of the monsoon season. Tomorrow is the third anniversary of the war! It seems like the *thirty-third* to me!

I do hope you are all well. How I should love to see you, my dears, but it is no use wishing – it will happen one day.

Cheerio and God bless you.

Your loving

Vera

૭

Ahmednagar
India
20.9.42

My Dear Mother and Father

It is very pleasant here just now. The rains are just finishing and it is cool and sunny. There are flowers everywhere, the trees are green, and the countryside looks very fertile. Really it is quite English here, and quite like dear old Essex. It will be sad to see everything dry up when the heat comes.

We are very busy here now and the hospital has settled down to hard work. Our long idle months in Bombay have faded from our minds and it is nice to feel we are no longer useless. It seemed then as if we would never have work again, but now we are working, and much happier. I have quite a busy ward, surgical, and a pleasant one, for just now we have plenty of flowers to make it bright and cheerful.

Our off-duty time is spent quietly, as there is little to do and nowhere to go, but I do not mind as I have plenty of letters to write and books to read. We do a lot of cycling, and it is quite pleasant to ride into the bazaar – four miles, or visit the bank, six miles. We all keep very well and I think most of us look better than we did in Bombay.

There seems to be little news to tell you I am afraid, so this will be a shorter letter than usual. Will you please send me Geoff's new address.

Cheerio my dears for now, and I will write again very soon. God bless you always and keep you safe. I am always thinking of you and hoping you are not having too many raids. They are always on my mind. I was sorry to hear about the mental hospital being bombed and think I know which one you mean.

My love to all.
Your loving
Vera

ఞ

Ahmednagar
India
23.10.42

My Dear Mother and Father
I am very sorry to hear that you are having to pay duty on my parcels. It is a great shame. A number of people send them regularly, and are all under the impression that they arrive free of duty. I sent one about six weeks ago or more, so it will reach you soon. It would be better as you say, that I do not continue to send the parcels of food, as I do not want you to have to pay for them. If at any time the duty is no longer demanded let me know. I am thankful to hear that you are managing to get enough in the way of food, and do hope you always will.

I have ordered several pairs of stockings for Mother and Muriel from Bombay, and when they come I will send them immediately. Also there are two pairs on the way, for Mother. I am very glad you have written to say that they will be acceptable. I will send them often, to keep you supplied. Please let me know of anything else you would like me to send.

It is sweet of you to insist that I do not send you any more cheques, and I suppose it is really of little use to you if you have no coupons. I feel there is not much I can do to help you, and we are not rationed at all here, while you must be finding life really difficult. That is the bitterness of war! I will leave it to you to let me know what sort of things you need, as time goes on. In a letter I sent you recently, I enclosed a cheque for Father for Christmas. There are two parcels on the way. Mother's birthday present will come rather late, I am afraid, but it is on the way.

I was very pleased with the book Muriel sent me. It is called *The White Cliffs*. I am writing to her soon so will thank her.

I am keeping very well. We are busy all the time here. The rains have finished and we can see the grass withering and the earth becoming more parched. It is intensely hot here during the day, especially between 1 p.m. and 5 p.m. In the very early morning it is lovely – for it becomes very cool and there is quite a 'nip' in the air when we go to breakfast at 7 a.m.

Life is quiet here when we are off duty, for we are so much in the country. I enjoy the peace after Bombay. There is a cinema in the camp where we go sometimes, and where the pictures are not always quite so old and well-worn. Most of the films which come here were made during the 1920s! We also have an Officers' Club where we go to dances and where there is a library to which we belong.

We are all keeping well, and look well here, and I think it must be a healthy place.

I have much pleasure in looking after the chapel. We are having new altar frontals made for it, in Bombay. One is green and will have IHS embroidered in the centre, in gold letters. The other is to be white, with a gold cross in the centre, and will be in use for the first time on Christmas Day. I have had new green curtains made to hang at each side of the altar on the wall. We have very nice curtains of gold and green behind the altar. We put the new ones up recently and they look very attractive and add colour to the church. On our way to India we lost some of our chapel furnishings, including our olive wood cross and candlesticks. Recently we ordered new ones from Jerusalem, and are expecting them soon. A new padre has come to the unit, and he is very good and very keen. He had to leave Burma on foot, and has had some terrible experiences for he was in charge of a number of wounded men and they had to evacuate them 400 miles through the wildest countryside, which is also very mountainous. He is glad of a hospital chaplaincy in quiet surroundings for a change. We all like him very much. He is George Tidey.

I am glad to hear that Geoff is well and happy. I am writing to him soon, and will address it to you, so that you can forward it on as I do not know where he is now. It will be very nice to have a photo of him, and as I often tell my friends about my handsome brother in the RAF it will be nice to have a photo to show them too.

Well, my dears, I am afraid there is little news to give you so I will say cheerio for now. I do hope you are well. I am always thinking of you and wishing I could see you again. It will soon be three years since I waved goodbye to you on Chelmsford station, and you said I would be turning up on leave again 'like a bad penny'! Do you remember?

I will write often and send plenty of airgraphs as they seem to be the best and quickest way of correspondence.

God bless you always and keep you safe.

Much love.

Ever your loving

Vera

ఈ

My Dear Mother and Father

It will soon be a year since we landed in India. How time flies. It seems amazing that another Christmas is almost here. I wonder what you will be doing this year. I shall think of you, and be with you in spirit. By the time this reaches you it will be 1943!

You write such nice long letters and there seems to be so little news for me to tell you in return. Life goes on in just the same way. We shall have some cooler weather soon, for which we shall be most thankful. I expect you would be glad to have some warm weather.

I have ordered a number of pairs of silk stockings from Bombay, and as soon as they come will send them off to you. Later I will send you some more, and please let me know of other things you need. As you say that you have to pay duty on food parcels, I will not send them if you wish it, but if ever you should want me to send them again, please tell me.

It certainly must be a very strange and hard life at home now. People who have just come out here, tell us all about it. I do hope the air raids are not so frequent or so severe.

The news is really good just now, and the future is really looking brighter for us. What a great victory we have had in Libya. Is it too much to hope that this time we can make it a lasting victory, and not be turned back again? There are many people who think that the war will end during this coming year. Who can tell? It is no use trying to speculate these days.

I am so glad your canteen is such a great success. You are doing wonderful work, and it must be greatly appreciated by the men. They love to have such a place to go to, and it does make up a good deal for the lack of home life. Please do not wear yourselves out. You are always so busy, and I am sure you do not rest nearly enough. Will you promise me that you will rest *every* afternoon for at least two hours, (Hitler willing)?

Well, my dears, please excuse this short letter. There is no more news to give you. Cheerio for the present. Another letter soon.

God bless you always. Much love to all.

Ever your loving

Vera

❧

Ahmednagar
India
17.11.42

My Dear Mother and Father

I have written to you several times recently, and have sent an airmail letter in reply to Mother's letter which was the last news I have had from you.

I hope my letters reach you in time for Christmas. The lettercard has been started here, and I have sent you one.

How good the news is now. Did you ring our church bell on Sunday? We read in the papers that the bells in England would be rung again because of our successes in Libya. Let us hope it will be a lasting victory this time.

I do hope you are all well. There is not much news for you I am afraid, as life is uneventful but busy.

Writing again soon. Much love God bless you.

Vera

❧

Ahmednagar
India
6.12.42

My Dear Mother and Father

I was delighted to receive a parcel from you a few days ago. I am so pleased with the books and card, and I think you made an excellent choice. They are both books which I shall love reading and always value very much indeed. It is a lovely present. How good of Geoff to send me the book about the RAF. I wish you could have seen my pleasure when I opened the parcel. It is a lovely big Christmas present, and I much appreciate it.

I have recently posted you a parcel. It contains six pairs of silk stockings and a Kashmir shawl, which I am sure you will like as it is so warm and soft. It will wash well, and become thicker after washing. Three pairs of stockings and the blanket are for Mother for her birthday, and the other stockings are for Muriel. I am so sorry the parcel will arrive so long after 18th December but I am sure you will understand, for we are so buried in the country, and far from good shops, and I have only just been able to get the parcel off to you.

I received an airgraph from Muriel a few days ago. It took only a month to come, which was good. I also had your cable telling me you had not had any answer to your cable of 22nd October. I am sorry I did not send one then, as I had sent one a few days before. Perhaps it never arrived. Anyway I immediately cabled back when this one came about a fortnight ago, so I hope you received it.

I am very sorry to have to tell you that I have been in hospital again for five weeks. I did not write about it before, as I knew it would only cause you to worry unnecessarily. It had nothing whatever to do with my appendix – that is all over and finished with. There is an infection which has become very common out East, and it has kept us busy in the hospitals. It is acute infective hepatitis, in other words, an acute form of jaundice which is infectious in its earliest stages. This is what I had, but I am now completely cured and out of hospital again. I must also add that I am feeling very well and have a marvellous appetite again.

I went off duty on 28th October and was sent to the Military Families Hospital in Poona on that day. Poona is eighty miles from Ahmednagar, and I made the journey by ambulance. We had no special ward for sick Sisters so that is why I was sent to Poona.

After a few days of feeling ill with a raised temperature and pain across my liver, I began to feel better and simultaneously I began to turn yellow! You cannot imagine how I looked – yellow from top to toe, including the whites of my eyes. I was a perfect imitation of a Chinaman, only I was afraid of being mistaken for a Japanese! I was not allowed up for three weeks, and I began to think I would never look British again. However, owing to splendid attention and treatment I faded from the colour of bright yellow to a nice primrose shade, and then in no time at all, I was myself again.

I had a nice room of my own with private bathroom attached, and the door opened onto a long verandah with a garden beyond. The hospital stands on a hill, so from the verandah when I began to get up, I had a wonderful view over Poona and the hills beyond. I used to sit for most of the day on the verandah and had my meals out there too. It was very pleasant.

This was my second experience as a patient in a military hospital, and once again I was treated royally and received every kindness and consideration. There is a new treatment now for hepatitis – it has only been used this year, and has met with a large amount of success. Insulin, the drug used to combat diabetes, is given as an injection every day for five days. I had this, and can testify myself that it was a step forward in medical science. I felt better as soon as the course was started. It is believed that insulin acts on the liver and stirs it up to activity again, for in hepatitis it ceases to function and the result is that bile is distributed in the wrong directions and enters the blood stream and tissues, thus causing the skin to turn yellow.

Colonel Cameron, who introduced this new treatment, came to see me twice. He is a very clever physician and one of the leading medical men in India today. He was with my unit in Jerusalem, so was therefore quite an old friend of mine. He recommended a change of climate up in the hills for my sick leave and advised me to go to Wellington – a military station in the Nilgiris Hills in South India. It is over 6,000 feet above sea level, and an ideal place for convalescents.

I left the hospital on 2nd December, and was given three weeks' sick leave. I therefore return to duty on 23rd December. I shall be on duty again on Christmas Eve. I am glad I shall be back 'home' with my friends for Christmas. I went back to Ahmednagar by train, a five hours' journey, on the day of my discharge, and spent one day there, collecting warm clothes, hot-water bottle, blankets etc, from the bottom of my trunk. The next day I left by train again for Wellington.

The journey is very long, almost 1,000 miles, and it took me a day and a half and two nights to do it! As I was on sick leave I had a free warrant and will also have one for my return journey, so I am very fortunate. I did not have to change until the next evening at 7 p.m. so had over twenty-four hours in the first train. I was very interested in the scenery which became varied as we passed across the width of India, from the Bombay Presidency to the East coast. At night I slept quite well. There are no special sleeping carriages on Indian trains, but in each compartment there are wide couches for four people and they are quite comfortable. I had breakfast on one station where we stopped for twenty minutes and it was very good, and also I was able to have lunch and tea at other stations. We reached Madras at 7 p.m. where I had to change to the Blue Mountain train. How exciting that sounds! I had time for dinner here, but not time to see anything of Madras as the train left in an hour. I slept quite well again that night, and when I awoke I found we were travelling through mountainous country and the air was crisp and cool. How refreshing after the stifling heat of the plains. We reached a little station beneath some very steep hills at 8.30 a.m. Here I had to change again, this time into a small train with the engine at the back pushing the train instead of pulling it. I could see the reason for this when we started, for we climbed thousands of feet up into the Blue Mountains.

I think this was one of the most beautiful journeys I have ever made, perhaps the most beautiful. The rail has been cut out of the mountainside, in places solid rock has been blasted away to make way for the rail. The hills towered above and all round us, covered with lovely green jungle. Wild flowers and plants grew on the banks at each side of the line. Monkeys darted across the track in front of the train and swung themselves into the trees nearby, from which they looked down on us curiously. I was lucky to get a seat in the front compartment and as there was no engine in front I had a perfect view. We climbed up and up and far above I could see the railway track. It seemed incredible that we should be able to ascend to such a height, but we did. Down below were valleys in which clear streams shone in the sunlight. There was a road below us but I was told this is not used much now owing to the strict petrol rationing. I arrived in Wellington which is 6,600 feet above sea level, at 11.30 a.m. Here my journey ended. I had left Ahmednagar on Thursday afternoon, and arrived in Wellington on Saturday morning. I was going to stay at the Sisters' Mess there, for they have taken an extra bungalow especially for the use of the Sisters on leave from other hospitals. The Matron came to meet me, which was very sweet of her, and took me by car to the Sisters' Mess. The bungalow is really delightful like an English country cottage with a pretty garden full of flowers. There are even *roses* growing round the verandah! I have been given a very nice room with a fireplace in which every evening I have a gorgeous wood fire. What a joy to feel the chilliness of the evening and to see the mist rolling down from the hills, and to come in and toast your toes before a real English fire!

Wellington is quite a small village in a lovely setting in a valley with steep green hills all round. There are trees everywhere mostly eucalyptus and pine trees. The scent of these trees is lovely. I have already been for some delightful walks and it is a joy to be able to walk without feeling hot and sticky. What an appetite one gets here too. We have very good food in the Mess. There are only seven Sisters here, it is one of the very small peacetime hospitals, and so of course there is a homely atmosphere among the staff and it is a change to be away from a Mess of our size – fifty Sisters. The Sisters here are all very friendly and have taken me out and are going to show me all the beauty spots.

I am feeling fine now, and I know this leave will do me a great deal of good. A change from the plains makes all the difference. Please don't let yourselves feel at all anxious about me, because by the time this reaches you I shall be back on duty again. I am full of energy now. I wish you could be here with me. I feel I am seeing something of the real beauty of India – it is so different from the places I have already seen.

I think we shall have a happy Christmas in Ahmednagar. I think I told you that we have a new padre. He is a fine person and has become most popular in a short time. Many of the men who had become lax, have returned to the church and become keen once more. All the Medical Officers and Sisters like him. I am afraid our last padre missed many opportunities and had very little personality. We are going round the wards on Christmas Eve singing carols to the patients, and we have a really good choir formed to sing in the church as well. I hope your Christmas will be a happy one. It will not be at all like other years I am afraid.

Well, my dears here I must stop or my letter will be too bulky. I will write again very soon. God bless you always.

Ever your loving
Vera

శ

Ahmednagar
India
28.12.42

My Dear Mother and Father

Thank you so much for two airgraphs which arrived on 23rd December. One was from Muriel and dated 9th November and the other from Mother dated 16th November. I was so pleased to hear from you, as our letters are not coming so often recently. I am writing a long airmail letter tomorrow to tell you all about the way I spent Christmas. I have had a very happy time. Your airgraphs were waiting for me when I arrived back from leave on the 23rd December, so they were especially welcome.

I thought about you often on Christmas Day and knew you were thinking of me. I kept wondering what you were doing. We decorated the chapel and made it look very beautiful. All our services were very well attended. On Christmas Eve we went round the wards singing carols, and the patients were so pleased and said how good it sounded. We gave the patients a very happy time I am glad to say. I will tell you more in my letter.

I am now very well and looking well too. I feel very happy to be back at work too.

Hope you are all well. God bless you.

Love from
Vera

Ahmednagar
India
4.1.43

My Dear Mother and Father

Geoffrey's photo has just arrived, and I am so delighted with it. I will write to him, but please thank him also for sending it. I am sure it could not have been better. How well and handsome he looks! The photo arrived while I was having lunch, and I passed it round the table for all my friends to see. They were most impressed and all remarked what a fine picture it was. There were many amusing comments directed at me, such as 'What a handsome boy, fancy him being your brother! What happened to you?' Is this good-looking person really a relation of yours?' I have shown it to many people already, I feel so proud of it! My patients all admired him and wanted to know what service he was in etc. I think, of all the admiring remarks I have heard, the most excellent tribute in true soldier language came from one of my patients – 'My! He is a smasher!' He certainly is. I should love to see him again just as I should love to see you all. I will have the picture framed, and put it beside yours, which stands on my bedside table.

I wrote to you a few days ago, by airgraph and told you I was writing this airmail letter. It is a little time since I heard from you, but we seem to get our mail here later than most places. I suppose it is because we are 'off the beaten track'. I hope you received my cables, one sent at Christmas and one for Mother's birthday.

I have now been back from sick leave for ten days and have settled down to work again. I arrived back on 23rd December, and was allowed to have the 24th off duty as I had had such a long journey back, nearly three days and two nights. I feel very well now and am quite fit again, and am glad to be back on duty. All my friends have remarked how well I am looking now after my pleasant stay in the cool climate of the hills.

I was very glad I came back in time for Christmas because we had such a happy time. It is much better to be with one's own friends at such a time. There was a friendly atmosphere and the pleasant Christmas spirit everywhere.

On the afternoon of Christmas Eve, I helped to decorate our church I wish you could have seen it, for it really did look beautiful. We managed to collect quite a lot of flowers, and ferns in pots to make it look pretty. We have added many new things to the church furniture recently, among them being new prayer desks, one for the padre, and one for the visiting Bishop, new altar rails, and a platform which raises the sanctuary, and is a great improvement. A photo was taken of the interior of the church, on Christmas Day, and I will send you a copy as soon as I get one. The greatest addition, however, is our new altar frontal which arrived for Christmas. It is of white silk-linen with a gold design, and a gold cross in the centre. It really does look beautiful and has been much admired. We also have a new green frontal, also with a gold design, and the letters IHS in the centre.

At 8.30 p.m., we went round all the wards singing carols to the patients. While I have been away the padre has organised an excellent choir and they have been practising hard for weeks, so the result was remarkably good. We went from ward to ward singing several carols on each one. The patients all seemed to appreciate our efforts very much. It reminded me so much of KGH, where we used to sing carols also, on Christmas Eve.

At 11.30 p.m., we had a midnight service of Holy Communion. The church was packed. It was a lovely and inspiring service, and once again we sang Christmas hymns with great enthusiasm. I wonder if by next Christmas we shall have peace again. It seemed strange to be singing *Joyful all ye nations rise* when the nations have already risen – in war against each other. This was the fourth Christmas of the war, but I think the spirit of Christmas is the same as ever, and war will never alter it.

On Christmas Day we gave the patients a good dinner, and each one received a present from the hospital. The dining hall, where the convalescents had their dinner, was prettily decorated and round the walls we had crayon drawings of Christmas scenes, the work of an artistic patient. I think the patients really enjoyed Christmas and probably had a much better time than if they had been with their units.

In the afternoon we had another carol service, which was also very well attended. I was off duty and able to go to this. Afterwards I went back to my ward, in time to get the Christmas tea ready. The men who were up had a fine spread on the table in the ward.

When I went off duty I found the Indian servants decorating our bungalow with coloured streamers and making it look very cheerful and gay. I thought it was a very friendly thought. Later they met us with garlands of flowers which they hung round our necks. This is an old custom of the country, and is practised on great occasions, shows respect, and is also considered an honour. There was a great deal of 'salaaming' and even a speech by the one who could speak the best English, wishing us a happy Christmas. I listened to the King's speech on Christmas night and though it very good. We heard it most clearly. Did you hear it also?

Altogether it was a very happy Christmas and New Year. I thought of you all, often and wondered how you were spending Christmas. It must have been quiet I am afraid. I am going on night duty at the end of the week. It will be quite a nice change, as I have not done night duty for a long time, as I missed my turn because of sickness.

I do hope you will receive the parcel of stockings which I sent on 2nd December. I am sending some more soon. Do let me know of any other things you need.

It is good to be feeling so well again now. I think 1942 was an unfortunate year for me. However, it is over now. There is much talk about this being the last year of the war. How can we know? It would be wonderful if we could have peace again before another Christmas.

Rosie Tredgett wrote to me recently. She has started midwifery at the Salvation Army Women's Hospital and is now at Morpeth which is the country branch. Matron of KGH also wrote me a very nice letter and sent a card. I cabled Christmas greetings to her.

Well, here I must stop. God bless you all. I will write again soon. With much love, your loving

Vera

Ahmednagar
India
6.1.43

My Dear Mother and Father

I received Geoffrey's photo on the 4th January, and have just written you an airmail letter to thank you for it. I am really delighted with it and like it more and more every time I look at it. He is certainly very smart and handsome in his uniform. The photo has been much admired by everyone. I am writing to Geoff to thank him.

I am now back on duty and feeling very well again. I had a very pleasant holiday and the cold climate did me a lot of good. I am going on night duty on the 9th. I have written to tell you about how I spent Christmas. We had a very happy time. I am sending you a cable today. I hope you received the last two I sent, one for Christmas and one for Mother's birthday.

I hope you are all well. Much love to all.

God bless you.

Your loving

Vera

Ahmednagar
India
8.1.43

My Dear Mother and Father

Yesterday I received a wonderful parcel from you. Thank you ever so much, you dear kind souls. I am just delighted with the books, magazines and Christmas carols. I really don't know how to thank you, for I think the books are so good and will be most interesting. I do so value the books you send me. I am writing to Muriel to thank her. It is such a joy to receive a parcel like that, and you really are much too generous, and should not spend so much money on me. I am so looking forward to reading the books. I have started *One Pair of Feet* and am thoroughly enjoying it, and have laughed heartily! My friends are anxious to read it too and they are always ready to pick it up and read a bit when I lay it down. I am finding the book true to life too, which is not usual in most books dealing with life in the nursing profession. This book cannot be bought out here yet, so I am very lucky to have it. The other two books have not arrived in India yet either. I know I am going to enjoy them too and I also like the little book called *Our Wonderful Women*.

Thank you also, very much for the Christmas cards. They are both very pretty. The RAF card is very impressive and colourful. I sent you a cable this morning thanking you for the parcel and Geoff's photo. I have the photo on my desk in front of me. I am writing this in my spare time on duty, as I am not so busy today. I show the photo to everyone who comes into the ward, for it is a thing to be truly proud of!

Your cable which you say you sent on 4th December or before has not arrived yet. They seem to be getting slower. I had a postcard from Mother today, dated 4th December, so it was quite quick. I am so glad to hear you are all well. Geoff will like being in his native county.

I wonder if you have received two parcels I sent in September. One contained a dressing gown for Muriel, and the other stockings and a dressing-table set for Mother. We hear that some mail sent in September found its way into 'Davy Jones' locker'. Tomorrow I begin a month's night duty. I am feeling very fit now.

More news in a day or two. Cheerio for now. God bless you all.

Your loving
Vera

My Dear Mother and Father

It is a short time since I heard from you, so I have no letter to answer, but expect some mail soon from England. You will be glad to hear that I am one of the few lucky people who has received Christmas mail. Many have never had either letters or parcels yet, but they may still come of course. Thank you again for the lovely parcel of books. It was a grand present. I have read *One Pair of Feet* and am just finishing *The Last Enemy*. Both are fine books. *One Pair of Feet* is so human and much of it is very like my own training. I wonder which hospital is described. It seems a pity the author left hospital after a whole year. She could not have been in love with her work, or else she would have stayed on in spite of everything. Nursing is like that, it either makes or breaks a person! If you are cut out to be a good nurse you will not give up. I had many a good laugh over the book, and so have my friends who have borrowed it.

I have so enjoyed reading *The Last Enemy*. Next I shall read *Pied Piper*.

I am now on night duty. I am feeling very well, and sleeping well during the day.

I am afraid there is very little news to tell you just now, so I hope you will forgive this short letter.

I will write again soon. My love to Muriel and Geoff.

God bless you.

Your loving

Vera

My Dear Muriel

The Christmas parcel arrived safely at the beginning of the month. I was so delighted with it. It has given me hours of pleasure. How very sweet of you all to send it. I do so like the books for they are just the kind I would have chosen myself, and they are all so newly published too. Thank you very much indeed. – and thank you especially for the book *The Last Enemy*. Have you read it? It is a grand story. I could hardly put it down once I started. I have always had a great admiration for the RAF, but have more now since reading this book.

One Pair of Feet is most amusing, as you told me it would be. The author certainly has a fine sense of humour. There was a great deal in it which reminded me of my training. Her chapter on night duty was very true to life. She discusses the awful weariness of it, the long hours of darkness during which the patients' symptoms are magnified a hundred times, the great race against time in the morning in order to 'get done'. Her part about private patients is also realistic. It is so true, what she says about that perpetual scramble to 'get done'. How often with one eye on the clock, I have rubbed Mrs A's back, and thought about still having Mrs B's dressing to do; remembering at the same time that Mrs C and Mrs D are due for injections at twelve o'clock! Then other thoughts have come crowding into my mind; there is that cupboard to tidy, those bandages to wash, that linen to put away, etc etc etc. It is a great life all the same, and those who are made for it, stay on and love it. Those who are not, leave, because the discipline is too much, the hours too tiring; in fact, the training altogether is not happy for them, as it should be. One of these was Monica Dickens, who strangely enough stayed a whole year, and probably passed her Prelim Exam but did not even wait to see!

It is a very entertaining book, and I have often wondered which hospital she is discussing. My friends are also enjoying reading it. I am now going to start *Pied Piper* which I am sure I shall enjoy. Thank you very much for the *Auckland Weeklies*. I have a New Zealand friend here, who likes to read them also. I was also glad to have the *Church Times*, and I have very much liked the little book, called *Our Wonderful Women*. It was indeed a lovely parcel and you were very good to send it.

I am one of the few people who received a Christmas parcel. Our mail is being delayed somewhere and the arrivals of letters and parcels are becoming more and more infrequent. An MP has asked the House of Commons to do something soon as the troops are becoming very fed up about it. It is India which is affected, not so much the Middle East. A cable arrived yesterday – 17th January from you. It was sent I think on the 2nd December. It has been therefore about *six weeks* coming! It was to wish me birthday and Christmas greetings. Mother has written an airgraph since – on 4th December, and it arrived long before the cable. Actually I am much more fortunate than most people, but the general opinion is that the mail question is very bad for the morale of the troops.

I am now on night duty. You will probably have received my letter sent on 6th December, telling you about my stay in hospital at Poona, with hepatitis. Well, I am now very well again and glad to be back on duty. I have been on night duty for a week, and am glad to say I sleep well during the day, which makes all the difference. Here we have only one Sister (myself) on night duty and on each ward there is an orderly. I have to do a round three times at least during the night to visit all wards, so, as the hospital is quite scattered, I have quite a lot of walking to do. I have just been out now to do my 2 a.m. round. There is a full moon shining, and it is a lovely night. We are having a spell of quite cold nights just now, so it is pleasant to be on night duty.

How good the news is now. I wonder if the war will end sooner than expected. It is hard to say. Churchill does not give us much hope for any early peace. He is wise, for it is useless for us to expect too much. We must finish the thing properly this time.

Life must be very hard for you people at home. The rationing is becoming severer we hear. I am sending some more stockings soon. I have ordered them but they take some time to come from Bombay. I hope you receive the last parcel I sent. It contained six pairs of stockings and a Kashmir shawl. I shall be so sorry if it is lost, but will send some more instead. Also I sent two parcels before that, so hope you received them.

I was so glad to have Geoff's photo. Please let him know that I am writing to thank him for it. He certainly looks fine in uniform.

There does not seem to be any more news just now. Thank you for writing so often. I do like your letters. Cheerio for the present.

Much love from
Vera

෴

Ahmednagar
India
20.1.43

Dear Geoffrey

Thank you ever so much for the book you sent me. *So Few* is just the kind of book I like and I am finding it extremely interesting. I was so pleased when the parcel arrived. It is a grand present and you could not have given me anything which I would have appreciated more. I am most interested in the RAF, and especially since you joined it, so I shall value the book very much indeed. I received another parcel a short time ago. It contained your Christmas card with the RAF plane on it. I like it very much. Thank you.

I wrote to you about the middle of November. It was an airmail letter-card. I wonder if you have received it yet? Mails are being delayed very much lately. Today I had your birthday card to me. It was sent on 15th October so has been over three months coming. I had a cable from home recently, which took six weeks to come! Thank you also for the birthday card. You have all been very good to me, sending me such lovely parcels. Thank you ever so much for your photograph. It arrived safely, and not damaged at all, as it was well packed. I am thrilled with it, and think it is a very fine photo of you. I must say you look extremely smart in your uniform and it does suit you. All my friends admire the photo and I have shown it to lots of people. I am so glad you are enjoying life. I hear you are now in a certain very nice town in your native county.

We have a quiet life here for we are right in the country. We make our own pleasures in the unit. There is a small cinema which shows rather ancient films; we have a choir in the church, and are starting a small choral society, so have practices to pass the time away. There are some good singers in the unit, and they did very well at Christmas when we sang carols in the wards. There are lectures and debates quite often, and football matches which I quite enjoy. We also have cycle rides round the country and go for picnics. I spend a lot of my free time reading and writing letters, to say nothing of darning stockings! Altogether Ahmednagar is not a bad place, isolated as it is. I am now on night duty, so do not do very much apart from working and sleeping.

Did you ever receive some cigarettes I sent you some time ago? I sent them to Blackpool, but you had left there by the time they should have arrived. I am afraid they may have been lost. Would you like me to send some more? I would like to do so if you would like them, and if you will not have to pay duty on them. Let me know will you, and also please tell me if there is anything special I can send. I would like to send you something but it is difficult to know what you would appreciate most. Perhaps money would be more help. Anyway write when you can and tell me.

Well, there does not seem to be any more news so I will say cheerio.

All the best, and much love
Vera

❧

Ahmednagar
India
27.1.43

My Dear Mother and Father

I had a postcard from Muriel a few days ago. It was written in November, and took two months to come. Apart from that it is some time since I heard from you, but I know it is because the mails are so much delayed. Some people have not had letters for months, many have heard from people at home who say they cannot understand why they do not get letters from India. The cable system is in a bad condition too. A cable you sent me with birthday and Christmas greetings was six weeks coming, and an airgraph which you sent afterwards arrived about two weeks before the cable. It was a good thing the cable was not urgent; some people have had urgent cables sent and that of course is much worse when they are delayed. I am so sorry for the troops, they do so love their letters and it makes so much difference to their happiness. An MP, who is on service in India, had requested Parliament to attend to the matter as soon as possible. Airmail letters are often taking longer than sea-mail. The last batch of airmail letters was three months coming! Among them were a birthday card from Muriel and Geoff and a letter from Muriel, posted on 15th October.

I have written to them both. I have so enjoyed the lovely books you sent me. Thank you so much for them. I loved reading *One Pair of Feet*. It was most entertaining and very true to life. The other two books *The Last Enemy* and *Pied Piper* are very fine stories, extremely well written. I wish you knew how much I appreciate you sending them, although you should not spend any money on me when life is so hard for you at home. I have lent the books to my friends and to some of the patients and they have given many people hours of pleasure. I have one patient with a badly fractured jaw. He has been in hospital for nearly four months and is very patient but tired of his long illness. I have lent him a lot of books, and when these came I lent them to him also, and he has much enjoyed them.

I am reading *So Few* – the book Geoff sent me. It is very good and most interesting. I also read *St George or the Dragon* with great pleasure. You have chosen very well, and you are very generous indeed.

I am still on night duty. I have about ten more nights to do. I am quite liking it, as I sleep very well during the day, better than I have ever done on night duty. We have had some lovely moonlit nights, and it is quite pleasant walking round the wards at night. I am the only Sister on, so have to do a tour of the hospital at intervals during the night. We have had quite a menagerie in the ward tonight (I don't mean patients!). A baby mouse played round my feet in the kitchen; a lizard came running down the wall after a moth, and when he had swallowed it, stopped to smack his lips, which was most amusing to watch. A few minutes later a baby frog and a large frog came hopping through the open doors. One of the orderlies came in with his dog, and a pet mongoose which follows him everywhere. The mongoose is very friendly and faithful and a good companion for the dog. It was funny to watch Joey the mongoose following the orderly down the path in the moonlight. It was like a very thin shadow sliding swiftly along.

I must stop now. Lots of love to all. God bless you. I am very well. Hope you are.

Your loving
Vera

ও

Sister V K Jones
QAIMNSR
No 5 India Base General Hospital
Deolali
India
11.3.43

My Dear Mother and Father

Thank you so much for your airgraph received today. I am glad to know you are all well. How disappointing that the parcels I sent have never arrived. Really it would be safer to send a cheque. Then it is better for you to have a parcel as money cannot buy these rationed goods. I am very pleased that Father received his cheque, and was able to buy a comfortable armchair.

I feel very sad to think that the parcels must have been lost. You have had nothing from me for Christmas, and your parcels reached me safely. The one sent on 1st December may still arrive, as it is only two months ago, and the parcels invariably take three months. I have ordered more stockings from Bombay and will send them as soon as they arrive. I am sure a lot of mail was lost at the same time as my first parcel was on the way.

I know you write to me often, and I write to you every few days. I do not worry when mail is delayed as I realise it does not all reach us.

I was sorry to hear about the raid in which eight people were killed. I remember hearing about the severe raid on your part of the country. I was on night duty in Ahmednagar. I felt very worried and was afraid you were having a bad time. I became so anxious that next morning I sent you a full-rate cable so that I would soon have a reply to set my mind at rest. Your answer came in four days, which was excellent, I was so glad to know you were all well, but felt you had suffered in some way through it. Now I hear today that you had to deal with the injured, which must have been very sad. Did you ever receive my letter sent on 6th December in which I described my sick leave in the hills following an attack of jaundice? I am sorry if the letter was lost, as I wrote about the journey there and described the beautiful scenery of the hill station. I had a very pleasant time, and the memories of the cold crisp climate up there are very good, now that we are having such hot dusty days here on the plains.

I am very happy here in my new job. I have been here just a month on what is known as 'temporary duty'. I may remain for several months, and I am glad, as it is a very nice hospital and the Sisters are all charming. I like Matron very much indeed. I am about 120 miles from my unit at Ahmednagar. I have a very nice ward – all officers, and there are medical and surgical cases. The ward has over forty beds, and they are seldom empty. As soon as one man is discharged another takes his place. We are busy all day, and the hours fly by.

It is becoming very hot and dry here, the temperature is today about 105 degrees in the shade. I am afraid it will be much hotter later on.

Do not think we are short of food here. The reports you have heard are wrong. The lower caste Indians are suffering a shortage of rice and cereals which are their main foods. There is a certain amount of hoarding of sugar going on, as well as some other commodities, but we are very well fed. In our Mess we have excellent food. I feel guilty to think that I have never had to bear the hardships of rationing.

Please let me know if I can send you more food parcels. I should very much like to if you will not be made to pay duty on them. The Army and Navy Stores in Bombay will send them for me.

Well, my dears, there is no more space, so I will close now. Will write again soon.

Fondest love to Geoff and Muriel. How is Peter? As lively as ever I hope. God bless you.

Much love
Vera

୬

Deolali
India
17.3.43

My Dear Muriel

Thank you very much for your airgraph, dated 4th January. I have not written to you lately, but I did send you an airmail letter-card for Christmas. I wonder if it reached you.

I am enclosing a cheque for you, also some photos of our little hospital chapel at Ahmednagar, and one of myself. It was taken outside the church just before I was transferred here. It is quite good, considering I was feeling very hot and sticky having just finished dusting the church, and doing the flowers ready for Sunday. I am having one taken of myself in uniform as I have not sent you one for a long time, and I will let you have a copy of that also.

I have ordered a book for you from Bombay but it has been a long time coming. I will send it as soon as it comes. I am afraid it will be late for your birthday. I hope you will be able to make good use of the cheque.

I was very pleased to receive the cable to say that the stockings and Kashmir shawl have arrived. I was most relieved, as I had begun to think of them as something at the bottom of the sea! I am afraid the first parcel sent in October will never reach you. I do love the books you sent and will always value them as they are the kind which can be read again and again. I have lent them to my friends who also enjoyed reading them.

How sad it was that Richard Hillary was killed in January. We heard about it during the news from London. The announcer spoke of his book, *The Last Enemy* and said he had died in action, as he had wished. It is a great book. One of my patients, an RAF officer, worked with him at an RAF station in England, so he knew all about him. He spoke very highly of him, and was most sorry to hear of his death.

I have been in my new station, Deolali, for just a month, and like it very much. I may be here for some time as it is a very busy hospital, with over 1,300 beds. We are always full of patients, and never have empty beds for long. I have thirty-five officers in my charge. We have quite interesting cases among them, as well as the ever prevalent cases of malaria and dysentery, and other tropical diseases. I have gained many good experiences by nursing in the East.

Our Sisters' quarters are pleasant and comfortable. I have my own little room which I have made very homelike. My favourite books stand on a small writing table, on which I also have the family photos. Geoffrey in uniform, now looks very handsome in a brown leather frame, and he is much admired by everyone.

We have to spend our off duty quietly as there is little to do here. It is just a vast camp with a small Indian bazaar. Our one place of recreation is the Officers' Club, where we have dances twice a week, and where there is a fairly good library. It is very hot now, so we do not feel much like going out often, as it is cooler indoors with a fan!

There are only eight Sisters here, and we are all friendly with each other. They are all very nice girls. One of them is Vera Pannell, who was about a year junior to me at KGH. I could hardly believe my eyes when I saw her on my arrival here. She knew me immediately and was delighted to see me again. We have had many long talks, and she has told me a lot of news about people I knew at KGH.

We are about twelve miles from Nasik. I hope to go there sometime as I should like to meet the Bishop. The padre at my unit has written to him to tell him I am here. Everyone likes him. I believe he is a fine man, and I have a book written by him.

I was very interested to hear about the Nativity Play. I would have loved it I am sure, and can imagine that you did your part very well.

Please let me know if I can send some more parcels of food as there is a shop in Bombay which undertakes to send them.

Mother says she hopes to send photos of herself and you in uniform. I shall look forward to having them.

You people at home are certainly giving all to the war effort, carrying on with never a grumble, doing the work that is nearest and having the hardship of rationing and the horrors of raids to bear at the same time. We all take off our hats to you on the Home Front!

How I should love to be home with you all. It is nearly three and a half years now!

Well, my dear, here I must stop, but I will write again soon. I wonder how long this letter will take by air.

All the best, and God bless you.

My love to Father, Mother, Geoff and Peter.

Your loving

Vera

 споча

Deolali
India
16.4.43

My Dear Mother and Father

I have received several letters from you recently so feel quite up to date with news about you. One letter from Mother was dated 30th December so was quite old, but it was an interesting letter telling me all about the Nativity Play. I had an airmail letter-card from Mother written on 18th March and it arrived in less than three weeks. It was as usual full of news. You mentioned about the parcel which I had sent and which did not arrive intact owing to it being of cardboard, and so badly damaged. I cannot remember sending a cardboard box at all, as I am always careful to send things in tin boxes. It may have been a parcel of food which I ordered about last September, but surely you would have received it long ago. I cannot think what it can be. I suppose you will have heard more about it by now.

The quickest letter I have received from you for a very long time, was an airmail letter-card from Father. It was sent on 23rd March, and arrived in just fifteen days. I don't know anyone who has had a letter in less time than that. It was such a newsy letter too, and I was so pleased with it, as I really feel that the postal arrangements may be improving. I am sending you a cable to let you know that the photos have arrived. I hope you receive the cable I have sent for Father's and Muriel's birthdays.

I will certainly send you some material, and will wangle it through the post so that you do not pay duty if possible. Some more stockings will be coming to you in due course. I will try to get lisle this time if possible.

I am so glad to hear that Geoff is an LAC. He has gained promotion in very good time, according to several RAF patients in my ward, who have told me much about the RAF.

It is very hot and dusty here. Could you possibly send me a bottle of pure, fresh, English air! It would be wonderful. Next month is going to be hotter, but in June we shall have the monsoon.

Well, my dears, here I must stop. Much love to all, and a big kiss for Peter, right on the white line between his eyes!

God bless you.

Your loving

Vera

My Dear Mother and Father

You are very much in my thoughts today and I am wishing I could be with you at this time. We all think with longing of Easter at home, it is never quite the same abroad. There are no lovely flowers such as daffodils, jonquils, narcissi etc and the churches at home are always filled with them. I wonder if you will be allowed to ring the church bells – it would be wonderful! Somehow I think you will all be feeling very joyful today, not only because it is a great day, but because the news is so good. We have not felt so optimistic about the war for a very long time.

I am receiving your letters so much more regularly now, especially letter-cards. I feel I am in much closer contact with you, as the news is so recent when letters only take fifteen to twenty days. I seem to be 'letting the country get me down' as the troops say. For the third time in less than a year I am a patient! I am now convalescent and feeling quite well again, but I have had diphtheria. I thought I had better tell you as I shall be going away on sick leave again and you would want to know why. I don't know how I picked it up, but if there are any odd germs flying about, I seem to be the one on whom they settle!

I was taken ill at the beginning of this month and I had an infection of the middle ear which gave quite a lot of trouble and I had the drum opened twice. The diphtheria had spread there from my throat, but I had large doses of serum and my ear improved, and it is now quite better.

I have been very well looked after and I am in the Military Families Hospital. I shall be here for another two weeks or so and then I am to have four weeks' leave and I will go to the hills. This is the best time of the year to visit the hills especially as the heat here is becoming really awful.

Recently I received one letter from Mother in which she said she was glad I had recovered from infective hepatitis, and had I decided what I was going to have next! That arrived one day when

I had just had a painful injection of serum in my seat, so I was not amused!

I am *not having anything else*. This is absolutely the last wretched dose of sickness India is going to give me! I am sure Palestine suited me much better.

Tomorrow the Bishop of Nasik is giving me Holy Communion. He is preaching at the Garrison Church today. He is much loved by all.

I received some magazines, *Reader's Digests*, from Muriel yesterday. They were most acceptable and very interesting and could not have come at a better time, just when I needed books to read. I will be writing to her to thank her. I told you in my last letter that I received the photos of the play and was delighted with them. I am looking forward to hearing about your Passion Play.

I have had two handbags sent to you from a famous leather firm in Madras. One is for Mother and the other for Muriel. The one with the metal fastener and zip inside is Mother's and it is made of cobra skin. The other is of python skin. Don't tell me I am being extravagant, because I want you to have these gifts and I know they will last you for ages. You do not get many extras in your hard lives. I only hope they arrive safely. I have been told there will be no duty to pay at all, or I would not have sent them.

I will send your material as soon as I can get it when I am out of hospital. I shall probably get better material when I go up to the hills. Also stockings will be more easily obtained there I think.

I am going to Wellington again, I think, as I liked it so much and made friends there. Also it suited me so well.

How is Geoff? Give him my love please. I am writing to him. I wrote some weeks ago.

My love to Muriel and both of you.

More news soon. God bless you.

Your loving

Vera

ა

My Dear Mother and Father

I have recently sent you and Muriel airmail letter-cards, and I am going to send them always, and airgraphs as all other letters take so long to reach you.

I received a cable from you yesterday to say you were all well. I was so pleased to receive it and am sending one back tomorrow.

By the time this reaches you, you will have heard that I have been in hospital with diphtheria and ear trouble, but now I am very much better and getting up again. I hope to go on leave again to Wellington in about a week's time. I am sure it will be very pleasant up in the hills just now, for we are in the hottest month of the year, and this is the time when anyone who is not in the army goes up to the hills to escape this inferno of the plains!

I hope to travel in an air-conditioned coach when I take this train journey, for it will take nearly two days and two nights and the train will pass across the Deccan, one of the hottest parts of India. I would have liked to go to some other part of the country for a change, but it would mean taking much longer journeys to other hill stations – and Wellington is one of the nearest. You have told me to try to visit Agra, but at this time of the year, it will be blazing hot there, and it is certainly not the kind of place in which to convalesce. Wellington is delightful, and I am sure it is the wisest plan to go there. Also I have made friends of the Sisters and Matron there, and shall be able to stay with them again.

Your letters are coming much more quickly now, and it is so cheering. In Mother's last letter, dated 8th April (airmail letter-card) she says that two of my airmail letters have taken four months to reach you. She said that one letter had been opened and 'Ahmednagar' blued out. That surprises me very much because we are allowed to give that address, so it must have been someone who was being officious. I wonder why I forgot to censor that letter.

I have not forgotten that you have asked me to send material and stockings to you, also socks for Father. When I leave hospital I will be able to send them. How strange it must seem to have no railings round the garden, I hope the cows don't get in and eat your vegetables.

The news is wonderful now Tunis and Bizerta have fallen! I think it is our one really great and triumphant campaign of the war so far. The troops in North Africa must be at the top of their morale. Now the Germans will be having their 'Dunkirk' and I hope we give it to them hot and strong during their evacuation.

How is Geoff keeping? I have your photos in my room in hospital and everyone admires them. They all think Geoff is just grand, and needless to say I agree!

Cheerio for now. God bless you dears.

Fondest love

Vera

෯

Deolali
India
14.7.43

My Dear Muriel

I was so delighted to receive your two airmail letter-cards, dated 22nd June and 29th June. How quickly they came. We are eternally grateful for airmail letter-cards out here, for since they became used, we have felt much nearer to all our dear ones in good old Blighty!

I was so very interested to hear all about your lovely holiday in Wales. What a grand experience it has been for you. You certainly made the most of your short stay there. Your descriptions of Wales are beautiful. Why on earth don't you write a book, my dear. It would take the world by storm! Even the war would be a second thought in people's minds! Seriously though, you have a great gift. How I should have loved to be with you. After the war we must have a similar holiday together, in Wales, or perhaps, Scotland. I shall look forward to it. I am so very glad you were able to have your holiday, as you must have needed it, and you certainly deserved it. The little church at Harlech must be beautiful.

You certainly did very well to climb Cader Idris. I can almost see that lovely panorama you describe. I hope now you are feeling very fit after your holiday. It must have been such a joy to get away from the raids and all the troubles of life during this weary war on the Home Front. I am sure you will have returned to your job feeling much refreshed.

I returned to duty on 24th June and have now quite settled down to work again. I am feeling quite well again, in fact I am better than I have ever been in India. During my leave I had a course of fourteen liver extract injections as I was very anaemic after my illness. They did me so much good and made my blood count quite normal again. Since I finished the course, I have felt much brighter altogether and have so much more energy. I have mentioned in some of my letters that there was a possibility that I would be sent home as I have been out some time, and have been ill for long periods. Well, there was, at one time, a very *strong* possibility. I was almost certain of it. Before I went on leave, I was recommended for a passage home in charge of patients who were being sent on either a hospital ship or a troopship. I was told that if the need arose for a Sister for this duty I would be able to go. It is very difficult to get home from India these days. Somehow, it has not materialised, this chance to return. There are so many others who should be sent back, and cannot go, that I must not complain. After all, I am very well now and so thankful for my restored health. I came back to duty looking so much better, and I have gone to work again and am glad I can be useful, and work as hard as ever. It would have been very wonderful to come home. I cannot say how overjoyed I would have been to see you all again. I will write more in my letter home, which I am sending to Father and Mother today. Will write to you again soon.

Lots of love.

Your loving

Vera

&

My Dearest Muriel

Thank you ever so much for your lovely photo which came two days ago. I am so pleased with it, and I think you look very good in your uniform. It certainly is a good photo, and I was excited when it arrived. I now have photos of the whole family in my room, including Peter, without whom the family would not be complete.

Thank you again, very much. I am going to get a lizard-skin or snake-skin photo frame for it and you will look very nice indeed in it.

Thank you also very much, for the magazines. I was very glad to have them. The parish magazines were most interesting. I am always glad to have the *Reader's Digests* also, for the articles are so good. Your choice is excellent and it is such a good idea to mark the stories and articles you consider are best.

I am so looking forward to having a copy of your play. I do hope it is printed for publication.

We are just as hectically busy here. I like my ward very much, and we have some interesting cases. We are never slack at all, but go hard at it, from noon till night, and we have very few empty beds. I am feeling fine, and looking very well too.

I had thought I would be going back to my own unit when I returned from sick leave, but it seems now that I shall be here for a while longer. We are in need of all the Sisters we have and we urgently need more, so I shall not be allowed to go back yet. The Matron here is very sweet, and has been so kind to me, that I could not possibly ask her to let me go back to Ahmednagar. I should feel I was deserting her, and she always says she would be very sorry to lose me. This is a happy place, and the Mess is pleasant, so I am quite content to be here. I often feel I should love to go back to the 60th, however, for all my old friends are there, and we have such a fine, well-equipped hospital. Also, I should love to be able to appreciate our beautiful little chapel again. Having looked after it for so long, I miss it very much now.

I am so glad you enjoyed reading Cronin's *Keys of the Kingdom*. How lucky that it reached you just before you went on holiday. I am so glad you were able to read it while you were away. It certainly is the best of all Cronin's books, and lacks that cynicism present in his others.

I often look at your python-skin handbag, and think how you will love it one day. I only wish you could have it now, but I do not want to risk losing it at sea. I remember the beautiful dressing gown which went to the bottom!

Please give my fondest love to all. I will write again very soon. Lots of love and God bless you dearly.

Your loving
Vera

⤫

Deolali
India
31.7.43

My Dear Mother

This is a special letter for you, but I am writing an airgraph to Father also, so that he will not feel left out of it!

I have just received Father's airgraph in which he tells me that you have been in hospital and had an operation for the removal of a lump at the top of your leg. I am so very sorry, and feel most anxious about you, my dear. I do hope you are now quite well again. Father describes the lump as a 'Thelma' but I am sure he has got it wrong, and means either a fibroma or a lipoma, which are innocent lumps of fibrous or fatty tissue which have to be removed. I have seen quite a number of them, and I know that they are easily dealt with.

I do hope you were well cared for in the nursing home, and had the very best of attention, for nothing is too good for you the world's sweetest mother! Please tell your doctor from me that I am glad he is looking after you well, and I hope he will keep a steady eye on you, and see that you don't go rushing round as you have been doing. Please write again as soon as possible and let me know just how you are. It is such a good thing that our mails will soon start coming to us quicker than ever, when the Mediterranean opens again.

What grand news it is about the campaign in Sicily. How good that Musso has caved in! The tide is surely turning in our favour.

I am keeping very well and very busy on my dysentery ward. I have some interesting cases. Since coming abroad I have done so much dysentery nursing that I think it is time I was awarded the Diploma of the Order of the Bed Pan!

The rain continues to pour down as if it means to go on for the duration! There is deep mud everywhere. The mosquitoes are worse than they have ever been. We have all been given mosquito cream to smear on our legs and arms to try to discourage the little devils from biting us. The atmosphere is very damp. One buys a box of matches, only to find that it is so damp, that the matches will not strike.

I was so pleased with Muriel's photo and have put it in a lovely frame. I have all the family framed now, including Peter who looks very proud of himself.

Will write again very soon. Take care of yourself.

Fondest love

Vera

❧

Deolali
India
2.8.43

My Dear Mother and Father

I have just received Mother's letter dated 14th July. I am so sorry to hear that you had not at that time, received any letters from me for three weeks. I have written many. On checking up in my little notebook in which I record all the letters I write, I find that I have written to you twelve times during July, four airgraphs and eight letter-cards. I do hope that by now you have received some of them. In June I also wrote very often. You have not heard yet that I returned here on 24th June and have been very busy on duty since. I told you in my letters that my leave was not extended by HQ although the medical staff at Wellington wanted me to have it. However, I have felt very fit since my return and I look well too. We have been very busy all the time. All the troops in Deolali seem to be developing dysentery and coming in to my ward! I am sending you an airgraph today and also a cable to let you know I am okay, and to tell you I am receiving your letters.

I wrote an airgraph and a letter-card yesterday to answer your airgraph (from Father) in which you told me of Mother's operation. I was so relieved to read in Mother's letter today that she is feeling better and making a good recovery. I wrote immediately I had the airgraph and gave Mother some sound advice to take things more quietly in future. I hope that letter arrives.

The lipoma may have been caused by a knock, hardly noticed at the time. I have nursed several such cases. The lump is nearly always in that same place, and is successfully treated. I am so glad people have looked after Mother so well, and I know they will see that she does not dash about so much from now on.

Do let me have more news soon. I am so glad it was not a serious matter, and that Mother did not have to stay away from home for long. I shall be very pleased to hear you are away on holiday in Devon where you must have a complete rest, both of you.

I am so glad Muriel enjoyed her holiday. I was so pleased with her photo which I have put in a nice brown leather frame. It stands on my dressing table. I am very proud of all my family photos and people always admire them. Muriel looks so nice in her uniform and it does suit her. I am so glad she was at home and able to look after Mother.

I did not know Canon Ottaway is leaving Ilford. Is he retiring, for he must be getting quite old? I wonder how long the parcel I sent will take to reach you. It contained dress materials. I hope you will not have to give up coupons for them. I will send to Bombay in a day or two for some more material and send it off soon.

Deolali is just the same, full of mosquitoes, flies, ants, cockroaches and donkeys which 'hee-haw' all day long and most of the night. The mud is deeper than ever, and the rain continues to pour down continuously. It is Deolali-on-mud now. Everything is very damp, and all linen has to be well aired before we can put it on the beds.

More news soon. God bless you.

Fondest love, your loving

Vera

∾

My Dear Muriel

I received a long airmail letter dated 28th April, recently. It took nearly three months to come. It was so interesting and I much enjoyed reading it.

I was so interested to hear how you wrote the Passion Play. It must be very beautiful indeed for you were certainly inspired to write it and it is a wonderful thought. I am so looking forward to reading it, and hope you will be able to send me a copy.

You will be pleased to hear that I have lent the books you sent me last Christmas, to many people, and everyone has enjoyed them so they have given pleasure to others as well as myself. I lent *One Pair of Feet* to a Sergeant-Major in my ward who needed cheering up, and he chuckled all day and brightened up in no time.

I do hope the materials I sent you will arrive safely. There is green linen for you, which I am sure you will like and some blue material for Mother. When I go to Bombay, as I hope to do at the end of this month for two days, I will buy some more material for you. It is not possible to get it in Deolali. I am going on night duty next week, and when I come off I shall have three days off, so will be able to go to Bombay as it is quite near.

How I should love to hear your gramophone records. They must be wonderful. What pleasure you must have from them, and what relaxation in these strenuous days.

I was so very sorry to hear of Mother's operation, but am

thankful it was not more serious, and that she is feeling better now. What a good thing it was that she was able to come home after three days. I am so glad you looked after her well. I am sure you will insist that she does not work so hard now, and takes more rest. Please let me know how she is as soon as possible.

It is very wet and windy here. There has been quite a gale blowing for days. It does not deter the mosquitoes, however, for they are with us in their millions. I think this must be the mosquitoes' HQ! They are almost as active during the day as at night. Next week on night duty I shall need to wear two pairs of stockings and possibly my wellingtons as well, to protect my legs.

I do hope you are receiving my letters more frequently now, for in Mother's last letter she says that you had not heard from me for three weeks. The mail must be held up somewhere, for I have written very regularly, and I expect you will receive a batch of letters at once.

No more room, so cheerio. I will write again very soon. Lots of love to all.

Ever your loving
Vera

෨

Deolali
India
8.9.43

My Dear Muriel

Thank you very much for your most welcome letter just received. I am so glad you are receiving my letters regularly. I keep a record of all those written and received, and when I hear that you have received letters sent on certain dates, I can look back in my notebook, and say to myself, 'They will soon receive two letters and an airgraph. How nice.' Then I see that I have written to you and I can be glad that you have probably just received that letter. I always know which of my friends owe me letters, and can look forward to hearing from them.

I have just sent you a parcel which also contains something for Father. I won't tell you what your Christmas present is, as it will be disappointing if it is lost at sea. I just hope very much that you receive it, as I am sure it will be most acceptable.

I am anxiously waiting to hear if your parcel containing material has reached you. It will be so disappointing for me as well as you if it does not arrive.

It is becoming difficult to get material even in Bombay now, but I have ordered some more. I just cannot get stockings of even fair quality, and I am afraid most of them have been in stock some time and become perished, as you say some I sent you wore out in no time at all.

I am keeping very well and as busy as ever. I am now in charge of a large medical ward, full of malaria and jaundice cases, fevers of every kind, and other medical diseases. It is a very pleasant ward as it has been redecorated, and is clean and cheerful and very spacious.

I saw the film *Random Harvest* while I was in Bombay, and I much enjoyed it. Have you seen it? It is very well acted, and very fascinating. Recently I saw *The Moon and Sixpence* from the novel by Somerset Maughan. It came to our garrison cinema. I enjoyed that also. It is rather sordid in parts, but the plot is good, and unusual.

The news certainly is wonderful. It seems hardly possible that we are actually fighting in Europe. We have the right men leading our armies now.

By the beginning of next month I shall commence my fifth year of service!

More news soon. I do love to have your letters, for you give me lots of news.

Cheerio. God bless you.

Much love

Vera

Deolali
India
18.9.43

My Dear Mother and Father

Thank you very much for Mother's letter of 29th August, received yesterday.

I am so glad to hear that Mother is feeling much better now and do hope she will be even better still after your holiday. I am longing to hear how you have enjoyed yourselves and I often try to picture you in North Devon, and Torquay, later. Doesn't it seem years and years since we were all so happy together in Torquay, the summer before the war?

I have sent off three parcels which I am so hoping will reach you for Christmas, also cards. Another parcel has yet to be sent, I am still waiting for some material to arrive from Poona. It is lovely navy-blue silk for a dress for Mother, and I will send it off the very day it arrives. I am so sorry to hear that parcels are being stolen in the post offices. It is very disgraceful. I am still going to send them, however, and hope fervently that they reach you. I will not cease to make the effort just because parcels are being stolen. It will be just giving up hope altogether, and I would much rather try to get things to you and if they are lost, well, I will have tried!

There is not much news to tell you. Life goes on much the same from day to day. We are working very hard and have nearly twice as many patients as we are supposed to have (on paper)!

A lot of new Sisters have just come out from home, and some have come here. They are nearly all very young, and just finished training. I feel quite old and experienced in comparison! They look at me with awe when I tell them I have been abroad nearly four years. I feel something more than awe when I think of it!

I have become very fond of embroidery work lately. I made an afternoon tea cloth just after I left hospital when I was on sick leave, and gave it to Matron who was very pleased. Now I am embroidering a linen dressing table runner for Mother. It has quite an intricate border of spring flowers all round it and it is fascinating work.

Well, my dears it is time for duty again so I must stop. I shall be able to post this on my way.

How are Muriel and Geoff? I wrote to them both recently.

More news soon.

Fondest love as always, your loving

Vera

ॐ

Deolali

India

25.9.43

My Dear Mother and Father

Thank you so much for your most welcome letter-card received two days ago. It came in fourteen days. I am so happy to hear that you were in Devon when that was written having such a delightful change and rest.

I wish you could know what pleasure it gives me to know that you really are away from work and worry, and enjoying lovely scenery, sea air, and best of all, good food. I feel so relieved that you have taken this holiday, and that it is all that you hoped for. How wonderful for you to have such lovely teas again. There certainly seem to be some parts of England which have fared much better than others. I am glad your room was so comfortable and you met nice people.

I wonder where you are now. I believe Father said you were returning on the 18th and going away again probably to Torquay. If so you may be in Torquay now. How well I remember that lovely countryside and those pretty walks along the cliffs beside the sea. That holiday of ours in 1939, seemed to be full of lovely surprises, for each place we visited seemed to be more beautiful than the last.

I well remember the place near Torquay where we had as many cream buns, and as much jam and cream as we could possibly consume for the small sum of about a shilling.

Oh dear! My imagination is taking me right back to Devon and I have come down to earth with a bump – right in the dust of

Deolali! I am so looking forward to having more news about your holiday.'

I have sent off the material about which I told you in my last letter. It arrived from Poona two days ago, and I packed it up and sent it off the very next day. It is lovely navy blue heavy crepe, four and a half yards. It is for Mother's birthday, and I do hope it reaches you in time. The parcel is done up very securely and registered also. It should help to keep it from thieves. I *do* so hope it reaches you safely as I am sure you will love it.

There does not seem to be much news to give you. The work continues to pile up. The army gets bigger and bigger! My ward is always full, but it is a clean and pleasant ward to run so that is half the battle.

Please give my love to Muriel and Geoff. I wrote to Muriel recently and to Geoff at the beginning of the month.

More news later. Lots of love, and God bless you.

Your loving

Vera

⁇

Deolali
India
7.10.43

My Dear Mother and Father

Your last letter, (from Mother), was written on 14th September and received on 30th September. I wonder if you are now back home again, or if you went to Torquay. I am so thankful you have had this holiday for it is a rest you have long been needing. I hope the rain stopped before you left, for you say in your letter that some days were very wet.

We are having very hot and sticky weather with lots of rain and storms just now. Last night there was a terrific storm and the rain was so heavy that we could not hear ourselves speak. It is always like this in October, at the end of the monsoon.

I have asked Matron here to do her best to send me back to Ahmednagar, and although she was not anxious at first to let me go, she has realised how much I want to, and has promised to write to HQ, and to my Matron at the 60th. I am full of hope about it and feel all may be well. I have had some happy times here but it is not like my own hospital and I miss my old friends.

I do so hope you receive the parcel I sent three months ago. It was, after all, only sent at the beginning of July, so you may not have it until four months afterwards. I have sent four other parcels for Christmas and will be very happy when I know you have received them. It is just four years (on 5th October) since I was called up. Do you remember how I telephoned you from Plaistow to tell you?

My ward is still as busy as ever and I nearly always have about 88 patients. Twenty of these are convalescent and are in a small ward nearby.

I did receive the letter in which you told me you had seen Mrs Murchison, but I did not have the one in which you told me of your talk with Matron of KGH and where you gave me news of many of the nurses. That is the only one I seem to have lost. Mrs M was so delighted to see you and wrote and told me about it.

Please give my love to Muriel and Geoff. I am keeping very well now and I do hope you are all well too.

No more news just now, but I will write again very soon.

God bless you and keep you safe. Lots of love to you both as always.

Your ever loving
Vera

❧

Deolali
India
19.10.43

My Dear Mother and Father

Thank you for your two airmail letters received today. They were written on 30th September and 5th October, so were very quick. I was so glad to have them as I had had no letters for nearly a month. There must have been a hold-up somewhere. I also had a lovely long letter from Muriel written on 28th September.

I am very pleased to hear you went to Torquay as I was afraid you wouldn't, after having so many rainy days in North Devon. I could easily picture you sitting on Babbacombe beach as I read your letter. I could just see those lovely red cliffs with the deep blue sea in contrast, and you two sitting on the sand with your backs against a rock, reading! Or were you in deckchairs? I wish you knew how much good it does me to know that you have really had a good holiday. I love to think of you sitting down all day by the sea with no parish worries, no meetings, no sick people to visit, and no canteen to run!

How I should have loved to be with you! Still it is no use yearning for the impossible. I must wait for those special pleasures until after the war!

We little dreamed when we had such a happy time in Torquay in 1939 that the war-clouds were so near, and that we were so soon to be separated. It seems so long ago.

I am very glad my parcel of tea, etc has arrived. I sent it in June, and the other parcel of material, I sent in July, so there is every hope of it reaching you. It may still take another month or more. I do hope my Christmas presents arrive for you before December, as I sent them in August. There is more dress material for Mother on the way, for her birthday.

I have sent in an official request to the Principal Matron in Poona, for me to be sent back to the 60th. I am anxiously awaiting her reply. I have done all I can now; and if I am unsuccessful I must just settle down and forget my old unit, if I can! One does become fond of one's own hospital and although my special friend there has been posted away to Calcutta, I still want to go back very much.

Don't worry at all about our food situation, for the Bengal famine is affecting the native population and we are not at all short. It is a tragic thing. Hundreds are dying daily in that area.

I wonder if Geoffrey will go overseas, and if so, where. Perhaps it will be Canada. I do hope so. I should not like him to go too far away from home. He will probably not have to be away for long anyway.

I have often wondered if you have received requests from the

229

General Nursing Council for my yearly, retention fee of 2/6d. Have you been paying it? If you have not heard, my name may now be off the register as a reprisal! Please let me know and I will write about it.

More news soon. Lots of love dears.

Ever your loving

Vera

❦

No 60 British General Hospital
India Command
31.10.43

My Dear Mother and Father

As you see by my address, I am now back again in my own unit, much to my joy! I applied officially to the Principal Matron for this transfer, and within ten days my orders to return here arrived. I left No 5 IBGH on the 27th and reached _____ on the 28th at 1 a.m.

We are still in the same place, but it would be better I think if I did not mention the name as regulations have become stricter.

I am so glad I have come back. It is eight months since I went away, a very long exile. The hospital looks so nice, for all the wards have been redecorated, and painted cream and green, and new sinks with running water have been installed. That is very unusual for country districts in India, but then my unit always does things well, I am proud to say. Better even than sinks, we have *chains to pull*, so are considered quite ultra-modern, and as the Indians would say, 'pukka'.

The whole hospital looks very clean and well organised and well equipped. The countryside is very fresh and green and there are plenty of flowers about, though the monsoon is finished now.

It has been grand seeing all my old friends again, and they made me feel very welcome. One is always worried against asking for any changes in the army, as most people say that the change often proves disappointing, but that has certainly not been so in this instance. I am more and more thankful every minute of the day that I have been able to return here.

I had a grand send-off from No 5 IBGH, and Matron gave a dinner party in my honour. It was great fun. I was so sorry to leave the Matron there, for we were very good friends, and she was always so good to me. She helped to make life much more pleasant, for we were working under difficult conditions, and it made all the difference having an understanding and helpful Matron. I now have my old job of looking after the church here. It is lovely to be able to come back to it. We are starting our carol practices again soon, and hope to sing carols round the wards on Christmas Eve as we did last year.

The padre is as keen and popular as ever and he still has the church very well attended. We have a Celebration every morning and several services on Sundays.

I will send you a cable to give you my new address. It will help my letters to reach me much more quickly, for if they have to be readdressed from No 5 IBGH they will take as much as a week longer to come. The inland posts are most erratic.

I had a very nice letter from Geoffrey before I came here, and am answering it very soon. I will write again soon.

Lots of love to all. God bless you always.

Your loving

Vera

_ᔓ_

No 60 BGH
India
8.11.43

My Dear Mother and Father

Thank you so much for your welcome letter-card received today. A few days ago I sent you a cable to tell you my new address. I hope you have received it.

I am so delighted that you have received my parcel of material safely. Please don't worry so about the cost of it. It gives me the greatest pleasure to send you anything and I never expect you to attempt to send me presents, for I know how difficult it is for you to buy anything. Remember, prices here have soared since the war and I do not consider the material at all expensive according to present day prices. Please don't mention your anxiety about cost when next I send you a parcel. It gives me as much pleasure to send it as it does you to receive it. I only wish I did not have to state the cost of the contents on the label. Now don't you dare mention prices to me again!

I wrote to you a few days ago to tell you I am now back in my own unit. It is very good to be back, for mine is a fine unit and I have realised this more since I have been away for eight months.

You seem to be busier than ever in the canteen. I wish you would not work so hard for you will soon feel tired again if you do.

When I come home I shall rule you both with a rod of iron. My patients never dare put *one foot* over the side of the bed when they are not allowed up. They know me too well!

Talking of coming home, it seems too good to be true, but after serving abroad for five years, we are allowed to return home, we are what is known in army terms as 'repatriated'. If this is still official next year we may well expect to see dear old Blighty in another twelve months' time – if not before. It seems like something too wonderful to contemplate, I just cannot say how overjoyed I would be to see you, and England again. So many new people are coming out that we often think we could easily be released for Home Service, but they seem to want to keep us in India, and many of us who have become seasoned members of the Service, are being sent to the worst places on the Burma border.

I do hope you are all well. I wrote to both Muriel and Geoffrey a few days ago.

I am very well and people say I look fine.

Lots of love dears. God bless you.

Vera

෴

My Dear Mother and Father

I have sent you a Christmas airgraph, and this is my Christmas letter-card. We have four free ones, and are not allowed to send EFM cables as greetings this year.

I have just received a number of copies of the *Church Times* and *Punch*. Thank you so much. I was very pleased to have them and am so glad you sent them. I am handing the *Church Times* on to our padre when I have read them. He will be glad to see them too. One of my patients comes from Chelmsford and he gave me a three month old copy of the *Essex Chronicle* to read, the other day. It was interesting, but made us both feel homesick, reading about the familiar places. We often discuss Essex, and when I see him I greet him with, 'Hello Chelmsford', and he says 'Hello Maldon', or 'Hello Heybridge'. These lads love to meet someone who knows their own county.

I have a surgical ward now. It is the one on which I worked just over a year ago, and it has been very nice to come back to it. I have been doing medical work for a long time so am glad to do surgical for a change.

We are having quite cool weather just now, and at night we need blankets on our beds. It is pleasant to go for cycle rides, for the early evenings are lovely. I went with another Sister to a lake, four miles away, a few days ago. It was a very enjoyable ride and we sat under some trees by the lake and watched the sun go down, and listened to the songs of the various Indian birds. It is a delightful spot and so peaceful. We hope to go again soon and take tea and stay there much longer.

I will try to get two days off together before Christmas and go to Bombay as I want to get my photo taken for you. I promised to send you one, also one to Geoffrey, but the one I had taken in Deolali was no good at all. I should like you to have a nice one, and you will be able to see how well I am looking.

Well, my dears there is no more news, so I will say cheerio, and a very happy Christmas. I hope you will not be having any air raids at that time. I shall be thinking of you a great deal.

Fondest love to all. God bless you.

Your loving

Vera

॰

No 60 BGH

India

30.11.43

My Dear Mother and Father

Thank you very much for your letter-card of the 9th November. I was delighted to have it. You should by now have received letters from me to tell you that I am back in my own unit. I am surprised you have not received the cable I sent giving my new address, but perhaps it has now arrived. I sent it about the 1st November.

Today, St Andrew's Day, I have thought of you all very much. We had our new red frontal on the altar in church in honour of St Andrew, and we had a special prayer 'for the priest and people of the parish of St Andrew, Heybridge' It is really very wonderful, and I am sure you and the people of our church will be glad to know, that in our little church here in Ahmednagar we remembered you on the day of your patronal festival. It was a link, joining us with you.

I have an orderly working on my ward, who comes from Oxted, near Colchester. His wife is there, and his mother lives in Witham. He has waited many months for mail and is very anxious for news from home. I told him that if it was possible you would be glad to go and see either his wife or his mother, and then write and let me know that all is well with them. The mail for the troops seems to go astray far more than ours for there are many more of them, and they are constantly on the move. That is why letters are delayed and lost. He has not yet given me the addresses, but when he does I will send them to you. I know it may not be possible, owing to lack of transport for you to visit them, and he realises that you will probably not have a car now. I expect you gave it up some time ago. However, let me know, please, if anything can be done.

I am so pleased to hear you are both keeping well. Now please *don't* overwork. You *must* take care of yourselves.

Thank you very much for paying my General Nursing Council fee. It was a relief to hear that news, as a warning has been sent round to nursing Sisters about this and I am very grateful to you for paying mine.

I am keeping very well. We are preparing for Christmas and already I have quite a store of crêpe paper for decorations in my ward. I shall be writing again very soon.

Fondest love to you all, and God bless you always.

Your loving

Vera

め

No 60 BGH
India
5.12.43

My Dear Mother and Father

I wrote to you last on 30th November and I wrote to Muriel two days ago, so I have not much news for you.

Before this arrives you may have a letter from me asking you to try to visit a woman living in Colchester, the wife of an orderly who works on my ward. I explained that he has not heard from her for a long time and he was anxious to know if all was well. I fear now that all is *not* well, for a letter has come to him from his mother to tell him that his wife has gone away with an American soldier! I am writing this to ask you not to do anything about it after all. There is nothing to be done. It is just another instance of a shattered home and we are getting quite accustomed to hearing of troops' wives deserting their husbands for other men and the 'other men' are not often Englishmen. I am terribly sorry for this man and he is broken-hearted about it and cannot understand his wife's unfaithful actions at all. She cannot have been worth very much to treat him so, but he could not look at it in that way. He feels he has lost everything. He used to talk to me so proudly of her, and of his children. I wonder who will care for them. Not their mother, when she has a new interest to occupy her time. I was afraid, when I wrote to you before, that this had happened, for I have met several similar cases recently, and it was always the same trouble to begin with, no mail coming.

We are having such lovely weather just now, sunny days and cool nights. It is fresh and crisp in the early morning and there is such a chill the air that we go on duty wearing cardigans or capes. I think December and January are the healthiest months of the year in Ahmednagar. There are plenty of flowers about too. It seems as if we are to be blessed with lots of flowers for church decorations at Christmas. Asters are particularly lovely, in pinks and mauves, also yellow daisies, and hollyhocks. We hope these will still be blooming for Christmas, also if we are very fortunate there may be some sweet peas. So you see it is quite a fruitful place at this time of the year. Looking round at the gardens, the flowers, the ferns in pots, the green trees and hills, it is hard to believe we shall be living in a barren dusty land again in a few months' time. I am so glad we have all the flowers at Christmas time.

More news soon. Lots of love to all. A very happy and maybe victorious New Year.

Your loving
Vera

๛

No 60 BGH
India
13.12.43

My Dear Mother and Father
I had a very nice and welcome letter from Mother a few days ago. It arrived at 11.45 a.m. one day when I was off duty, and I had answered it by midday! Wasn't that a quick reply?

We are having very cold weather here now. Our climate goes from one extreme to the other. We shiver as we reluctantly leave our beds in the mornings, and we all appear at breakfast wearing woollen cardigans. When we leave on our bikes for the hospital we wear our heavy grey greatcoats buttoned up to our necks, and some of us have gloves on! At night we have three blankets on our beds. Perhaps we are so used to the heat now, that we cannot stand up to colder weather. I wonder how I should cope with an English winter now!

We are enjoying these pleasant days and have much more energy. I go for long cycle rides and some of the Sisters play hockey. This is said to be the coldest winter in this part of the country for years. The temperature, they say is just over fifty degrees, which is not really so very cold compared with what one would experience at home, but to us it feels bitter! It is at least fifty degrees less than the climate we usually have here.

Christmas will soon be here. I have lots of coloured paper which the patients are cutting into pretty streamers to decorate the ward. We have a colour scheme of red, yellow and green. Each bed has a lamp above it, and this will be covered with a yellow or a red shade. The shades have silver stars cut out of silver x-ray paper, pasted on them. The lights in the centre of the ward will have yellow shades. We are putting streamers across the ward and hanging from the fans. When one walks down the centre of the ward there will be an arch of coloured streamers above, coming down from the fans to the mosquito net wires which run along the ward at the ends of the beds on either side. It all sounds rather intricate to you probably, but I will tell you in detail how the ward looks at Christmas time. I think that it may be the prettiest of them all.

We are practising hard for our carol singing on Christmas Eve. I am so looking forward to going round the wards singing carols. It was lovely last year. We are having Holy Communion, with Christmas hymns, and the *Gloria in Excelsis*, *Agnus Dei* and Lord's Prayer will be sung, at midnight on Christmas Eve. The choir and congregation have been learning Merbecke, and now sing it well. This will be a lovely service I am sure. Last year the church was packed to the doors.

Lots of love, dears,

Vera

No 60 BGH
India
16.12.43

My Dear Mother and Father

I wrote to you a few days ago, on the 13th to be exact. Today, being my birthday I thought I would write, next best thing to being with you.

To think that I am twenty-seven today, and I was twenty-two when I joined the army. It is possible I shall have to spend another birthday abroad, but certainly not my birthday of 1945. We are all hoping we shall be home again after another year, if not before, for then we shall have completed five years.

Most of the members of the 60th are the original people who came out in 1939. We were the first complete hospital to be sent to the Middle East and we are proud of that fact. We think that the 'balloon will go up' in Asia 'ere long and the sooner the better, for then we can get things cleared up and go home where we belong.

I shall be thinking of Mother on her birthday and hope you receive the cable of greetings and especially the book I sent for Mother's birthday. We have finished making our ward decorations, and now all the patients are anxious to see them put up. We should have a very gay and festive ward for Christmas. The Indian sweeper, that is the boy who washes the floor etc, has shown himself to be quite artistic by cutting out a perfect copy of the RAMC badge from stiff silver paper. He has pasted it onto red paper and we are going to hang it over the ward door where it will be seen by all.

21st December

I am very much afraid I have delayed writing this letter for I did not have time to finish it on the 16th. Life is very busy these days. We are going to decorate our wards tomorrow, and the church on Friday. I have bought presents for all the orderlies on my ward, and I am sure they will much appreciate them, and they certainly deserve a little reward for their hard work.

Thank you so much for two Christmas airgraphs just received. How attractive they are. I was so pleased to have them so near Christmas, and will answer them more fully in my next letter. I thought of Mother very much on her birthday.

More news soon my dears. God bless you all. Lots of love from,

Your loving
Vera

ക

No 60 BGH
India
28.12.43

My Dear Mother and Father

Thank you so much for your two airgraph letters of greeting. They came on the same day, 24th December. One was from Mother dated 18th November and the other from Father and was sent on the same day. Wasn't that grand, that they both came at the same time and on the best day, Christmas Eve, just in time for Christmas. I have also had three letters from Muriel recently. Her latest, dated 6th December, came yesterday. I am writing to thank her for them. I was so sorry to read in that letter that Mother has had influenza and do hope she is now quite well again. It is most disturbing to have such news, and I am most anxious to know if she has made a complete recovery. Do please let me know as soon as possible. There seems to be a lot of influenza about just now in England. You must take great care of yourselves, all of you, please, and don't work so hard, and dash about so much.

I am so pleased that my Christmas parcels to you have arrived, and that you were pleased to receive them. There is still a birthday present, material for Mother, to come, and I hope by now, it has arrived.

We hear that most of the mail posted in England between 30th September and 20th October has been lost, so I have made up my mind that my parcel from you will probably not come, as you sent it on 27th September. One can always hope, though, especially as some people have received parcels which they know were posted between the dates mentioned.

I thought of you very often at Christmas and wondered what you were doing. I hope Geoffrey was able to get leave, for it will have made a nice family gathering – minus me, if he did. I am looking forward to hearing all about your Christmas, although we have read in the papers that the festive season passed very quickly and there were few extras to be had to celebrate the great day. The spirit of Christmas is always the same though, I think, for it is the Birth of Christ we are remembering and that is always full of wonder and joy and cannot fail to inspire us, no matter where we are, or what our circumstances may be!

We have had a very happy time here, and to me it has been a really lovely Christmas. I will describe it all from the beginning. On the 23rd, we decorated our wards. I had a number of convalescent patients who were able to help to hang coloured streamers, so we spent a hilarious afternoon decking the ward with most attractively made streamers in red yellow and green. I had as much fun as the patients. When the streamers were all up, we made an archway of green branches in a doorway which separates our section of the ward from another. I arranged a number of coloured lights, red, green, yellow, blue and orange, all round the archway, so that it looked like fairyland and how the men loved it. The British 'Tommie' does appreciate simple homely things like these! At night my archway with its dainty coloured lights looked very pretty and added to the Christmas air of festivity. In the bazaar, I found a cardboard manger scene, very finely made, in soft colours, and with the Holy Family, shepherds, wise men and animals all there. I hung this in the centre of the archway with a blue light glowing behind it and a red one in front, and the effect was very good. Everyone admired it.

My ward was unanimously voted the best decorated in the hospital, you will be pleased to hear!

On Christmas Eve, we decorated the church. The padre's wife, Rosamund, who is a very dear friend to me, arrived, accompanied by a tall, bushy cypress tree which was transported from a nearby garden by a tonga (similar to a rickshaw). We planted this in a large green box and stood it in the middle of the aisle so that all could see it on entering the church. We decorated it with silver tinsel and little silver balls, and tiny white candles. These were lit on Christmas Eve and Christmas Day, for the services. The tree looked so attractive and home-like and the men all admired it and said how grand it was to see a Christmas tree like those they remembered at home. It was not possible to get a real Christmas tree, but our substitute was extremely successful.

As I thought, I have not been able to write all I have to say in this letter, so I will continue in another letter-card, and post it at the same time. I hope they arrive together.

Much love.

Your loving

Vera

ൟ

No 60 BGH
India
28.12.43

My Dear Mother and Father

I have just finished writing you an airmail letter-card, but could not write on it all that I wanted to, so am continuing on this one. I hope these two cards arrive together, so that you can read the first one before this.

I have told you about my ward decorations for Christmas, and about our Christmas in the church. How I wish you could have seen our little church when we finished decorating it on Christmas Eve. The altar wore its beautiful white and gold frontal, and was a mass of white chrysanthemums and asters. I arranged two large vases and two small ones at each side of the cross. In the sanctuary we had more vases of white flowers, and on either side of the altar we placed a large green fern. All down the aisle were more ferns in pots, some green and some red, these were all very pretty. There were flowers everywhere, and all the windows were decked with green branches. Over the altar we affixed on the wall a large silver star, which shone brightly at night when the lights were on. The church looked very lovely and very joyful. I think it has never looked more beautiful on any other occasion.

At 8.30 p.m. on Christmas Eve, our carol singers met and started out round all the wards singing carols. We sang all the well-known hymns, such as *Hark the Herald Angels Sing*, *O Come all ye Faithful* and *While Shepherds watched their Flocks by Night* etc, as well as *Good King Wencelas*, *Good Christian Men Rejoice*, *The First Nowell* and many others. The patients very much enjoyed it and from all the wards, patients have sent messages thanking us most fervently.

The great favourite of the troops is *Silent Night, Holy Night* which we sang again and again. We had a special request for it on almost every ward, and I am sure we were as deeply moved as our listeners when, on one occasion we stood outside the Isolation ward, (which we are not allowed to enter unless on duty), and sang it with a star-filled sky above us, and deep silence all around!

After our carols, at 11.30 p.m. we went to our midnight Communion Service in the church. This was the most beautiful part of Christmas for us. The church was packed to the doors, and extra seats had to be provided. It was one of the most inspiring services I have ever attended. It was great to see such a crowd of men, so wholeheartedly joining in, and one could tell from their expressions, how glad they were to be there! We sang *While Shepherds watched*, and *O Come all ye Faithful* and Merbecke's music to all the responses, *Agnus Dei*, Lord's Prayer, *Sanctus*, and *Gloria in Excelsis*.

A number of my patients attended, including one who has been lying on his back with a TB spine for fifteen months, and now is up just in time for Christmas. He sat in a wheelchair and looked so happy.

On Christmas Day we had great celebrations. Matron and the Colonel visited the ward, as well as Colonels from regiments stationed here, and all the men had their pals in to see them. Every patient had a stocking with gifts in it. We served dinner at a long table set at the top of the ward. Some patients sat at tables in the centre and the beds of others were pulled round in a semi-circle so that all could see. I will not describe the dinner, for it would not be fair to you, but it was a good one. Two of our doctors carved and wore chefs' hats. The patients had a very good feed and there was lots of fun.

In the afternoon we had a band to play to the patients and afterwards a grand tea, and the members of the band joined in. The orderlies went off duty at 5 p.m. and another Sister and I cleared up the litter and settled the patients for the night. Some were soon asleep, like happy children. They all enjoyed themselves very much and said so again and again. Even the ill ones were able to have a little dinner.

I am sure the relatives of these men would be glad to know how happy a time they had, even though they were in hospital.

There is no more room so I must say cheerio.

Lots of love to all.

God bless you.

Your loving

Vera

ॐ

No 60 BGH
India
30.12.43

My Dearest Muriel

I have three letters in front of me, all from you, and all awaiting answering. One is dated 31st October, the next 22nd November, and the third 6th December. It is high time I wrote. Thank you so much for these letters, all of which were most interesting and welcome.

You should by now have received a Christmas airgraph, and Christmas letter-cards, a letter containing photos (though I am doubtful about this as it was sent by ordinary airmail), and a letter to you, which I sent on 3rd December. I am writing more frequently these days, so there is a lot of mail on the way.

I am so pleased that the Christmas parcels have arrived safely and that you are so glad to have the undies. You will be pleased to hear I had some nightdresses of that material and I had worn them on the three occasions I have been in hospital, and had them washed and washed and I am still wearing them. If you could see our Indian dhobis, or laundry men, beating the clothes against the stones and jumping on them, at the big stone coppers in which they do their washing, you would indeed marvel at this. However, the laundry always comes back snow white and nicely ironed, so we do not worry about the process through which it has passed!

I am very glad Mother likes her book which I felt sure would please her, and I hope Father's socks fit, as I have worried about that. There is a parcel for Mother's birthday too, so I hope it arrives safely.

I thought of you all very much at Christmas, and longed more than ever to come home. Actually I always feel a greater nostalgia during the New Year, for I think of another year coming and I am still away from home. We hear that some members of our unit who were sent from us to other units in the Middle East, are being allowed to go home, as they, like us, have done four years abroad. It is sad that we cannot do likewise, but we are in India, and it is much more difficult to arrange repatriation from here than from the Middle East.

I have written to tell Mother and Father all about our happy Christmas here. Our carol singing round the wards was deeply appreciated, and we loved singing to the patients. How dry our throats felt when we finished our round at 10.45 p.m. and made our way to the chapel for our midnight service. But here we raised our voices joyfully again in *While Shepherds watched their Flocks by Night* and *O Come all ye Faithful*. We also sang the chants and responses to Merbecke's music which sounded lovely, and during the Communion we sang that beautiful hymn *Let all Mortal Flesh keep silence*. The church looked lovelier than I have ever seen it, decked with white chrysanthemums and white asters. We had a fine cypress tree in place of a Christmas tree and it was a good substitute, and stood so proudly in the centre of the aisle, adorned with tinsel, silver bells, and little white candles, which were lit when the congregation came in to the service.

The patients had a lovely time during Christmas. My ward was so festive, with its decorations of red, yellow and green streamers, little coloured lights, and coloured lamp shades. Even the most ill patient had a small dinner on Christmas Day, and it seemed to do him good! On Boxing Day at 7 p.m. we had a carol service in the church and again it was packed to overflowing.

I do hope you enjoyed your trip to London to see the pantomime. It is a very kind thought of yours to take the Prowse children. I am anxious to know if Mother has quite recovered from her attack of influenza. I am so sorry to hear about it, and shall be glad to have more news soon.

Our padre gave me a very good book for Christmas. It is called *The Problem of Pain* by C S Lewis. I am much enjoying it for it discusses a big subject. I gave him a book of Studdert Kennedy's poems, and to Rosamund, his wife, who is also a good friend to me, I gave a copy of *Ave Maria* like the one I sent Mother.

I will write again soon my dear. I often wish I had your company. We could have such pleasant times together.

Lots of love. A happy year to come.

Vera

༉

No 60 BGH
India
5.1.44

My Dear Mother and Father

Thank you so much for your letter dated 12th December which arrived today.

Yesterday I went for a picnic with the padre and his wife, one of our Medical Officers and a Sister. We went on our bicycles and took tea. It was a special excursion as we visited a famous old landmark, the tomb of Salabat Khan. This is a circular tower built in 1560. It stands on a hill about four or five miles from our hospital. We had a lovely ride and the weather was just right, cool and sunny, with a pleasant breeze. This is the best time of the year for cycling. When we reached the foot of the hill we left our bicycles and followed a track round the hillside which gradually brought us to the top.

The tomb is most interesting. It is a vast building of solid stone with three floors. In the vault lies the tomb of Salabat Khan. As one enters the building on the ground floor one sees a vast circular room with a great dome at the top. On one side round the wall is a winding staircase of wood, built in recent years to enable people to reach the upper floors. The old stone stairs were in a state of decay and had to be walled up. We went up the wooden stairs and found ourselves on the first floor. This is a wide circular stone place with windows of Tudor style and large stone window seats. It reminded me rather of a castle. On this floor we found a narrow stone staircase with deep stone steps, worn with age. This must have been part of the staircase which was walled up. We followed these steps up to the next floor which was similar to the first one, and from there we went up again to the top of the building which was a flat roof. Here we saw the pillars which were to have supported yet another floor of this strange building.

We stood, looking down upon a most wonderful panorama of the countryside for many miles around. Brown fields and green fields, hills and streams, roads white with dust and curving into the distance, villages and camps, lay far below us. Little clouds of dust rising here and there above a road showed where an army truck was moving. We watched bullock carts toiling slowly along towards a village. A lake which I know and have visited, lay still and shining in the sunlight. The scene was very peaceful. We sat down and in silence studied every detail. The tinkle of bullock bells came up to us faintly from the hills below.

I will tell you the history of Salabat Khan's tomb. (Ahmednagar is full of interest and has a long and exciting history. In the year 250 BC it is said to have rivalled Cairo and Baghdad in splendour). About the beginning of the 16th century, King Hussein, the ruler of Ahmednagar, had for his Prime Minister a good and just man, Salabat Khan. It was he who supervised the building in stone, of the vast Fort which still exists here, and who built the aqueducts which gave the water supply to the city. He lived for many years as PM and not until he was seventy, was he allowed to retire, for the King valued his services. Salabat Khan built the great tomb first as one of his residences where he is believed to have lived richly and luxuriously. After his retirement, he grew tired of life, and not wishing to live to a great age in idleness after so full a life, he prepared three cups of poison, one for himself and one for each of his wives. He asked them to drink it so that all might die together. One drank hers immediately, but the other hesitated. To the one who drank without flinching he assigned the honour of being buried with him in the tomb, but the other for her few moments of doubt and fear, was buried at his dying order, outside the tomb, on the terrace, together with her child and his pet dog. This wife's grave lies there, covered with a great stone slab, in front of the entrance to the vault wherein lie the Prime Minister and his favoured wife.

We were only allowed to peep into the sacred room where the two slabs lay side by side, covered with red and gold cloths, for the Hindus will not consent to people of other Faiths, polluting it by their presence.

In 1803 when Wellesley captured the 'City of Ahmed' he was in favour of using the great round building, once so full of splendour and colour, and then empty and useless, as a temporary convalescent home for some of his men, and he even bricked in some of the windows to make it less draughty. No one seems to know what prevented the carrying out of his plan, but it never materialised. Whether the Hindus prevented his interference, whether the water supply was insufficient or whether the ghost of Salabat Khan appeared in great wrath to put him to flight, is not known!

It stands to this day, a relic of ancient and turbulent Indian history. As the saying goes, 'If only those walls could speak!' They looked down upon many battles after the passing of Salabat Khan, saw Chand Bibi, the Dowager Queen of Bijapur, defend Ahmednagar against the army of the Emperor Akbar, who brought his forces from Delhi; and saw many other battles raging on the plains below, before the final battle in which Wellesley was victorious, and thus the British came to Ahmednagar.

The sun was sinking in a blaze of glory and the walls of the tomb were tinted pink, when we started back from our picnic. We rode home in the dusk singing carols, and feeling very happy and pleasantly tired.

Well, I really must not write much more, or this letter may be too heavy. I am writing you an airmail letter-card tomorrow, as this may take some time to reach you.

Lots of love to all, and God bless you.

Ever your loving

Vera

∾

No 60 BGH
India
17.1.44

My Dear Mother and Father

I wrote to you a few days ago and sent a snap which I hope reaches you safely.

I have just received some news which came like a 'bolt from the blue!' I have been 'posted' on permanent duty to a hospital in Secunderabad, (further south), as *Assistant Matron*! I can still hardly believe it. I do not want to go at all, for you know how happy I was to come back here from Deolali and having been back just over two months I am now departing again.

Why have I been promoted? I know the answer. The Matron and Colonel at Deolali sent in a report and a recommendation for promotion to HQ, and this was mentioned to me by Matron when I left there, but I did not think any more about it.

The order has come from New Delhi, so there is no hope of trying to arrange for someone else to go. It means I shall have to leave the unit of which I have been a member since October '39, and there will be no return for me as I am permanently posted. I am very sad about it for I shall have to leave my friends, who are many, and our little chapel which has meant so much to me.

I know one must expect such upheavals in army life, but having just 'done' eight months away, I felt sure I would not be moved again for a time. However, this is definitely a break with the dear old 60th and I cannot feel any glow at all at the change to a higher status.

People say what an honour has been shown me, and talk of

increase in pay etc but I only want to stay here where I have been so happy.

Secunderabad is on the plains further south, and near Hyderabad. You will find it on a map of India. It is said to be quite beautiful in parts. It will take me about two days to get there.

Well, my dears I will write to you again as soon as I arrive at my new post. I leave here the day after tomorrow.

Lots of love to all.

Ever your loving

Vera

ക

No 127 IBGH (BT)
c/o No 17 ABPO
India Command
22.1.44

My Dear Mother and Father

I wrote to you a few days ago telling you that I have been posted to another unit as an Assistant Matron. I have now arrived here and my new address is above.

I cannot tell you too many details about this part of the country as censorship is very strict, so I may not mention the name of the town where I am stationed. However, you will know, by my last letter sent from my old unit.

I am sure you must have been very surprised to hear my news of my new appointment. By the time this reaches you my last letter should have arrived, so you will know. No one was more surprised than myself. I was simply staggered when I heard. Although I have been in the Service for over four years I am only a reservist, and also I am only twenty-seven, the youngest member of my old unit! It is something unusual to be given such promotion, so you can imagine how amazed I was!

This post has been given to me on the recommendation from the Matron at D! I did not know about this until my new orders came. Although I did not want to leave my old unit and friends at all, and was very sorrowful about it, I am going to do my very best here, and try to be as helpful as possible. I now have three 'pips' instead of two!

The hospital is a very fine place – quite the grandest I have seen since I came abroad. The wards are even nicer than our wards in the 60th, and that is saying something. They are solid stone buildings of a cream colour, with most pretentious entrances, wide steps and massive stone pillars of Georgian style in front of each main doorway. They are such handsome buildings that I still gaze at them in amazement for they might almost be paintings of a group of beautiful Georgian mansions! The gardens round each ward are very pretty and there are hundreds of plants, ferns in pots everywhere.

The interiors of the wards are just as fine as the exteriors. Each one is wide and lofty with shining polished floors, and large windows. The equipment appears to be very good. It is really a joy to walk round them as I have to do, and to be in charge of one of them must be very pleasant.

Our Mess is delightful. It is very large, for there are a large number of Sisters here. We have a big comfortable sitting room, and the dining room is most pleasant, with a long polished table and high backed chairs. Our rooms are very nice. I am especially fortunate in having not only a bedroom but a sitting room and bathroom as well!

I go on duty at 8.30 a.m. (breakfast 8 a.m.). During the morning I help Matron in the office where there is a lot of writing to be done. Then I do rounds of the wards. In the evenings there are more ward rounds to do, more writing etc. There are many details which I shall pick up as I go along for it is not an easy job, and it is a responsible one.

I still feel quite dazed at my sudden jump into a new kind of life! Only a few days ago, I had no idea this move was pending, and now here I am far away from my old friends, and sadly missing them. The padre and his wife came to see me off at the station. I did appreciate that. They have been great friends to me and have asked me to go back and stay with them at any time. They are also hoping to come here and see me.

I shall have to write to all my friends giving my new address.

Perhaps you could let Mrs Murchison and Matron KGH know. I wrote to them a few weeks ago. I do hope all are well. Longing to hear from you. My letters will be taking longer now as they will have to be readdressed.

Lots of love to all. God bless you.

Your loving

Vera

ൟ

No 127 IBGH (BT)
India
1.2.44

My Dear Mother and Father

Thank you so much for your most welcome letter received two days ago. It was dated 6th January and had been sent on from · the 60th. As it was the first I have had from you since my arrival here I welcomed it joyfully.

I am so very glad you have received the blue dress material. It gives me great pleasure to know that you will be able to have two new dresses now for the spring. I hope Muriel has been able to have a pretty dress made of her material. There are much better shops here and there seem to be lots of good materials so I am going to get some more to send on to you. I am sure Mother will look 'smashing' in her blue dress and she will be able to wear the pearl necklace Muriel gave her, with it.

It really does give me so much pleasure to know that all my parcels have reached you safely. I am afraid your parcels to me will not come now for I think they have gone down in that ship which was sent to the bottom before Christmas. We heard that most of the mail posted between 30th September and 20th ¯ October had been lost, and I see in one of Muriel's letters that you posted your parcels on 27th September.

Some Christmas mail is still arriving, so maybe they will come yet. Never mind. – I am very thankful my mail reached you safely.

I am very glad Geoff was at home for Christmas and I am pleased you had a happy time. Your Air Force ring and cigarette case must be very nice indeed.

I hope you have received my letters telling you about the happy Christmas I had.

I am settling down in my new job and liking it very much. It is so different from being a ward Sister and really much more difficult for there is lots of responsibility and a great deal of 'brain' work to do in Matron's office. I find it more tiring in many ways than running a ward. I am really rather young for such a position and I find I have to spend a lot of time – when I am off duty – alone, for one cannot be just 'one of the girls' any more when one is placed in a senior position.

Our Mess is very pleasant and comfortable, the best I have seen in India. I have a lovely room and a sitting room attached. I have plenty of shelves on which I have arranged all my books. It is like having a nice little flat all to myself. The countryside is very pretty and at present pleasantly green. It is quite hilly not like Ahmednagar which is rather too flat. I often go out for long cycle rides.

We have a little chapel attached to the hospital not nearly so big as our St Bartholomew at the 60th but very nice all the same. I can go there every Sunday to Holy Communion and on Feast days for it is so near and there is plenty of time to go before duty. There is also a lovely big church near here, called St John's. I went to Evensong on Sunday, and much enjoyed it. There is a large choir of little Indian and Anglo Indian boys who sang very sweetly.

I miss my old friends and my old unit very much. I am afraid the break with them is final this time for I have left them permanently. I suppose I was lucky to be left with them for four whole years!

I am writing to Muriel and Geoff very soon. Please give them my fondest love. I do hope you are all well, and that Mother has recovered from her bronchitis, or rather influenza. I am keeping very well. More news soon my dears.

God bless you always. Lots of love.

Your loving

Vera

10 127 IBGH
India
12.2.44

My Dear Muriel

I wrote to you two or three days ago in answer to your two lovely long letters which came together. I could not say all that I wanted to, however, so promised to write again.

First of all thank you all very much for the very welcome cable which came yesterday congratulating me upon my promotion. It was sweet of you to send it and it gave me a great deal of pleasure. I am so very glad you are pleased.

I was very interested to hear how you spent Christmas. It must have been very pleasant, though quiet and I am sure that there were lots of things you could not have. Your friend sounds a very nice girl. I am glad you were able to go up to London together to see a play. How smart you must have looked in uniform. I feel very proud to think we are all doing something in this war. I wish I could have been there with you in my QA uniform. You must have some lovely records now. I hope to hear them played one day.

I have told you in my other letter that I am sending you some green Kashmir wool material which will make a very nice dress for cool days. Actually I think you might almost wear it any day at home, for your climate is so much cooler than ours. I am sorry I have chosen green again like the linen I sent, but it was the best colour I could find and I am sure you will not mind. I am enclosing with the material some green sewing silk, some needles, and also hairgrips, as these will probably be useful. You must be very short of such things.

I shall be sending a parcel to Father also very soon, for his birthday. I had my photo taken a few days ago, and if it turns out well I shall be sending an enlargement home. I had it taken in uniform. I do hope it is a good one. There are some good photographers here. The town is very large and there are plenty of shops, such a change from Ahmednagar with its tiny, dirty bazaar.

I am cherishing great hopes of coming home next year, for at the end of this year I am entitled to apply for repatriation. It is a wonderful hope, and I think I have every chance of returning to Home Service. The new Sisters who come out look at me in amazement when I say I have been abroad over four years. They say *they* wouldn't stay all that time and they would *die* if they had to. I tell them they will have no choice in the matter, and ask them if I look like dying! They tell me I look amazingly well and have a nice complexion, which surely ought to be yellow and wrinkled after so much exposure to tropical sunrays! So there you see, I do look well in spite of my periods of illness.

I like my new job and am learning a lot. It is by no means easy and I am kept very busy. I am glad I have been given this fine chance of gaining more experience. It will all be a great help to me in the future.

I am still overwhelmed at this great change in my life. Nothing so unexpected and so exalted has ever happened to me before.

I do hope all are well at home. Please give my fondest love to Father and Mother and to Geoffrey, when you write to him.

I will write again soon.

God bless you.

My very fondest love,

Vera

❧

No 127 IBGH
India
17.2.44

My Dear Mother and Father

Thank you so much for your most welcome letter which came today. It took only days, very good, isn't it? I am so glad you are so pleased to hear of my new appointment. I was delighted to receive your cable. Thank you very much for sending it.

I am working very hard and doing my very best. Every day is a busy one, and I find my job even more tiring and exacting than being a ward Sister.

I have not become a 'regular' as I believe you think. I am still a reservist, and am one of the very few reserve Sisters who hold this position. I do not wish to join the regular army, although I have enjoyed my army life and gained such good experience. It is a great privilege for me to have such a post, and I am terrifically anxious to do my job really well. All other Assistant Matrons I have known have been 'regulars' so I feel quite awed that I, just a reservist, should have this job!

I still hope to put in for repatriation to the UK at the end of this year. Having then completed five years abroad. I shall be entitled to Home Service. No matter how much England may have changed for the worse, I am longing to see it again. All of us out here, from a Private to a senior officer, live for the day of our return home. It is the one hope which keeps people going. Without that hope, there would be nothing to fight for, would there? I have heard much about social and political changes at home, about the breaking up of homes, intermarrying of English and foreign people, as well as the awful tightening up of rationing and all the other hardships of the war. I cannot begin to realise what you poor people have to go through, and I feel very humble knowing how brave and persevering you all are. It must be a great strain, and it has gone on for so long. The raids must wear one down. How can I understand how awful they are, who have never been in an air raid?

It will all end though, but when we have won this war, England will be very different; it is *now*, as you say. I could not bear it if I thought I was going to settle somewhere else and never live in England again. I have no desire to go to New Zealand or Australia or any other dominion. Reconstruction will take years, there will be so much damage to repair, in more ways than one, and it will not be a happy country for a long time. But I want to be there to see the changes take place, just as hundreds of other people I have met, want to be there, in their own country to clean up the ravages of the war. The men out here think and talk a lot about England after the war, it is inspiring to listen to them, for many of them have sound ideas. England's future will have more hope when they return. I believe that after fighting for England, after long years in countries which cannot *compare* with dear old

'Blighty' they will go home and a new order will and *must* come out of the chaos. One must look to a bright future, even if we have to slave for it. It is because all, or nearly all the youth of Britain is overseas and the foreign element is so strong in England taking possession of our land, that England has so changed. It is only the thought of home and peace, back with one's own kith and kin, which keeps the whole army in action! That is why you must not write and say that England as we knew it has gone for ever. There *is* no peace to compare with England, even with all her faults, and it is because of that, that we keep up the fight until we have won!

Now I really must stop giving you my sentiments about such a big subject. There is still more news to give you.

Today I have sent off a photo of myself to you. I had it taken here a few days ago, and I think you will like it. I am in indoor uniform, and the photo is very clear, and altogether rather good.

I have also sent some dress material to Muriel for her birthday. I am so glad you went to see Mrs Murchison. She must have been most delighted to see you. What a nasty raid they must have had. I am so sorry your raids are just as bad as ever. I am anxious about you often. They must be very nerve-wracking.

I am writing another letter-card tomorrow to finish this.

Lots of love dears. God bless you.

Vera

♈

No 127 IBGH
India
18.2.44

My Dear Mother and Father

I wrote to you yesterday, but did not say all I wanted to, so I am writing again today.

Thank you very much for your nice letter of 1st February. I was also most glad to receive your cable. How thoughtful of you to send it.

I am liking my new station very much. It is pretty and interesting, and there are lots of shops and cinemas and a fine Officers' Club. After the funny little bazaar at Ahmednagar it seems like a great city. There is even a good hairdresser, but I have got so used to washing and setting my own hair that I don't think I will go to a hairdresser. It is strange to see wide streets, pavements and houses, just like an English town. I think it is much better than Poona, which is really very over-rated!

We are very close to another very large and important town but I cannot tell you its name. The senior Prince of India lives there. He is the richest man in the world. Everywhere in the town one sees portraits of him dressed in a rich looking long blue cloak and a turban on his head. He is getting old, and his sons have married two cousins from the Persian aristocracy. They are most beautiful women. People say it makes them gasp to look at them when they are present at some public function. I have seen portraits of them in a photographer's studio. They certainly look very lovely – with fine features, dark hair and large dark eyes. There was also a portrait of one of their sons, a sweet little boy of about six, sitting on a fine white horse. The Prince's palace is said to be very splendid. He has, I believe, nearly 200 wives and some of the more favoured ones have palaces of their own. The sons may have only one wife each, the Persian cousins, for when they were married the Shah of Persia insisted that if either brother took another wife the two Persian girls would return to their own country.

It is quite hot here now, and as the heat has started earlier than usual, we expect an especially hot summer. The birds here are beautiful. I have seen some bright green ones, some vivid red, others of mixed green and red, and some blue. Some sing very raucously, and have a monotonous note, but there are others which are very pleasant to listen to. We hear the brain-fever bird often. He shrieks, in a high pitched alarming note something which sounds like, 'You're ill! You're ill!' I used to hear him outside my room when I was in hospital in Deolali, and I was ill too. It did not make me feel any better to be told I was!

I have sent my photo off to you today. I told you all about it in yesterday's letter.

I am kept very busy in my job. I like going round the wards

and seeing the patients. The wards are very scattered so I cycle round from one to another.

Matron does not ride, and it is a little late for her to start learning, but she wants me to teach her. She has been in the army twenty-six years!

How is Geoff getting on with his course? I am writing to him soon. I wrote two letters to Muriel recently. Would you like me to send off the two snake-skin handbags I have been keeping for you. I do think it is a long time to wait yet until I can bring them home, even if I can get home next year. I can send them if you like and will pack them very carefully.

Lots of love to all. God bless you. Please take every care in those nasty raids.

Your loving
Vera

✌

No 127 IBGH
India
28.2.44

My Dear Mother and Father

Thank you so much for Mother's very nice letter which was written on 12th February and took only *twelve days* to come. It is so nice to have such recent news from you.

I wrote to Father yesterday by ordinary airmail and enclosed a cheque for his birthday. I have also written two letters to Muriel recently. I shall also be writing to Geoff soon.

I really feel glad you may be moving soon, and I do so hope you will go to a much safer district further inland. You have never had any peace from air raids where you are and you must be utterly worn out with them. I shall be most relieved when I hear you are away from the South East coast. I always feel so awfully worried when I read in the paper of widespread damage caused by raids on East Anglia. I see those reports much more frequently lately, too.

I hope you go to a quiet country town and have a very nice house and church. It will be pleasant if you can be near the

Gilbeys. You will be able to write me a nice long letter describing it all in detail.

How I should love to see the snowdrops, and the daffodil buds in the churchyard. I am just longing to see a snowdrop again and I have not seen a daffodil since I left England. You cannot imagine how we miss English spring flowers out here.

I think you are quite right in saying that you think I am here for a purpose. I feel the same, but cannot explain why. I know that this is meant to be, and feel sure I shall understand why some day. I do believe that these changes are ordained for some hidden reason, and I was not surprised when you said the same thing in your letter.

I am settling down better now, and do not feel so strange and lost in my new job. I am learning a lot and find it interesting. It is still very difficult in certain ways, but I feel I am overcoming the obstacles which troubled me most when I first came.

It is not easy when one is young and one's superior is so old, and so prejudiced about young people, and so inclined to doubt their capabilities. I am sure it is quite a new thing for her to have a young reserve Sister in a senior position, and she does not like such changes. In the regular army, promotion is very slow. However, life has already become much easier and smoother for me, and I am determined that this prejudice which I am up against *will* be broken down, and give way to appreciation and complete trust.

I am working with the most senior Matron in the QAIMNS so if I can really please her it will be a great achievement.

I have lots of encouraging and praising letters from my friends. I often hear from the padre and his wife at Ahmednagar.

I went to see *Mrs Miniver* here recently. I expect it sounds very much like past history to you, but it has just arrived in India. I did enjoy it so much. I am glad you liked *The Lamp still burns*. I hope to see it one day.

I am very lucky to be in such a pleasant station, and our quarters are most comfortable. I have a pleasant bedroom and sitting room.

It is getting hotter every day. We are now up to 96 degrees in the shade, and it is only February.

God bless you dears. Lots of love to all.
Your loving
Vera

❦

My Dear Mother and Father

I had a very nice long letter from Muriel a few days ago. I am answering it soon. Please tell her I hope she has received my two letters of 13th and 21st February. I also had a lovely long letter from Geoffrey which I have answered.

I do hope Muriel is better now. I was so sorry to hear she has had flu and tonsillitis. She must certainly not go back to nursing until she is quite well again. I am sure the war must cause you all to have a low state of health and you must take great care. I shall be anxious until I hear she is quite well again.

I am very sorry to hear you are having a lot of bad raids, but I feel sure you will be looked after. I know you take every care. I shall be thankful when I hear you have moved to another part of the country, for I am sure it must be a great strain for you living where you are. London seems to be suffering again too.

I am keeping very well, and working hard at my new job. I am settling down better and learning a lot. I think I am overcoming my earlier difficulties and feel more sure of myself. It is a responsible post, but I am getting used to it and feel sure I shall soon be quite accustomed to the new work. The Sisters here are a very nice crowd, hard workers and most pleasant always.

We are having very hot and humid weather, with a lot of thunder and lighting every night. It gets hotter every day. Soon the monsoon will break, as I believe it comes earlier here than in Bombay.

I have bought a gramophone – a very nice HMV. It is of a deep red colour, and has a good tone. I am so pleased with it, and had saved up for it. I have some very good records, among them being *Overture 1812*, *Tone-Poem Finlandia*, *The Warsaw Concerto*, *Hear My Prayer* (our old favourite) and *Ave Maria*. I have endless pleasure out of listening to my records, and am looking forward to getting some more in the future, when they arrive in the shop. I have ordered Beethoven's *Symphony No 5 in C Minor* and *Fingal's Cave* by Mendelssohn. I expect you have some of the records I have mentioned. Muriel would love them, just as you would, but they are not Geoffrey's taste! There are two good music shops in the town and I have already spent two pleasant afternoons listening to records being played, before choosing.

I don't suppose you have received my photo yet. I have sent one to my friend who was with me in the 60th and is now in Assam, and I also sent one to the padre and his wife at Ahmednagar. They liked it very much indeed, but said I looked too serious. I do hope you will like it. I am sure you will.

I love looking after our little chapel here. It is very sweet and homely and our padre is very well liked. He knew Padre Tidey who was with us in the 60th, and worked with him in Burma.

I have recently been taking orderlies' examinations, both written and oral and it was interesting. I am giving lectures to them soon. No more space so I must stop.

Lots of love dears. God bless you.

Ever your loving

Vera

భ

No 127 IBGH
India
27.3.44

My Dear Mother and Father

Thank you so much for your two lovely letters which came today and were dated 13th March and 14th March. How very quickly they came. It is really grand to have such recent news from you.

First of all I must hasten to tell you that I am winning through here and am much happier. Since I last wrote, I have made great headway, and feel much more confident. Matron is changing a lot towards me and I feel she is trusting me and understanding me at last. We have had several long talks and she has said several things which give me every reason to believe she thinks far more of me than I was given to understand. We are also good friends off duty too, and have been to the cinema together often, also we go to Evensong every Sunday evening. Two months ago I felt sure we should never work happily together, but how different it is today! I am sure that the big prejudice was that I am so young to be promoted, and not a regular. She is senior to even the Matron-in-Chief, London, by her years of service, for she has been in the army for over twenty-six years, so she is proud of her regular army in which promotion is so very slow. If, at last I have pleased her and shown her I can do this job, I have accomplished something great!

What should we do without prayer in this life? I am convinced that I have been helped all the time in answer to many fervent petitions, and how strengthening it is to one's Faith to know that God is guiding and showing the way, through all the difficult days!

I was very interested to hear more about your hoped for move. I think it will be a very good thing for you to have a change. It will be so much better for you to have a quieter parish, and a safe one for you have certainly had a very anxious and trying time in Heybridge. It will be good to have a change from the canteen. Is Muriel glad about it too? I wonder where you will go. The Welsh Sisters here tell me that Hereford is very pretty and a nice county, so you would probably be happy if you go there. I am sure you would soon feel less tired and weary of the war if you settled in a quieter place. It will be strange to come home to a new place, and I shall look forward to seeing it very much. I do hope Muriel is now quite well again. I was so sorry to hear she has had flu and tonsillitis. I had a letter from her recently and shall be writing to her very soon. I hope she received my last letter safely.

I wonder if my photo has reached you yet. As I sent it by parcel post I doubt it.

I have heard from my friends the Tideys at Ahmednagar, very often since I left. Now the unit has moved, and the padre has gone with it, but Mrs Tidey was not able to go too, as they have gone on active service. She is going to nurse in a mission hospital. It is sad they have had to be separated but they quite expected it and have been glad they were together for so long.

I am afraid I have not been able to get any Easter cards this year, as none of the shops here are selling any. However, I will send you a cable at that time instead. I do wish you all a very happy Easter. I shall be thinking of you all at that time very much, and shall be wondering if there are snowdrops in the churchyard.

I am keeping very well, and this climate suits me. It is getting very hot now.

I will write again soon my dears. God bless you, and lots of love as always.

Ever your loving
Vera

ço

No 127 IBGH
India
Good Friday
7.4.44

My Dear Mother and Father

Here we are in another Holy Week. It really does not seem so very long since last Easter.

I have been wondering what you are doing today. I have just returned from the Three Hours Service. Matron and I went off duty at 11 a.m. and went to church at midday.

We stayed for the whole service, and very much enjoyed it. It was held in St John's Church, which is a lovely parish church near here. The addresses were most inspiring and moving, and we sang all the well-known Good Friday hymns.

We spring-cleaned our hospital chapel on Tuesday and tomorrow I hope to decorate it for Easter Day. I have tried hard to get lilies for the altar but they do not grow in this climate. However, I am sure other white flowers will help to make the chapel look joyful and festive for Easter. There are many frangipani trees round here. They have no leaves, and their branches are laden with the loveliest white flowers with delicate petals. The scent of them is beautiful and almost as heavy as that of Madonna lilies. I hope to have some of these flowers in the church.

It is very hot now and we just ooze perspiration day and night. I am thankful for my fan which keeps a little breeze round my bed in the night. As for the mosquitoes, they are on the increase and more vicious than ever. It often happens that I settle down to sleep having just put out the light and tucked my net in round my bed, when I hear the familiar, high pitched note of a mosquito, close by my ear, and I know he has dived under the net at the same time as me! I then have to get up, put on the light, and pursue the unwelcome visitor round the net until I catch him and kill him in a corner.

Not far from here is the house in which Sir Ronald Ross discovered that malaria was transmitted by the anopheles, or female mosquito. There is a tablet there to his memory, 'a benefactor of mankind'.

> *This day relenting God*
> *Hath placed within my hand*
> *A wondrous thing; and God*
> *Be praised. At his command,*
> *Seeking His secret deeds*
> *With tears and toiling breath,*
> *I find thy cunning seeds,*
> *O million-murdering Death.*
> *I know this little thing*
> *A myriad men may save.*
> *O Death, where is thy sting?*
> *Thy Victory, O Grave?*

I sent you a cable yesterday and I believe it was sent GLT. At any rate, I was told it would reach you in forty-eight hours so let me know if you have it in time for Easter.

Have you any more news about your move? I shall be interested to hear.

There is not much news to tell you I am afraid, so I will stop now. How wonderful it will be if I am home with you for next Easter! It is quite likely.

I hope you are all well. I am keeping fine.

Lots of love to all.

Your ever loving

Vera

᠊ᢀ᠊

No 127 IBGH

India

16.4.44

My Dear Mother and Father

I have not had a letter from you for about two weeks or more, so expect one any day. I wrote to you last on Good Friday, 7th April so I must write this today, for it is over a week since that letter was sent. I do hope you have received my cable safely. I sent it on Maundy Thursday or maybe it was Wednesday, the day before, and I was told that as I sent it GLT rate it would reach you in forty-eight hours just in time for Easter. I am afraid I could not get any Easter cards at all this year.

I thought of you such a lot at Easter, and tried to imagine what you were doing. I wonder if you had some lovely spring flowers in the church. I very much enjoyed decorating our little chapel. On the altar I put white frangipani. I wish you could see what a lovely delicate flower it is. I cannot describe it well enough. It grows on a tree and has an exquisite scent. There are numerous blooms on each spray and the petals are white with pale yellow centres. They look so fragile and lovely that one might imagine them to be made of wax. They looked beautiful in the brass altar vases and so expressive of the joy and triumph of the Easter festival.

There are many frangipani trees round here. In the evenings when I am doing my ward visits, riding round on my bicycle I pass one of the trees and the lovely scent of those flowers in the warm evening air is something to remember. We had lots of other flowers in the church also, and some ferns in pots, so it really did look very joyful. There were many people there. I was amazed at the number of people who appeared there for the first time, people whom I never realised were Church of England Communicants. It seems to me very strange that they should come just this time and perhaps at Christmas, and never give it another thought for the rest of the year.

We are having very hot weather now. The shade temperature has been round about 112 degrees on several days lately. We are not looking forward to May, the hottest month.

There is a severe shortage of water and the taps are turned off at the main for several hours every day. We are told how much water to use for a wash, and how much for a bath.

I have been here for just on three months now, and have quite settled down and am very happy. I don't worry now as I did when I first started here and I *know* that I am appreciated and relied upon a lot, which makes all the difference. Isn't it amazing how one is faced with what seem like insurmountable obstacles, and in time they don't seem nearly so big, or it is that one learns to persevere harder and climb over them? I never thought I was going to find life so much happier and easier, when I first came, but I have done and I am very glad I came here.

I told you in my last letters about my gramophone. I now have two more records *I Know that my Redeemer Liveth* soloist Ernest Lough, and *The Hallelujah Chorus* sung by the Royal Choral Society with the London Philharmonic Orchestra. I am very lucky to be able to get them here.

I do hope you are all keeping well. Is Muriel feeling better?

I will write again very soon.

All my fondest love.

Your ever loving

Vera

&

My Dear Mother and Father

Thank you very much for Father's airgraph which arrived two days ago. I was very glad to hear that his letter and cheque arrived safely and that he is putting the money towards a new suit. I am so glad it is a useful present for him and that he is so pleased to have it. It was several weeks since I had heard from you, so I was very glad to have the airgraph. We have reason to believe that some of our outgoing mail has been lost, and I do hope my recent letters to you have not gone, or you will be anxious if you do not hear from me.

I thought of Father and Muriel on their birthdays and wondered what you were doing and wished so much that I could be with you. I just *long* to be home more and more as the time goes by, and I am so hoping that this year may be my last abroad. There could be nothing more wonderful in the world than seeing you all again!

It is blazing hot here now. We just drip all day long and the nights are not much cooler. One awakens in the darkness feeling hot and sticky with an oppressive heat all round, and with the electric fan keeping the air moving a little. How lucky we are to have fans, for they do help. I am really more used to the heat than the other members of the staff who have all come to India recently, but I do not like it any more than they do. Lately the temperature has stood at 112 degrees in the shade. The birds seem to be the only creatures who revel in it, for they sing gaily all day and sound very happy. The brain-fever bird raises his voice above the others and seems to carry on cheerful conversation with other brain-fever birds on neighbouring trees. Then there is the copper-smith bird (I expect the Indians have another name for him). He has a most monotonous note, not at all beautiful to hear, but he is a bird of most exquisite colours, a red breast, blue wings and a yellow head.

The trees also show their full beauty in these hottest months of the year. I have told you about the frangipani tree with its delicate white flowers. There is another tree known as the Flame of the Forest. It has flame coloured flowers. There are many of these trees here, they are like splashes of red all over the countryside. The bougainvillea creeper, pink and mauve in colour, adds beauty to many gardens, and shades the verandahs of many bungalows in the district. The grass may be dry and shrivelled and the hills brown, but we are compensated by the colour and beauty of these tropical trees and flowers.

I am keeping very well and enjoying my work so do not worry. I do hope you are all well too.

Cheerio for now. God bless you.

Lots of love as ever.

Your loving

Vera

&

No 127 IBGH
India
28.4.44

My Dear Mother and Father

I have already written to thank you for Father's airgraph of 4th April, and now I have received two lovely interesting letters from Muriel. They came on the same day and I did so enjoy reading them.

Please tell Muriel she may certainly wear my taffeta evening dress, and that I had quite forgotten I had such a thing. I do want her to take anything in the way of clothes or anything else she may find useful of mine and keep them. I don't think I left very much behind but they are all hers now, and I am so glad the dress fits her and that it will be just right for the wedding.

How I should love to see the churchyard full of daffodils. The church must have looked beautiful for Easter. I tried to imagine it, a mass of gold and white. I am so longing to see an English spring, there is nothing in the world like it. We have many exotic brilliant flowers out here, but what are they compared with daffodils and snowdrops! I feel so much nearer home now that we know that after five years we may definitely be transferred home. An order has come out recently confirming this and in just another *six months* I hope to send my name in!

It is very hot indeed here now, but I am thankful to say I keep very well and am more or less used to it.

Everyone looks damp and tired with the heat and even the candles on the altar in our chapel curl right round in a semi-circle and become quite warm and soft. Can you imagine anything more dejected than a candle which has bowed its tall figure over in weariness until its top has touched the bottom of the candle-stick? Now I have to store the candles in a cool cupboard between the services.

I have started a course of lectures to nursing orderlies. I give a junior one on Tuesdays and a senior one on Thursdays. It is interesting and keeps one up to scratch in one's knowledge. The preparation takes some time as the whole lecture has to be thought out and written down, like a sermon! Cheerio for now. My fondest love to you both and Muriel and Geoff. God bless you.

Your loving
Vera

ൟ

No 127 IBGH
India
5.5.44

My Dear Mother and Father

I was very pleased to have Father's letter of 11th April a few days ago. I am receiving news from you very regularly, and hope my letters are reaching you safely also.

I am getting news from lots of other people also, friends everywhere, and it takes me all my time to keep my correspondence up to date. I seem to have a very busy life, but it is good to be busy for time passes so much more quickly. This year seems to be speeding along.

I wonder how the Bishop's visit 'went off' and if you have heard any more about a move. He ought to offer you a very nice parish after the long time you have spent in Heybridge and all the hard work you have done. What a busy Easter Day Father had. I hope you were able to go to a play in London on Muriel's birthday as you had hoped. I am sure it was a very nice change for all of you.

We are having intense heat here, and it seems to be getting hotter as the days go on. The sun is so brilliant that one must wear sunglasses or the eyes may easily become inflamed, and it is possible to get sunstroke through the eyes if they are exposed too much to the sun. Nearly everyone has prickly heat, a nasty irritating rash due to the heat and excessive perspiration. I have had it recently – it looks like measles, but fortunately does not affect the face, or one *would* look a mess! There is a very good lotion for it and it helps a great deal. As soon as the monsoon breaks, the prickly heat vanishes which is something to look forward to. We expect the monsoon in the early days of next month, about the 10th.

My friend Pauline Arthur who joined up with me from Plaistow, is in Italy, and she says in her letter that she has been halfway up Mt Etna, to where the snow starts, and she waded through inches of snow. How lovely to think of cold white snow in this blazing heat. She has had some varied experiences in Iraq, Egypt, Tripoli, and now Italy. She is a very faithful friend and writes often. Mary Insley is also a regular correspondent and she is in Naples, and has worked hard during a typhus epidemic. We are extremely busy here, but I cannot say any more about it!

Everyone seems very sleepy this afternoon. All the Sisters who are off duty in the neighbouring rooms are lying down, and the Indians are curled up under trees or in any shade they can find. The Indians are able to sleep at any hour, they just stretch themselves out and go unconscious and they take some waking! In the afternoons India goes to sleep, except for those white people who have work to do – hence the saying 'Mad dogs and Englishmen go out in the noonday sun'. I never sleep in the afternoon, and feel just as hot lying down. More news soon, my dears.

Lots of love to all

Vera

　　　　　　　　　　　　　　ｓ

No 127 IBGH
India
14.5.44

My Dear Muriel

This is my second letter and I hope the two letter-cards reach you at the same time as yours did to me. It is so nice to have two letters from the same person at the same time.

Thank you very much for the encouraging things you have said about my new job. Yes, I feel sure those difficult first weeks were sent to try me and how thankful I am that I stuck it out and now can say with confidence that I do not need to feel apprehensive any more. It is difficult to describe things such as this in a letter, I hope I may be able to explain it to you, when I come home which I so much hope may be at a not too far distant date. I was nervous and anxious at first because I knew before I came, with whom I should be working, and she is well known all over the country! I found that the reports I had heard were not untrue, but I was determined not to let my spirit be broken as has happened to others. It was not easy to be sent, on one's first appointment on promotion to such a task, and I often longed to be back in the old 60th. As I have said before I prayed harder than I have ever done about it all, and I began to see a new side to her, a human side, and I saw her as one who needed a friend. She was lonely and inclined to be bitter. I have *made* her like me and although I am just a reserve member of the service of which she has been a regular member for twenty-seven years, she has come, incredibly, to treat me in a very friendly way, in fact I sometimes think she is quite fond of me! Certainly she relies upon me now and discusses everything with me. She seems glad to have my company and we often go to the town together, or to the pictures, and always to Evensong on Sundays. It is strange that we were so much apart and so different in age and seniority when I came, but she has come to appreciate me more than I ever dreamed possible. She is so senior too, senior even to the Matron-in-Chief by years of service.

It is very hot indeed here now, the temperature ranges between 110 degrees and 112 degrees F but of course we are lucky really as it is not as hot as some places. One perspires profusely all day and even at night. Even the fans cannot seem to bring much air into the atmosphere.

We are extremely busy, but that is all I can say about it. The monsoon may make a break for us next month, at present there is no lull at all – it seems that we are having a race with the rains, in the hope of making good consolidated positions before the monsoon.

How beautiful the church must have looked at Easter, all white and gold. I should have so loved to see the daffodils in the churchyard. How good it is to remember that those things last for ever, will always come again with each spring as they have done ever since Wordsworth wrote those immortal lines you mentioned. I am just longing to see an English spring again. After all, exotic and brilliant as some of the Indian flowers are, my heart too will fill and *overflow* with pleasure when I see once more a bed of daffodils. There is no flower so lovely as our English daffodils, snowdrops, primroses and narcissi.

Well, my dear, here is the end of my space so I must say cheerio, but will write again soon.

All my fondest love, and God bless you.

Your loving
Vera

❧

No 127 IBGH
India
15.5.44

My Dear Mother and Father

I was so pleased to receive Mother's letter of the 24th April. It came a few days ago.

These letter-cards are coming through more quickly than ever. I had one from Geoffrey yesterday which took fourteen days, and today I had one from an old Plaistow friend, now nursing in the north of England, and it took only *nine* days!

Another came from Iris, which took ten days. It is grand to have such recent news from home.

I wrote to you a few days ago so there is not really very much news. We are working extremely hard, but possibly the arrival of the monsoon will bring a lull for a time. It is extremely hot and sticky. May is the worst month. Even the nights are very hot and one can hardly bear to be covered by even a sheet.

You seem to be in a state of tension at home at this critical time. We all know why of course. There was quite a lot about it in the paper today and we are told that there is one subject of conversation on everyone's lips, one question, when will it be? It must be a strain for you all, but it will mean another step, and a definite one towards victory. I wonder how long the struggle will continue out here, I am afraid after the war with Germany is over. If it were not for the heat, disease, and the monsoon, it would be terminated much more quickly I am sure.

I am so pleased that Mother has been able to get one dress made up. I should love to see to see her in it. I hope she will have the other one done soon, as well. It must be very difficult to find a dressmaker.

Geoffrey's letter was such a nice one, full of news and humour, I do love to hear from him. I am sorry he has been disappointed about his leave.

I am glad you were able to go up to London to see a play. It must have been a pleasant change. What a shame Muriel could not go too. I wonder if my photo has reached you safely. I hope by now that it has. I am anxious to know how you like it.

I am glad the Bishop's visit was so successful and you had such a well-attended service. I do hope now he will do his best to move you to a very pleasant parish, as I am sure a change is most essential for you.

I am keeping very well and the heat seems to affect me very little except to give me a prickly heat rash, from which most people seem to be suffering. I am quite happy and liking my work and learning a lot. More news soon dears.

All my fondest love. Have written to Muriel.

Your loving

Vera

My Dear Mother and Father

I received a very nice letter from Geoffrey a few days ago but have not had any recent ones from you. I have answered your last one, from Mother. I expect I shall receive one any day now as there has not been a large English mail for some time.

There is not very much news to give you. The heat goes on, increasing daily, but we expect the monsoon in about two weeks time, so probably when you receive this the rain will be flooding us out here, and new grass will be springing up and everything looking fresh once more. We have had several cases of heatstroke recently. It is a very acute condition and everyone on the ward concerned has to work very hard to save the patient. All the cases have recovered. The temperature rises as high as 110 degrees F, which in England must sound impossible! It is reduced by giving iced spongings, and iced water is poured over him. He is also given lots of fluid to drink with a large amount of salt. If he is unconscious he is given fluid intravenously. It is dramatic work and very worthwhile. At the finish everyone is drenched with perspiration owing to the continued exertion, but how glad they are that they have not worked in vain and the patient's temperature is down to 101 degrees F!

I am still giving lectures to orderlies and like it very much as it is interesting teaching people, and keeps my knowledge up to date also.

I am keeping very well. This climate seems to suit me, in spite of the heat, and it is more healthy I think than Ahmednagar. I do hope you are all keeping well. You must be hoping for a warm, fine summer at home, for June is nearly here.

My gramophone is a great joy to me. I have not very many records yet, as I am careful not to spend too much on them, for they are quite expensive, but in time I shall have a nice collection. My latest record is the *Moonlight Sonata* by Beethoven. It is beautiful. Have you got it too?

I hope Muriel receives the two letters I sent her safely. I wonder if you received the cable I sent you for Easter. I hope so. Please tell Geoffrey I am answering his letter very soon.

I am sorry there is little news to tell you, but life is quite uneventful, though there is plenty of work to do. More news soon.

Cheerio my dears. God bless you.

All my fondest love,

Vera

∽

No 127 IBGH
India
4.6.44

My Dear Mother and Father

Thank you so much for Mother's very nice and welcome letter received a few days ago. As usual it came very quickly, in twelve days. I also had a very interesting letter from Muriel sent on 23rd May. It came yesterday. I am answering it, and hope Muriel has received the two letters I sent her on 15th May.

I am so pleased to hear you have received my photo safely, and that you like it so much. It gave me great pleasure to know that you are all so pleased with it. If Father would like one for his study as well, I will send another copy.

I had a letter from Horace Crook recently. He has been in Burma, and in action against the Japanese. He was wounded slightly by a bullet in his arm and has been in hospital. Now he is at a convalescent depot in a very nice place and is quite fit again. I wonder if his family knows.

The monsoon has not yet broken and it is still very hot. There are strong winds now, which usually precede the monsoon. We expect the first rain in about a week's time.

How dreadful the clothing situation must be for you! How few coupons you are allowed. I shall certainly take your advice and bring a good supply of clothes home when I come. We have had a number of new Sisters, recently out from home, so I know from them just how things are.

Today is Trinity Sunday I have just come back from Evensong. Matron and I go together and it is quite a pleasant walk to the church and takes us about half an hour. I always think of you very much on Sundays, it is because the church is like ours in Heybridge and so my thoughts are with you. I imagine what you are doing – five hours behind our time.

I am glad to hear that Geoffrey is in a station nearer home, and that he has done well in his exam. I wrote to him a short time ago.

We shall all be glad when the rains start and we lose our 'prickly heat' rashes. Some people look as if they have measles! It is strange how it starts. One feels very damp and hot and then the skin starts to feel prickly. On looking in the mirror there is the most frightful rash all over one's neck and chest! There is not much to be done, except hope for an early monsoon.

Well, my dears, I am sorry I have no more news to give you and no more room. Writing again soon. God bless you.

Fondest love,
Vera

ço

No 127 IBGH
India
11.6.44

My Dear Mother and Father

I have not had a letter since I last wrote to you a few days ago, so probably as soon as I have posted this, one will arrive. We are quite expecting that from now on our letters will not come so quickly owing to the invasion of Europe, and we have been very lucky to have had them so regularly for such a long time.

We heard the great news of our attack on France just about twelve hours after it began, and everywhere people were crowding round wireless sets in great excitement listening to every news bulletin.

What a vast invasion force it is and how thrilling to know that we are back on French soil, on the offensive this time, with so much power and strength to meet the enemy. As Winston Churchill said, 'Everything is going according to plan, and what a plan!' It is hard to write down just what one feels about this great thing. We are all keyed up with excitement, and thirsting for more news, out here, so *your* feelings at home, so close to the Front Line can well be imagined. One thing is true. We all wish we could be in England at this time, which may well be the great turning point of the war. We feel so much apart from these important events. We must remember of course that we all have a job to do and that there is a Front in Burma and that it will not cease to be a Front because of the invasion of Europe. It is just that one feels so stirred and so impressed by the news from home that one wishes to be there at this vital hour. I am longing to have news of you but of course there will not be much you can say.

The monsoon has not yet broken here, but it has started in Ceylon so we should have it soon. The heat is typical of that which comes before the rains, heavy and oppressive and humid. The sky becomes black in the evening, and there is thunder and lightning, but still no rain. It will be a relief when it comes.

I am keeping very well and happy and always busy. Please let me know if there is anything you would like me to send you. I feel there is so little I can do, and you must need so many things, so let me know what I can send.

I hope you are all well, and not having too many raids and that they have not increased since the new Front opened.

More news soon. All my fondest love. God bless you always.

Your loving

Vera

ও

No 127 IBGH
India
23.6.44

My Dear Mother and Father

I received a very welcome airgraph from Father a few days ago on the 19th and it took only twelve days to come.

This is the greatest record of all, however. A letter-card came from Muriel on the 21st, having been written on the 13th so it took only *EIGHT* days which is just wonderful. How very lucky we are to have our mail in such quick time especially when a new Front has been opened and shipping must be greatly needed. It proves how well organised our postal services have become and we are very grateful. I am glad to hear that my letters are reaching you in good time also.

We are following the news with great excitement and interest and it is very cheering and hopeful. How wonderful that the King and Churchill have both already visited Normandy! Our positions must be fairly well consolidated for that to be possible.

I was very impressed by what Muriel said in her letter about the masses of planes roaring overhead on the eve of the invasion. You must have guessed what it meant. How I should love to be at home at this time.

There is not much news to tell you about myself. Life goes on much the same from day to day. I am quite settled and happy here and like the station very much indeed. I feel so very glad that, in spite of the worry and difficulties which I encountered at first, I have proved to Matron that I can fill the position successfully.

The heat is still rather trying, but certainly the temperature is lower now. The monsoon has started but not in real earnest yet. We had a downpour of heavy rain on Sunday evening just before church, and the smell of the rain is delightful. Already new grass is springing up.

Well, my dears, I will say cheerio for now. My fondest love to you both. I am so pleased Geoffrey has done well in his exams.

God bless you.

Your loving

Vera

My Dear Muriel

Thank you so much for your two very interesting and welcome letters. One was dated 23rd May, and the other 13th June. Both arrived very quickly, but the second one has created a record here which no one has yet been able to beat. It came in *EIGHT* days. That is simply grand, and quite the quickest letter I have ever known. I could hardly believe it when I opened it on the 21st, and saw it was dated the 13th.

I am so pleased to hear you had such lovely presents for your birthday. You deserve them of course and I only wish I could have been there to present you with mine personally. I have read the *Song of Bernadette*, and loved it. It is a most unusual and fascinating book. I am glad you have it for it is the kind of book you will really appreciate.

How thrilling it must have been for you to be awakened by that great mass of planes passing over, just at the beginning of the invasion. I am sure you must have realised what it meant and felt relieved and thankful that the liberation of Europe and the final defeat of Germany was about to begin.

The news is wonderful and we are all following it with deep interest and great hope.

I have added some more snaps to my collection in my big album recently. I now have a grand number and they are most interesting. I am so looking forward to showing them to you one day. I only hope I shall not be prevented from bringing them home with me for the authorities can be very strict about those things. Do you know of anyone who has brought snaps safely home?

The good news has come out in Indian Army Orders, to say that all army personnel who will have completed five years service abroad by June 1945 should now apply for repatriation! As my 'time' is up in December I should be quite well up the list, so I am putting in my application immediately.

Of course it may be many months before my turn comes, but what a *wonderful* thing to look forward to! Isn't that fine news? I feel so much nearer home already.

I am so glad Geoffrey did well in his exams. I wonder where he is now. Can you give me any clue?

All my fondest love to all.

More news soon.

Lots of love as ever,

Vera

ഄ

No 127 IBGH
India
5.7.44

My Dear Mother and Father

Thank you so much for Mother's letter received yesterday. It was dated 23rd June. I wrote to Muriel a few days ago.

I am afraid I do worry about you a great deal, for the raids have increased a lot and we hear that those wretched pilotless planes are adding to your troubles. It is good news that we are bombing their bases and dealing with them as they come over. You are all in my thoughts all day long and I feel so anxious about you. Anxiety is an awful thing – it gnaws at your heart and makes you wonder all sorts of things. How I wish I were not so far away and must remain so for a while longer yet. I would give *anything* to be with you. Being out here in a part which has never been touched by the war makes one feel in a guilty way that one has escaped and lived comfortably away from all raids and other horrors. Can you understand the feeling? I want to be at home and take my share of the suffering. It is a futile feeling of course, because I must go where I am sent and do the job I am given. You must be having many very disturbed nights which are most trying. I don't like the idea of you going up to London.

You don't know how proud I am of you all, Father doing a grand work, enough for at least two or three people, Mother being the best Mother on earth, of course, and doing many other good deeds day by day. Muriel putting all her energy into the First Aid Post, the hospital, and goodness knows what else and Geoffrey in the RAF doing so well and how proud I am of him and I let everyone know it! Yes I am very lucky to have such a family, all of you making such a superb war effort. Churchill should be told about you!

I am sending you a parcel of such things as elastic, hair clips, press studs and other haberdashery. Let me know what other things you need please as I shall be so glad to send you anything. I am so glad the check blue frock looks nice.

It would be wonderful if I could meet some of the men who went to your canteen. It is quite possible here, and I must make enquiries from some of the patients.

The rain is not nearly as heavy as it should be. Usually we have the ground flooded by now, with the ditches overflowing. The humidity is rather trying – one feels damp all the time.

I am keeping very well. More news soon, my dears. Keep smiling. You are always in my thoughts and prayers.

All my fondest love,
Vera

ॐ

No 127 IBGH
India
13.7.44

My Dear Mother and Father

I was so pleased to receive Father's very welcome and interesting letter dated 3rd July today. I am very glad to hear you are all well and that although you have had many disturbed nights and anxious times, the town has been very fortunate. I do hope this is still so. I am feeling very anxious about you, and read the papers very carefully every day for news of this new 'blitz'. You are constantly in my thoughts and prayers. It is so hard to think that after all you people at home have had to bear, this new terror in the air has come to reap more destruction. We hear that people are calmly going on, as they always have done, and taking to the deep shelters again, when they can leave their work. I know you will all take great care when there is danger. Please don't run any risks.

I have just had three days off duty. It is called 'station leave' because one is on leave but cannot go away from the station. Most of the staff have had it in order to rest for a bit as they have all been working hard. I felt quite ashamed when I had Muriel's letter in which she told me she worked twenty-four hours on and six hours off with no day off at all!

I do not expect to have any leave this year, however, and it is over a year since I was on sick leave, so I was very glad of that break. I don't really want any leave and feel very well and coming to a new station has been a pleasant change. I wrote ten letters during the three days! One of them was to Geoffrey, enclosing a photo, as he asked for a copy for himself.

I have actually filled in my application form for repatriation! A special army order has come out recently, to say that all personnel who will have completed five years abroad, by June 1945 should apply now. As my five years will be up in December I think I should stand a good chance of an early repatriation soon after the end of the year. I feel I have really taken a good step forward now, and there is an excited feeling inside me every time I think of it. On the form it says in one column that one should state the approximate date on which one wishes to be repatriated, and I was longing to write *TOMORROW* in block capitals, but had to put, 'as soon as possible after end of 1944'. This year has not dragged for me so far, so let's hope the rest of it passes quickly, then 'Blighty is the place for me'.

We are having quite a cold spell now. The climate has done funny things this year. It has been the hottest summer for this town on record, and now when it should still be hot with the humidity high, it has decided to become English, so we have rain, cold winds and leaden skies. Consequently everyone, almost, has developed a cold because of the change, myself included.

Lots of love dears. God bless you. More news soon.

Ever your loving

Vera

No 127 IBGH
India
21.7.44

My Dear Mother and Father

I have just received Muriel's very nice and welcome letter of 9th July. I am writing to her also and have two of hers to answer. I wrote to her last on 2nd July, so she should have that letter by now. I received Father's airgraph on the 13th and answered it the same day.

I do hope my letters are reaching you regularly now as I am writing often. I think I shall send an airgraph between each letter to be sure you hear from me very often.

I am so glad you are all well but am sure you must be very tired and over-strained with all the worry and danger you have. I think of you all so much, and pray always that you will be kept safe and well.

I am sorry to hear that Mrs Gilbey has lost a cousin and a cousin's daughter in a raid.

While the Germans continue to send their diabolical flying bombs over England, they are slowly but surely having their country approached upon by three armies and each one is strong and well equipped. The Russians, in today's news are closing in upon Warsaw, which advance will bring them very near to Berlin. It is grand news.

I am so glad to hear Muriel's news about her hoped-for transfer as a Red Cross worker abroad. It is a great opportunity for her, and will be such an interesting experience. Her work will be very valuable and she is most suitable for that kind of job. I am longing to hear more about it. She certainly deserves to be accepted. How wonderful for her if she goes to France – she will love that.

The heat has decreased a great deal now and we are in the midst of the monsoon.

I told you in a previous letter that my application for repatriation at the earliest possible date has gone in to Headquarters. It is a good step forward, and now all I have to do is wait as patiently as possible.

There does not seem to be much news to tell you this time. I am kept busy in my job, and still enjoy giving my lectures twice a week to orderlies and correcting a big pile of books after each lecture. The exam will take place soon, and I am hoping the results will be better this time than they have been in the past, although on the whole they have not been bad. I have tried very hard to give them good lectures, and included practical demonstrations as well. Lectures help to give my knowledge a polishing-up as well. I often think I should like to be a Sister-Tutor one day.

I am glad Geoffrey is well and has been posted near home. I know you will all take every care in raids but I must beg of you again to look after yourselves, and not run any risks.

More news soon. God bless you.

All my fondest love

Vera

☙

No 127 IBGH
India
2.8.44

My Dear Mother and Father

I was so pleased to receive Muriel's very nice letter dated 17th July and Mother's equally nice and welcome letter of the 20th. I was very glad to know that you had by then received one of my letters. I answered your cable immediately so hope you received my cable in good time.

I am so sorry to hear that Muriel cannot be released yet for the job she so wants. It is a great shame and must be most disappointing for her. She so much deserves the change too. It is very hard that her hopes are frustrated at the last minute like that. I do hope you are having some quiet nights though it is a lot to expect I know. In the papers today we read that the flying bombs are being sent over in salvoes. I am writing a long letter to Muriel in answer to several of hers.

I am keeping very well. More news in a letter-card tomorrow. Cheerio for now.

Lots of love. God bless you.

Ever your loving

Vera

୭

No 127 IBGH

India

3.8.44

My Dear Mother and Father

I have sent you an airgraph yesterday and am now sending two a week between the letter-cards so that you do not have to wait long for news.

Tomorrow I am sending Muriel a long letter in answer to several received from her. She is so good to write so often and I love to have her letters.

I think about you all so often and do hope and pray you are not having too bad a time though. I see in the news that the number of flying bombs going over Britain does not diminish much. Each morning on awakening I wonder how many hours' sleep you have been able to snatch.

Our Matron is leaving for home very shortly, I cannot say when. She has been in India nearly eight years, as she is a Regular and so was here before the war. She is of course very glad to be returning and is longing to see her people again. We are giving her a very nice Indian silver cigarette box and ash tray to match as a farewell gift and I am sure she will like it as a memento of the country. Her successor is very nice indeed and I think we shall be very happy with her. I will enjoy working with her, I feel sure.

I went to see the film *Jane Eyre* recently. It was very good but not altogether true to the book as it often happens when a classic is filmed. Have you been able to see it?

We are having lots of rain just now and some very humid days, but on the whole the weather is much cooler.

There are thousands of insects about just now, little black flying beetles, and eye flies which are very small and which hover in front of one's eyes when one is writing or sewing and sit on one's eyelashes if you don't shake them off! The mosquitoes are very troublesome too.

My request forms for repatriation have been forwarded to New Delhi and I feel very satisfied and happy about it, for now all I must do is wait as patiently as possible for more news. I am glad I have sent in my application several months in advance for then my return home at the end of five years abroad should not be long delayed.

I told you in a previous letter that we are going to wear khaki now. Mine is being made at present and should look quite nice when finished.

More news soon. All my fondest love to all.

Your loving
Vera

❧

No 127 IBGH
India
4.8.44

No 1
My Dear Muriel

Thank you so much for your last letter which came on 30th July and was written on 17th July. I do love to hear from you for you write such interesting letters.

I am sure you must be feeling terribly tired out, working as hard as you do. I do so admire the way you go on with those long hours of duty and hardly any free time at all. You must always feel weary. Life is certainly a great strain for you all, especially just now. I wonder if the flying bombs are decreasing at all now that we are advancing on the Continent.

I am sorry you were not able to see *Jane Eyre*. Perhaps you will have another chance. It came here recently. I enjoyed it very much, except that I did not think Orson Welles suitable for the part of Edward Rochester. His speech was not easy to understand, as he mumbled rather, and his brusqueness was overdone, making him appear rough and too ill-tempered. The Rochester of the book was certainly bitter and hardened at the beginning, but not to such an extent. Most people said they could hardly hear what he said. Joan Fontaine as Jane, was extremely good and suited the part well, being gentle and timid and courageous, and her dialogue was good.

The story was changed in several places, Helen Burns was not portrayed as the fine person she was and appeared only for a short time, Dr Rivers, instead of being a clergyman was a medical man and came on the scenes at Lowood School as a kindly doctor, and when Jane ran away from Thornfield she went to her aunt's house again and was reconciled with her before her death. The Rivers family did not come into the story as the people to whom Jane went on leaving Thornfield. The atmosphere was good, however. That eeriness of the house and the air of mystery over the mad inmate were captured, and the mad woman's screams and ghoulish laughter were very thrilling. The portrayal of the dreary Victorian school was very good. I was sorry Miss Temple was absent, for she was a predominant character at the beginning of the book.

I have read a very good book recently, called *Honoria Lawrence*. It is about Indian history from 1837 to the Indian Mutiny in 1857. It is written as a novel, the story of a girl who goes to India by sailing ship to marry her fiancé in the Indian army. Their lives out here are very interesting telling of the places they visited, the primitive ways they travelled, the dangers they met, and the wars they went through. It brings in history all the time, the first Afghan War, the Sikh War, other skirmishes and political disputes, and finishes with a thrilling account of the Indian Mutiny. Honoria dies in 1854, and her husband is killed in the Siege of Lucknow. He asked for the epitaph 'He tried to do his duty' to be placed on his tombstone, and I am told it is there now, and the place is well preserved and shown to visitors to Lucknow. He was Sir Henry Lawrence and is well known in Indian history.

I am writing another letter-card now. More news there.

Lots of love

Vera

No 2

My Dear Muriel

I have just finished one letter-card to you and will post it and this one together, and hope they reach you at the same time.

I was very sorry to read in Mother's letter that you cannot be released from the ECC, for the post you want so much. I think it is a rotten shame, for you are most suitable and would do it extremely well I know. How rotten that when all seemed to be going so well, you were frustrated like that. I do hope that you will be able to go later. You have served in your present job for a very long time and they should appreciate that and be more considerate.

Let me know more about it when next you write. You deserve to be doing the job you want and to be really happy.

The heat is much less now since the rains started. Everywhere the country is looking green and fresh once more. The early mornings are quite cool, whereas not very long ago, we used to get up feeling like limp rags in an oppressive heat as early as 7 a.m.

I am now counting the months to the time when I can hope to have word about my coming repatriation. About December I should know more about when I may expect to have orders. Maybe it will be sooner, one never can tell. It depends upon shipping of course. My papers of application have gone to General HQ, and that is the most important thing.

I really feel proud to think I have nearly completed five years abroad and can now be eligible for Home Service. How I am *longing* with all my heart and soul to see you all again!

I am very interested in my orderlies' lectures and the coming examination. I have nearly finished the course now, which is fifteen lectures, one per week for each class, and as there are two classes, I shall have given thirty lectures. They write them out in exercise books and seem to take an interest all the time, and ask lots of questions. I shall be sorry when the lectures finish, but will start again on another course within a short time. The exam will be interesting for I shall then see how much they have learned.

I do hope you are all well at home. I am glad Geoffrey is so near and can see you often.

Cheerio for now. More news soon.

I will send an airgraph in a day or two.

All my fondest love

Vera

∽

No 127 IBGH
India
12.8.44

My Dear Muriel

I was so pleased to receive your letter of 1st August. I sent you two letter-cards on 6th August and an airgraph on 14th August and I hear from Mother that you have received these.

I was surprised to have news of Geoffrey being posted overseas. I suppose by now he has gone and you are awaiting news from him and wondering where he is. I am very sorry, as I was so hoping he would still be in England when I came home. Now I am afraid I shall have to wait longer to see him, unless he does not go far and can get home on leave. I shall anxiously wait for more news of him as soon as you can let me know.

The news is wonderful! Every day we read in the paper of a greater advance made. Now our airborne troops have landed in Holland, and the Allied Armies are in Germany. More and more cities are being liberated. This is a great time for Europe, after four years under Nazi domination.

The news that the flying bombs no longer come over Britain has been quite the best news of all. We knew that when the Calais area and other parts were captured that menace would be overcome, but we never realised it would be so soon. Very extensive damage has been done, and many lives have been lost, so we received that news with great relief. It seems hardly possible that our people at home are now considered safe from raids again. We can imagine your feelings now, or I wonder if we can! We cannot possibly know just what you have all been through.

I do hope now that you are having peaceful nights and can sleep undisturbed. You have been through a lot, having to stand by for all emergencies, on call night after night.

I am getting more and more excited at the prospect of coming home. I feel so much nearer you all, already. I have heard that my friends in the 60th think they may easily be home for Christmas, and we all came out together! It seems too much to hope for. I am afraid to bank on that in case I am disappointed.

Every month when I tear a leaf off my calendar my heart seems to bound with excitement, as I realise another of these slow months has passed.

My orderlies' exam takes place this week and I am hoping they will prove a credit to me. Most of them are good, and have shown a lot of interest in their lectures.

The new Matron has quite settled down, and it is such a pleasure to work with her. We are very good friends and I am very happy in my job here.

I have my khaki uniform now and it looks quite smart.

Well, I must stop now, as there is no more room. I will write again soon.

I am so looking forward to seeing you.

Lots of love as ever

Vera

ও

No 127 IBGH
India
14.8.44

My Dear Mother and Father

I was so pleased to receive Father's long and newsy letter on 9th August. I am sending more airgraphs now, and hope that these will keep a continual supply of news to you, coming between letter-cards.

I was glad to hear that Geoffrey's letter containing my photo arrived safely. I will certainly send one for Father, if he had any difficulty in getting one made from Geoffrey's, so let me know, and I will send one off.

I wonder if you will have news of a move soon, and where it will be to. It will be funny coming home to a new house, in a new place, and very interesting. What a lot I shall have to see and do and talk about. I often imagine our meeting again – how *wonderful* it will be! I am just longing for the day, it will be the greatest thing in my life, seeing you all once more. What a long five years it has been!

I was very interested in your account of the visit to the man in Maldon who has the lovely collection of antiques and fossils. How I chuckled at your remark about Mother not wanting, at first, to see any old fossils, for I remembered how she has always hated museums with dry and dusty exhibits, and how we could never get her to visit one during our trip home from New Zealand. Do you remember the museum at Naples where she was so bored? I shall be glad to go and see the man who said 'Bring Vera along' if we are still at Heybridge when I come home.

Are you able to keep the eggs your pullets lay? Do you have to sell them because of the shortage of eggs? I hope you can keep some.

Our new Matron has settled in and we all like her very much.

We are expecting VADs from home some time, to help in our hospitals, and how glad we shall be to have them! There is certainly a great need for them out here.

Yesterday I wrote a great pile of airgraphs to relatives of dangerously ill patients. It is my weekly job, and I love doing it because I know what a lot it must mean to a man's wife or mother to have direct news from someone who sees their loved one every day. The hardest thing is writing to tell of the person's death, because I feel that the airgraph will be treasured ever afterwards so I put my best into it. I often have such grateful replies.

I am keeping very well. We are having rather hot and damp weather again, which will continue until October.

Lots of love to all. God bless you.

Ever your loving

Vera

My Dear Mother and Father

I have not had a letter from you lately, but the mails from home seem to have been held up somewhere so we are all expecting letters soon.

What wonderful news we are hearing now. The European invasion is going forward very rapidly, with the Allies only twenty miles from Paris, and a large part of the South of France also in our hands now as well as Normandy. I wonder what the news will be when this reaches you. I saw the first newsreel of the invasion, at the cinema yesterday. It showed the landing on French soil, and the fall of Cherbourg. I could recognise parts of it quite well.

We have heard details of the flying bombs from people who have come abroad recently. I do hope and pray you are not in great danger, and that you have some quiet nights for sleep.

There is not much news to tell you. We have torrential rain every day and strong winds. The countryside is looking very green and pleasant again after the rain, so different to the dried up hills and fields we had become accustomed to all through the summer.

I have the *Ilford Recorder* sent to me quite often by old Mr Rand. He also sent the *KGH Annual Report* which was very interesting. I give the copies of the *Recorder* to a patient here who comes from Dagenham. He was wounded in Burma. He loves to read news of Ilford and the surrounding districts.

Well, my dears, here I must say cheerio for the present. I am sending an airgraph tomorrow.

Lots of love to all.

Ever your loving

Vera

My Dear Mother and Father

Thank you so much for your latest letter – from Mother, dated 16th August. I had not had news from you recently, so was most glad to receive it. I am pleased to hear that Muriel has received my two letters together.

What a good thing you are having a sunny August. How one longs for sun in England, and here we have it pouring down upon us all the year round almost. I was so happy to hear that Mother and Muriel are going for a short holiday to Burnham-on-Crouch. It will do them such a lot of good and it will be a nice rest for them. I wish Father could go too, but can see that you could not all be away together. I hope he will manage to spend odd days with you.

I am glad Geoffrey is keeping well, and able to get home for days off. What a difference that must make!

You are having so many raid warnings, and must have very few quiet nights. It must be very trying and I do wish you could move to a quieter place, for you have had an anxious time since the beginning of the Blitz. It would be a weight off my mind if you moved. In time it seems that we shall put a stop to the flying bombs when we regain the land on which their bases are situated.

I am keeping very well and very busy. The expected VADs are going elsewhere, so we shall not have them to relieve the present staff in their extremely hard work. However, it cannot be helped.

I told you in my last letter that we now have a new Matron. I wish I could give you some idea of the difference she has made here. Life is now much easier for all. We are very good friends and very happy working together in the office. I only wish she had come months ago. She is so kind and fair, and so full of humour and sympathy.

Tomorrow will be 1st September and on Sunday we come to the fifth anniversary of the war! The year is almost over and as the months pass I feel nearer and nearer to home. My old friends in the 60th have sent in their names for repatriation so perhaps we may all come back together, just as we came out together. The other night I had a wonderful dream in which I was back with you all. We were all talking nineteen-to-the-dozen! When I awoke and saw my mosquito net above me and the fan revolving overhead, I came back to India with a bump!

Cheerio for now. More news soon. All my fondest love to all, including Peter.

Your loving
Vera

◆

No 127 IBGH
India
6.9.44

My Dear Mother and Father

Thank you so much for Father's letter received today. It took nine days to come.

We are very pleased to read in the paper today that Southern England has had a long period of freedom from flying bombs. It is wonderful news and perhaps it means that the advance of our armies on the Continent has put a stop to them.

The news is amazing, isn't it? Every day the paper tells us of a new victory, another city liberated, of more people freed from Nazi domination. What must be your feelings at home, so much nearer to it all!

How different was our position this 3rd September, to that position in which we found ourselves on 3rd September five years ago!

I had a lovely long letter from Mrs Isbister yesterday. It is the first I have had from her. She told me all about the children who have almost grown up. Jock is quite an old soldier. Joan is only nineteen but a qualified teacher and elocution mistress. Ann and

Audrey, fifteen and twelve years, are still at school. I expect you have had all that news from them yourselves. I am writing back to her soon.

I am glad Muriel is now second in command at the FAP. She must be very helpful as she has been there so long.

We are having rain almost continuously just now. At the moment it is teeming down and making a terrific noise. This is the last of the monsoon, at least next month will see the finish of it. During the rain it is pleasantly cool, but later the sun comes out and one feels hot and sticky with the humidity. We have had a humidity of 90 degrees recently. In Assam it is 97 degrees.

I am so hoping that dear old Peter will still be hale and hearty when I come home. He is very old, but from what you say about him, I don't see why he should not still be full of life for some time yet. Somebody said the other day that dogs never forget a person they know well, so I am wondering if some memory of me will awaken in his doggy mind, when he sees me again. Keep jogging his memory and we will see what happens.

I get more and more excited at the prospect of coming home. I do hope I am not getting excited too soon, then find I have to wait for months after Christmas. My old friends in the 60th BGH have hopes of being home *for Christmas*, but I think they are being too optimistic. That is a little too much to dare to hope for.

Well, my dears, more news soon.

Lots of love to all.

I am writing to Muriel and Geoff soon.

God bless you.

Ever your loving

Vera

૭

My Dear Mother and Father

Thank you so much for Father's airgraph which arrived yesterday, having taken only ten days to come.

As you will see by my address, we are now allowed to give the name of this station. As we are a static unit this has been permitted when writing to a place outside India. So now you know just where I am and can look it up on the map. I am sending you a letter-card today as well, to give you more news.

I am so sorry Mother and Muriel were not able to get away together for a holiday. I hope Muriel has had a good rest and change, however, and I hope you will both be able to have a good holiday in Clevedon.

I wonder if Geoffrey has gone abroad. I suppose that means he may be away when I come home and I was so longing to see him.

More news in my letter. Cheerio for now. God bless you.

All my fondest love

Vera

P.S. I sent a cable to Connie.

No 127 IBGH
Secunderabad
Deccan
India
16.9.44

My Dear Mother and Father

I have just written you an airgraph in answer to Father's of 5th September.

I have written the name of this station at the top of this letter as we are permitted to do so if stationed in a unit which is static.

You can write either to this address above, or to No 17 ABPD. I should do both if I were you and see which letters come more quickly.

I was very surprised to hear that Geoffrey was recalled from leave prior to going abroad. I had so hoped he would be in England when I return so that I should be able to see him. Now I shall probably have to wait much longer, unless he only goes to France and comes home on leave. I do hope he doesn't come out here just as I am hoping for orders to return to the UK. I shall be very glad to hear where he has gone. I wonder if he has embarked by now. You will miss him so, after seeing so much of him on leave.

I now have my new khaki uniform. I had it made at the one English tailor establishment in the town, and it really looks quite smart and well cut. It seems so strange to be in khaki after wearing white all the year round. I must have a snap of myself in my new uniform and send it to you.

The news is really wonderful and we are now in Germany. We certainly have got the Boche on the run. I wish we had the Japanese making tracks for home too. It will not be long, however, before we can start on them in full force too. We know, out here that as soon as the European campaign is over, we shall have a much larger army available to turn on the Japanese. How glad the men on the Assam Front will be to launch a big offensive.

I am receiving such a lot of grateful letters from relatives of ill patients in answer to those I have sent to them. It is grand to hear from them. I write on an average sixteen to twenty airgraphs a week, sometimes more, and it is one of the jobs I like doing most of all. I receive all sorts of messages from the relatives to give to the men, and the patients send messages back through me. It must be so much better for the people at home to have definite news of their sons or husbands, for the War Office reports are very brief.

What a pity Mother could not go away with Muriel, but I am sure she must have been anxious to stay at home to be with Geoffrey. I hope Muriel has had a good rest and is feeling less tired. I am glad you are both going away to Clevedon. It will do you a lot of good and I am sure you need a change.

Who is this person who is going to look me up? Have I ever met him?

More news soon, my dears. Cheerio.

My fondest love to all. I am writing to Muriel.

Your loving

Vera

സ

No 127 IBGH
Trimulgherry
Secunderabad
Deccan
India
30.9.44

My Dear Mother and Father

I was very pleased indeed to have a long letter from Muriel a few days ago and am answering it. I sent you an airgraph soon after that and hope it reached you safely. Are the airgraphs as quick as the letter-cards?

I wonder if you know yet where Geoffrey has gone. I am very anxious to hear, but do not expect you yourselves will know just yet. I can hardly believe he has left England. I somehow felt he would still be there when I returned.

You must miss him very much as he has been home to see you so much.

I really feel very glad Muriel is still at home, for if she too had gone abroad, you would now be quite alone. I am most thankful you have her company and have not lost *all* your family.

There is a great deal of talk about repatriation, but so far I have not heard any more about myself. When I do it will only be very short notice – probably four days in which to pack and arrive at a port to join a ship! It is all very quick and very secret. I shall not be able to tell you I am coming, so I think I had better say now that if you receive a cable to tell you to stop writing until you receive my new address, you will know that I am coming! From then on, don't expect letters from me for you will know the reason why I cannot write. It may of course be some months before I leave, but it is difficult to say. I am amongst the people who have been out the longest, but a good deal depends upon shipping. I am *very* excited and happy about it. It is a *wonderful* thing to look forward to. I hope I have enough winter woollies with me because I am sure I shall freeze in England after all this heat. I have some warm things put away since my Palestine days.

I have been thinking often, lately, that I could be very happy as a regular Sister in the army, and I have considered joining up permanently. What do you think about it? I should like your advice. I am really very fond of army life and have learned a great deal, gained grand experience and made many good friends. Above all I have loved nursing the 'Tommies'. I wonder if I could be as happy in a civil hospital. After the war, at the earliest opportunity, thousands of Army Reserve Sisters will be demobilised and looking for civil nursing jobs. The Army Nursing Service will be in great need of regular Sisters. It will not be easy to find good positions in civil hospitals, for while we are away overseas, other nurses are being trained and they in their turn will seek trained nurses' positions. The new Rushcliffe rates of pay will draw many more girls to nursing from now onwards and the hospitals should never again suffer that acute shortage of staff as during my training.

There will also be the other nursing services to be demobilised, the Naval, the RAF and the CNR, so the rush for work will be tremendous.

My new Matron is very anxious to recommend me for the regular army, but I am not being persuaded only by her. I have given it a good deal of thought, and have not yet decided.

If you agree that it would be a good thing for me, I could apply almost immediately and would be appointed soon if I am accepted. Do let me know as soon as possible what you think about it.

I will write again soon. I am sending you Christmas parcels in a day or two.

Longing to see you soon.

Lots of love to you both and Muriel.

Ever your loving

Vera

❧

No 127 IBGH
India
2.10.44

My Dear Mother and Father

I sent you an airmail letter-card a few days ago.

I am keeping very well, and hope you are too. Have you any news from Geoffrey yet?

There is no more news about repatriation for me yet, but I am getting ready for that great day and becoming more and more excited.

In three days' time I shall have completed five years' service, 5th October 1939 was the date of my joining. How well I remember telephoning you from Plaistow to tell you about it. It seems centuries ago.

I do hope you are not having any more flying bombs now. The news that the long range guns of Calais have been captured is very good indeed.

We are having the last of the hot weather now, and it is very hot, and sticky. The nights are very oppressive too.

More news soon dears. Lots of love to all.

Ever your loving
Vera

❧

No 127 IBGH
India
7.10.44

My Dear Mother and Father

I was very pleased to receive Father's welcome airgraph dated 25th September. It arrived in nine days. One of our Sisters has just received a letter-card in six days! What a grand record that is.

I am so pleased to hear you have gone to Clevedon for a fortnight. It is what you need, and I hope you will both have a good rest and return feeling very much better, with new energy. I well remember the time you went there in 1938, and returned at the time of the Munich crisis.

I am thinking of you a lot and wondering what you are doing and if you are having good weather.

Muriel will miss you. I wish I was at home to keep her company. By the time you receive this you will be home again.

I have bought a supply of sheets, pillowcases, and towels for Mother, and have packed them to bring home with me. They are very nice ones, and I am very glad I was able to get such good quality. Will you please let me know what other things you would like me to get? There are certain articles which are unobtainable in England, I know, so write back and tell me what would be most acceptable. We can no longer send dress material by post, but I am getting some to pack away for Mother and Muriel. What else do you need for the house, and what does Father need?

I have a lot of haberdashery needles, cotton, tape, elastic, pins, hooks and eyes, press studs, and am sending those to you soon. I have also sent off a parcel containing tea, butter, raisins, currants, sultanas, almonds and cornflour. I hope it will arrive safely and in good condition.

I am glad you had such good harvest festival services. I tried to imagine the church decorated.

We had a wonderful service at the Parish Church here on 17th September – Battle of Britain Commemoration Day. I went to the evening service which was packed, mainly with RAF personnel and a good number of troops. It was most impressive. The sermon was based on the 6th Chapter of St Paul's Epistle to the Ephesians, verses 10–18. It was fine – and one never to be forgotten.

Well, my dears, there is no more news just now, so I will say cheerio. Much love to you both and Muriel. My love to Geoff when next you write.

God bless you and keep you safe.

Ever your loving

Vera

My Dear Muriel

Thank you very much for your interesting letter of 12th September. I am glad you received my two letters safely. I wrote to you again on 19th September.

I was pleased to hear you had a few days at Burnham, and hope you enjoyed a good rest. I wish you could have had a longer time. Now I expect you are alone at home as Father and Mother will be away at Clevedon. It must be lonely for you and I wish I could be there to keep you company.

I see by Father's last airgraph that he does not think Geoffrey has embarked yet. I wonder if he has gone now.

I have just sent you a parcel containing two books for Christmas. I hope you have not already got them. I don't think so, as you have never mentioned them to me. I am keeping the snake-skin handbag for you until I come home as I would rather not risk posting it. I also have one for Mother.

Is there anything you especially want that I can pack away for you? I am getting some dress material but cannot send it on as we are not allowed to send material not made up, now. I am sure you would like material for undies so I will get that also. Do let me know what you need. Stockings are unobtainable otherwise I would get some for you. I have some sheets and towels for Mother.

Yes, I am glad also that you have not gone abroad, for Mother and Father would feel very lonely without you. I am sorry for your sake as I know you would have loved the opportunity of new scenes and new work. I wonder if you are now quite free of flying bombs or if some still come over from the Dutch coast. We hear that Heinkals have been over and dropped flying bombs on Southern England.

It is very hot here these last few weeks. This month is always an oppressive one just before the cooler weather begins.

We have had our orderlies' exam and the results were very good and much better than last time. Twelve out of seventeen passed the senior, and three of the four juniors passed. A number of them were very clever and wrote excellent papers.

There does not seem to be any more news now, but I will write again soon.

Cheerio. Lots of love and God bless you.

Your loving

Vera

⁓

No 127 IBGH

India

11.10.44

My Dear Mother and Father

Thank you so much for Mother's letter of 26th September.

I was so glad to hear you are safely in Clevedon having such a complete rest and change, away from air raids and sirens. It was a relief to hear you were benefiting by the change of air and scenery and feeling better. You both needed it so much. How I wish you could have much longer there. By now you will probably have returned home. I do hope and pray that the danger of flying bombs has passed and that from now on you will have more peace. What a terrible time you have been through, these five years of war. You should really have months away at the seaside with nothing to do and nothing to worry about. It would be such a good thing if you could have a move soon to a quieter and safer parish.

I can well understand your sadness at Geoffrey's departure. I wonder where he is now. I am writing to him at the address you have given.

I am keeping very well, and longing to see you again. More news soon. Much love to Muriel and both of you. God bless you.

Your loving

Vera

My Dear Mother and Father

Thank you very much for Mother's letter dated 26th September. I received it on 11th October and answered it the same day. I had also sent an airgraph a few days ago before that.

Today I received your cable telling me that you agree with my idea about joining the regular army. How sweet of you it was to send an answer so soon by cable. I am looking forward to hearing more about your opinion of it all, in a letter. I have not taken any steps as yet, and have still not made up my mind definitely. The army calls me to its ranks very strongly, but I am not sure whether to make my application here, or whether to wait until I come home and decide then. Once I join, I have joined if you see what I mean, and it may be better to decide finally in England.

I have always planned to take my midwifery training, without which no nurse is really fully trained, and I should really do it after the war. Of course I am sure I could still do it by being released from military service for a time for that purpose. Another thing is that Iris Ridler and I always promised each other that we would work together after the war and I shall have to disappoint her. I wish I could decide, but I feel sure that it will all work out for the best, as the future always seems to do for me. Often when one is undecided, the issue is suddenly made clear. I am going to wait for a time, and know that all will turn out for the best.

I have a very strong feeling that my time out here is nearly finished and I may soon be on my way home. *How wonderful.* Recently I have been dreaming of England and home, night after night. I feel so much nearer to you all! Somehow the distance has become much less since I knew that I had such a good chance of repatriation. Another request was sent here a few days ago, for names of nursing Sisters who were due to go back to the UK. I am the only one here – there are two others who will be due in 1945 and 1946. The rest all came out last year.

Our new Matron is such a fine woman, and I am very fond of her. I could not have a happier job than this. We are such good friends. She has made a vast difference to the whole place.

I am longing to know where Geoffrey has gone. If he *does* come to India, I shall be able to get ten days' leave to go to Bombay to see him when he arrives. That would be grand! I shall not be able to get there quickly enough if I hear he has landed.

I have written to him so hope the letter reaches him soon.

I hope you are both feeling much better and completely rested after your holiday. I have been feeling very anxious about Mother, and do hope to hear soon that she is less tired and the change has made a big difference to her.

More news soon dears. God bless you. Love to Muriel and both of you.

Ever your loving
Vera

 confidences

No 127 IBGH
India
25.10.44

My Dear Mother and Father

Thank you so much for Mother's letter dated 7th October and Father's airgraph dated 12th October. I have also had a letter from Muriel dated 8th October and I am answering it.

I am so glad you have had a very good holiday and feel much better now. You needed it so much and I am most thankful you were able to go. Now you are back at home and still having a great deal of danger all round you. The report that flying bombs were no longer going to fall on Britain was indeed premature. I had a long letter from Mr Rand, in Ilford, who also told me that such an announcement has caused thousands of evacuees to return to danger areas. Duncan Sandys slipped up badly that time. Why do we make so many optimistic statements, and then regret them afterwards? We were all so glad about that report, so we feel very sorry indeed to think that the danger is not over at all. Let us hope and pray that those raids really will finish soon. You have all been through so much.

I wonder where Geoffrey is now. How interesting that he is seeing places he has visited before. That either means that he is going to Italy or the Middle East, or that he is coming to India. I have written and told him to send me a telegram if he lands in Bombay and I will get a few days off to go down and see him, (I should say 'up' not 'down'. How wonderful that would be!) All the same I don't want him to come right out here just when I hope to come back to you. I am longing to see him again, just as I am longing to see you all. There is a Sister here whose brother – a squadron-leader has left England at about the same time so we have both decided that our brothers are together and we exchange news about them. How nice it will be if they are, and then if they come to this country she will soon be seeing him.

I thanked you in my last letter for the cable you so thoughtfully sent. I was amused to read in Father's airgraph that 'in my mid-forties' I shall be able to retire on a pension if I join the regular army. Such a prospect fills me with gloom! Who wants to retire at such an early age? Who wants to look forward to retiring on a pension? How I chuckled at that! I am still thinking a lot about joining as a Regular, and will let you know when I have decided.

Looking forward to seeing you soon!

Lots of love to you both and Muriel. God bless you.

Your loving

Vera

❧

No 127 IBGH
India
29.10.44

My Dear Mother and Father

I was very pleased to receive Muriel's letter a few days ago, dated 8th October. I mentioned it in my last letter to you which I sent on 25th October.

I am feeling very excited today because I have heard officially that I am to be repatriated in the near future and have filled in, and sent off my application for a sea passage to the UK. I have not yet been given any definite date, except that the 17th December, I am told is the date on which I am due for repatriation. That means that I may leave earlier than that date! Just think of it! I can hope to be *on the way* at Christmas time! I sailed from Southampton on 18th December 1939, Mother's birthday.

The next news I may expect is a notification telling me to be ready to leave in two or three weeks, and when I get that I am sure I shall stop sleeping at night altogether! As it is now I sleep lightly and dream over and over again that I am at home. What a wonderful thing to look forward to! I cannot describe my excitement and joy at every thought of it.

There are quite a number of officers here who are all hoping for the same thing and every time we meet we compare notes. One of them teases me unmercifully and says he has already received his embarkation number and he is off in a short time. Why haven't I received mine yet he says, it doesn't seem as if I am going. Then someone else tells me not to believe a word he says, for he is not any further ahead than I am. So we go on pulling each other's legs and we have a lot of fun out of it. There is another officer who is a patient here, and every time he sees me he mysteriously murmurs 'Remember REPAT' as I pass his bed when I am doing my round of the ward. He hopes to go home as well and insists that we shall be on the same ship. Matron is very sorry about it all and seems so sad to think that I am going that I try not to discuss it too much with her, because she doesn't want to lose me. It is very sweet of her, and I shall be most sorry to leave here too, for she has been wonderful to work with and I admire her tremendously.

All the Sisters are very envious of me for they have, most of them, only been out a short time, so cannot hope to go back for a long while.

I am glad you are not sending me anything for Christmas. It is very wise of you. I have sent you a food parcel and two books for Muriel, but I am not sending anything else, but bringing things back to you instead.

I am so sorry you are still having such nasty nights with raids. If only you could have some peace from them. They seem to go on and on, in spite of the very over-optimistic promises that the menace was over.

How sudden was the death of the Archbishop of Canterbury. He is a great loss to the Church. I wonder who the new Primate will be.

Well, I am longing to know where Geoffrey is. I hope he received my letter safely.

More news later. All my fondest love to you both and Muriel. God bless you.

Your loving

Vera

෨

No 127 IBGH
India
1.11.44

My Dear Muriel

I was so pleased to have your letter dated 8th October. Today I have had one from Mother which has only taken five days to come! It is amazing. How lovely to have such recent news of you. It is quicker for us to get a letter home than to get one to someone in India. Inland letters take ten days or more from here to Assam, where one of my best friends is nursing.

I am glad you were not too lonely while Mother and Father were away. You must have had some awful nights and in Mother's letter today she says you are still being visited continuously by flying bombs, and also by 'other terrible things'. I do wonder what they are! We have not heard about them, but can guess, we think.

I was sorry to hear about the poor woman who died of shock in St Peter's Hospital, after the raid. Your description of the flying bomb is very vivid – how nerve-wracking it must be for you during those seconds after the engine stops and before the plane falls to the ground.

Mother says in her letter that you think Geoffrey is coming to India. I am expecting a telegram from him any time now, to tell me he has landed, and do hope there will be time for him to see me in Bombay before he is moved to his station wherever it may be. I shall certainly be able to get some days off to go to Bombay and will hurry there as soon as I hear from him. How wonderful it would be to see him! How we shall talk! It will be grand for him to land here and have his sister to meet again after five long years.

I am growing more and more excited about my hoped-for repatriation soon. In my last letter to Mother and Father I said that my return to the UK had been approved and that I had sent in my application for a sea passage. Now all I have to do is wait for orders to be ready to proceed within a certain time. I cannot possibly say when I am likely to leave, one can never tell, and anyway I would not be allowed to give any date. I really must not let myself hope for it too soon, but there is every chance that I may leave soon.

What do you think about my idea of joining the regular army? Do let me know when next you write. I was so glad to hear in Mother's letter today that you all advise me to apply. I have almost decided to let Matron put my name forward as she wants to do, for I may regret it later if she doesn't. Her recommendation would be excellent I feel sure. Should I change my mind when I come home, it would still be possible to withdraw, but I don't think I will change it. At present I am still thinking about it, but I want to do what is best. I could not be happier in any other job outside the army.

More news soon. God bless you.

Lots of love to Mother and Father and to you.

Vera

No 1

My Dear Mother and Father

I am sorry I have not written to you for more than a week, but when you hear what news I have for you and you know why I have been too much occupied to write, you will forgive me I know.

I have met Geoffrey and spent three complete days with him in Bombay! He arrived there on 25th October and wrote to me on the 26th telling me he only had about two weeks there and so did hope I could go there to see him as soon as possible. The letter took seven days to reach me. I guessed that he had no knowledge of the incredible slowness of Indian post offices, otherwise he would have sent me a telegram. The letter reached me on Thursday, 2nd November, and I immediately asked for a few days' compassionate leave and was granted it by the station commander in record time. I left here on the Saturday at 9.30 a.m. I had already sent Geoff an express telegram to his APO number, saying that I would arrive in Bombay on Sunday morning at seven o'clock, if he could meet me. I never thought it would reach him in time, so I contacted all the RAF officers I knew for advice about how to find him if he was not at the station. They all gave me the name of a transit camp so I knew I would trace him quite easily.

I set off, very excited and wondering all the time if he would meet my train. When I reached Bombay at the end of twenty-four hours journey I kept on telling myself that he could not possibly have received the wire so it was no use expecting him to be there. Imagine my joy when, as I was approaching the barrier to hand in my ticket I saw him hurrying towards me.

How wonderful it was to see him again after all these years. He really has not changed at all, and he says I am just the same. He thinks it is amazing that I look so young and well after five years in the tropics.

How we talked! From that moment until I returned we talked

continuously. How good it was to hear the real news of you all and to know that you were all well. It made me long more than ever to see you once more.

We had a grand three days. First of all when I arrived we had breakfast at the station, and then went to the Women's Services Club where I was to stay. When that was all fixed up, it was still only ten o'clock, so we took a taxi and I showed Geoffrey the sights of Bombay, all the famous buildings, the Marine Drive, the shopping centre, the Taj Mahal Hotel, the Gateway of India, and then the view of Bombay from Malabar Hill, which is just outside the city, and a big residential part. This view is simply wonderful, one can see the city, with all the domes and spires of the buildings lying far below, and the bay and port, blue and sparkling in the sunshine. He loved Malabar Hill, and the ride there. I took him to the Club for lunch and afterwards we walked along the Marine Drive and talked for hours. It seemed such a lovely long day. I saw him off on the local electric train to his camp, at 10 p.m.

Next day I went out to the camp to meet him at 11 a.m. as he was not free until then. His quarters looked very good, quite new and comfortable. The RAF personnel are well provided for in India. He was allowed a pass for the whole day all the time I was in Bombay. We spent another grand day on the Monday. After doing some shopping we had lunch at a hotel with a QA friend of mine and her friend who is an important person in connection with the docks. She had come down from Assam to see him for a few days. He is a very kind and generous person, always pleased to do all he can for the Sisters. He gave us a lovely time, we had lunch with them then went to the pictures in the afternoon. Afterwards we had tea, and then we said we must go, but he insisted that we had dinner with him in his flat. We did and had a very pleasant evening. Geoff liked him awfully and has written to him since.

The next day was my last, but we filled each hour with activity. We went and had our photo taken together and the prints are being sent on to me. If they are successful I will send you one as soon as they come. It will be lovely for you to see us together. We sent the telegram to you, telling you we had met. I hope it reached you. We had lunch at a restaurant overlooking the

Gateway of India and the harbour. All the time we talked. During those three days Geoffrey saw the whole of Bombay, for as I know it so well I was able to take him about. He came with me to the station in the evening and I took the 9.30 p.m. train back to Secunderabad. I will finish this in a second letter now.

Lots of love
Vera

❧

No 127 IBGH
India
13.11.44

No 2

My Dear Mother and Father

I have just finished one letter to you, and here is another as I did not get all my news into the first one. I do hope these two arrive together.

I have told you all about my visit to Bombay and what Geoffrey and I did each day while I was there. It was a wonderful time and I am so thankful I was still in India when he arrived to greet him and give him a good welcome. It is something I shall always remember and I am sure he will too. He was so wildly excited to see me again, just as I was to see him, and he was so happy all the time. We were very fortunate in being able to be together so much during my short stay. His officers were very considerate, allowing him to be excused all duties during my time in Bombay.

He looks very well and very brown after his sea trip. He had a good journey out, and travelled on a Sister ship to the one which brought us back from New Zealand.

He is with a good crowd of men and has some good friends. He introduced me to two of his pals when I went to call for him at his camp one day. They were both nice boys. While I was staying down there a number of his crowd were posted and he was expecting to go any day. He had no idea where to. I expect by now he has moved on and I shall probably receive his new address soon. Don't worry about him he will most likely go to a good training station and be quite happy. The RAF looks after its men well in this country. I gave him lots of advice, about taking anti-malaria precautions, being careful about drinking water, protecting his head from the sun, not eating fruit until it has been placed in an antiseptic lotion first etc. I taught him a few words of Hindustani but I don't really know much.

Altogether it was a wonderful few days and I would not have missed it for anything. It was a grand reunion. I was so afraid we would miss each other and that he would be posted before I reached Bombay, so I was very fortunate not only in meeting him but in having such a good few days with him.

I am sure you will be very delighted when you have these two letters and know about our meeting. You can well imagine my pleasure when I saw him waiting at the station for me after not having seen him for five long years.

There is no more news as yet of my repatriation but I do not think it will be long before my orders come. I am confident that I shall soon be on my way.

Matron is going away for ten days' leave next week, and I shall be in charge, so I expect to be kept busy.

I have bought Father a new pair of black shoes in Bombay. Geoffrey tried them on as he said Father and he took the same size and as they fitted him well, they should be all right for Father.

More news soon, dears. Lots of love to you both and Muriel. I had a letter from Muriel a few days ago.

Your loving
Vera

ॐ

Vera and her brother Geoffrey meet in Bombay

৯০

No 127 IBGH
India
20.11.44

My Dear Mother and Father

You will soon receive the two letters I sent you on 13th November telling you about my meeting with Geoffrey in Bombay. I have not heard from him yet to tell me where he is. He may not be able to say much, but I shall be able to get some idea of where his station is from his APO number. It was wonderful seeing him again and I shall always remember most vividly our happy three days together.

Matron has gone away on leave for ten days so I am in charge. It is very good experience and I am enjoying it very much.

I was so pleased to receive your Christmas cards and the birthday card from Muriel today. They are such pretty cards and I am delighted with them and with the lovely verses on them. I wish I could get such nice ones out here, but they are all very poor, mostly cards with silly Oriental pictures on them for the troops to send. I have sent you a Christmas airgraph and hope it photographs well.

I now have quite a nice collection of things for you and for the house. We shall have a lot of fun looking at them when I come home.

There is no more news of my return, but I do not think I have much longer here.

I wonder if you are still having a lot of trouble with flying bombs and rocket bombs. In your last letters you tell me you have very few peaceful nights. There is a lot in the paper today about the rocket bomb. It must be very terrifying to have the explosion before any kind of warning can be given.

I have a very large mail from relatives of seriously ill patients to whom I have written. It is so good to have such appreciative letters. They write to me like old friends inviting me to go and see them when I go home. The patients are always so grateful to me for writing. When I go round the wards one of them often says to me, 'Have you heard from my mother lately? She has written to me and asks me to give you her love.' I often have messages like that. One poor woman whose son died here, still writes. Matron and I went to the cemetery recently and took a photo of his grave. We hope it will turn out well, as we want it to send to her.

Well, no more news now dears, so I will say cheerio. I am writing to Muriel. Your Christmas presents and Mother's birthday present will be given to you when we meet. I would much rather do that, and not risk sending them.

Lots of love to you both and Muriel.

Your loving

Vera

P.S. The photos of Geoff and me have just arrived. I have three copies and will send one straight away. They are grand.

∾

23.11.44

My Dear Mother and Father

This is my Christmas letter-card to you. It is rather a pretty one isn't it with the Taj Mahal in the centre. I wonder when this will reach you, probably before it arrives I shall be on my way home. I have not forgotten about sending the cable to you when I leave here.

May you have a very happy and peaceful Christmas. How I hope I shall be there with you, or if not that I shall be with you in the New Year.

Lots of love
Vera

❧

No 127 IBGH
India
23.11.44

My Dear Muriel

This is my Christmas letter-card to you but I must say I am sorry about the luscious looking bananas, grapes, and pineapples, forbidden fruits to you, to make your mouth water! We all think it most unfair to have to send such letter-cards to England.

I was pleased to receive your last letter of 28th October and I wrote to you on 1st November. I am writing a longer letter than this of course, in a day or so, when I have sent off all my Christmas lettercards and airgraphs.

I have some lovely things to bring home to you, and am *longing* to give them to you. Among them are six pairs of stockings, and six for Mother. I have bought a new trunk to carry my extra luggage.

You will have heard all about my meeting with Geoffrey, and the lovely time we had in Bombay. I do not know yet where he has gone.

The photo of Geoff and me has turned out excellently and I have sent a copy home by airmail.

Lots of love and a Happy Christmas.

Vera

ॐ

My Dear Mother and Father

I was very pleased to have your letters – one from Mother and an airgraph letter from Father on 22nd November, sent on the 15th and 13th November. They are coming very quickly. We often receive letter-cards in four or five days, much quicker than the inland post here! I have noted your advice about bringing plenty of warm clothes home. I have quite a lot of woollen vests and a warm bedjacket but apart from those my clothes are all for a tropical climate. However, I shall be quite all right as I have two grey uniform costumes which are of thick material as well as a heavy grey overcoat, and scarf and gloves, and as I shall be in uniform most of the time, I shall be quite warm enough. I still have plenty of grey and black stockings left, as we wore them in the Middle East. I have had to have my costumes made much smaller as I am much slimmer than I was when I last wore them. It was a good thing I tried them on the other day. I laughed so much when I saw how funny I looked with the coat *hanging* on me and the skirt miles too big. There is a good English tailor in the town and he will alter them very well.

I have bought some Indian stamps for Father. They are only used by the State of Hyderabad which is ruled by India's premier Prince, the Nizam. They are very colourful and unusual looking. I don't know much about stamps but I think Father will like them for his collection.

I also sent some to Mrs Isbister to give to Audrey, as she asked me to send some if possible. I wrote her a long letter in answer to the one she sent me, and also enclosed a photo of myself.

You will love the photo of Geoffrey and me I am sure. It has turned out so well and is so clear. I sent it to you by airmail and hope you receive it for Christmas. Everyone here likes it very much. It will be lovely for you to see a photo of us together. I am sending a copy to Geoffrey, but am waiting first until I receive his new address which I should know at any time now. Letters take quite ten days from one end of this country to the other. I am writing regularly to Geoffrey. As soon as I know where he is I will send you word. You will probably have received my letters telling you of the grand time we had together. It was wonderful to see him again. I have not much longer here I am sure!

Matron returns from leave soon. I have enjoyed being 'chief cook and bottle washer'. It is good experience.

More news in a day or so. Lots of love to you both and Muriel.
Your loving
Vera

৯৹

No 127 IBGH
India
27.11.44

My Dear Muriel

Thank you very much for your letter of 28th October. I wrote to you last on 1st November and since then have sent you a Christmas card and Christmas letter-card. I wonder if you have received the two books I sent you yet.

I am longing to give you the things I have for you when I come home. I will not tell you what they are. They will be a surprise for you!

I am so very excited about my repatriation. All the Sisters are very envious, but they agree that I deserve to go after five years abroad, and they say they do not know how they will exist abroad for so long. I tell them I have managed it, and look very well too, and they have to agree to that as well. I am still in the dark about when I may expect to go. One is not given much warning, so I must expect very short notice.

Matron is away on leave at present but I expect her back in two days' time. I have enjoyed being in charge. It has been much easier than I expected, and is excellent experience.

Since I last wrote to you, I have done a lot of thinking about joining the regular army, and I was glad to have your opinion and advice in your letter. The urge is very strong, and I think when Matron comes back I shall ask her to recommend me. She will be awfully pleased as she has told me so many times that she would like to put my name forward as she considers me most suitable. Should I change my mind when I come home I could still withdraw my application as it will be wartime and there will still be a chance to be demobilised should I so wish. After all, joining as a Regular is not *so* binding, even if I were not desirous of remaining in the Service after I had joined I am sure I could be released. All the same, I don't think I shall change my mind. I have always found in the past that I have not made a mistake about a decision of that kind. For example, I left Plaistow to join the army, when I was about to take my midwifery training, and I felt I had to go. What could I have done better? I have never regretted it.

If I do not ask Matron to recommend me I may easily regret it when I am back in England, so I think I should not let the opportunity pass.

I am sure you will like the photo of Geoffrey and I had taken. It is on the way home now, by airmail. I suppose you are still having a lot of trouble with flying bombs and rocket bombs. You must all be so weary of them.

More news soon. Lots of love to you and Mother and Father.

Your loving

Vera

❧

My Dear Mother and Father

Thank you very much for Mother's letter of 26th November. I was also delighted to have Muriel's two letters – Nos 1 and 2 which came together today.

I am so glad to hear that you have received the photo safely, and I am very pleased to know you like it so much. It is a very happy one isn't it, with both of us smiling and looking in the best of health. I do not think it could be better and I am so thankful we thought of having it taken. I have sent a copy to Geoffrey, but do not know if he has received it yet. The mails in India get worse, it takes about eight days to get a letter to him whereas you receive mine in about six and yours have come to me in five. I had a very nice letter from Geoffrey today and in it he said, 'I have come to the conclusion that it would be quicker for me to write to you via England!' One of my letters had taken fourteen days to reach him! I am writing often, however, so hope he will get regular letters in future.

Geoffrey seems quite happy and settled in his new station. He has plenty of good friends and seems to be in quite good quarters. I am trying to find out from RAF personnel, where he could be as they may know by his address. I am so sorry he did not come out sooner as we could have spent more time together when I had leave. Now I shall feel sad at leaving him here when I come home. However, I am so thankful we had that wonderful three days together – it might have happened that I had left the country before he arrived.

Did Geoff tell you in one of his letters that I bought a frying pan and a saucepan in Bombay for Mother, as he told me how difficult they are to get at home. In his letter he told me to let him know when I get home if there is anything I want, maybe a couple of frying pans or saucepans, and he will send them. I do love his letters they are so full of fun. I am writing to him about the question of his allotment and will certainly advise him to have a certain amount sent home each month, as it is the best way to save, and this country is so expensive. It is true about the swindling bazaars, and I warned him about being careful in buying. I will see what I can do, when I write. He has saved so well, that it would be a great shame to stop now.

Geoffrey also tells me that Mother would like some curtain material, but he does not say how much, or what colour etc. Please let me know all the details as soon as possible so that I can get what you need. There is quite a good selection here.

I have not had any more news yet about repatriation but I know I shall hear something soon. I am so very excited and just *longing* to see you! I wonder if you will have moved when I come back. I am looking forward to hearing more about your move. I should like to live in Hampshire myself, but all three counties Muriel mentioned, are very nice, I believe. How strange it will be coming back to a new house. I shall like it, as I really don't know the Heybridge people very well, but I think I should have liked to see the house once more. I am sure you will be glad of this move as you have been in Heybridge quite long enough. A change of scenery, and people, and a new church will be so refreshing – almost as good as a holiday.

I sent you a cable a few days ago wishing Mother a happy birthday, and a happy Christmas to all. I hope you did not think it was the cable to let you know I am leaving here. I thought when I sent it that you would become excited when it arrived and then disappointed when you had read it. I was unable to get a birthday card for Mother. There does not seem to be one anywhere in the town. I am so sorry. I shall bring her present home to her.

Well, my dears I shall not be with you for Christmas as I hoped, but I shall have you all much in my thoughts, and shall have the joy of knowing that I can hope to see you soon.

A very happy and peaceful Christmas and God bless you.

Lots of love to Muriel and both of you.

Your loving

Vera

❧

My Dear Mother and Father

I have received Muriel's two very interesting letters which I am answering today.

So tomorrow is my twenty-eighth birthday! To think that I was just twenty-three when I last saw you. You will be very much in my thoughts tomorrow, even more than you are every day. How wonderful to think that I shall soon be with you again and we shall be able to talk about all that has happened during these five years. I remember writing to you a few months ago and saying that I hoped to be home for 16th December, but that was not to be and here I am still waiting for my orders. I am confident that they will come soon and I shall find myself at home in an English winter or at least towards the end if it.

How often I imagine my return and where I shall meet you. I do not know where I shall land, or if I shall be held up in transit somewhere miles from home, perhaps in Scotland, but it will not be for long, and then I shall have the thrill of a railway journey taking me to meet you. I may not be able to communicate with you until I land, and then how exciting it will be for you to hear that I am actually in the country. The best thing I think will be for me to telegraph you to ask where we should meet, as if you have not already moved by then, you may have done so when I reach England. However, I shall know more about your expected move by the time I leave here I am sure.

I shall be thinking of Mother a great deal on her birthday. How quickly these birthdays seem to come round, and yet how slowly the years of separation drag away!

I sent a parcel of tea, (best Indian), jellies, butter, and raisins and sultanas a few days ago. I hope you receive it safely. Has the other food parcel I sent, reached you yet? I have received such a lovely calendar and Christmas card from Muriel. They are really both so pretty and colourful. I shall be thanking her for them in my letter.

Thank you all so much for the very attractive Christmas and birthday cards you sent. They have all arrived safely and stand on the bookshelf in my room. I love to look at them and read the words on them. They make me feel homesick!

Well, my dears may you have a very happy Christmas and New Year. I shall be thinking of you all. Lots of love as ever.

Your loving

Vera

ço

No 127 IBGH

India

29.12.44

My Dear Mother and Father

Thank you so much for your Christmas airgraph. I was very pleased to have it on 22nd December, and to know that you are all well.

I shall soon be sending you the long promised cable! You will quite understand when it comes. I shall just say 'Stop writing. Am moving to new address.' How thrilled you will be when it comes. There will then be silence for a while from this end, until you receive another message from me by telegram.

There is no more I can say. One has to be so very careful. If you are moving when the telegram or rather, cable reaches you, it will be awkward, as I shall not know where to communicate with you. Could you arrange for one of you to stay in Heybridge should this cable arrive before you go. You will see what I mean by that I am sure. There is so much *I must not* say! When I talk about the cable, I mean the one telling you I am moving to a 'new unit'.

I am in a whirl at present, and don't know whether I am on my head or my heels!

I have sent several express letters to Geoffrey and an express telegram. He is longing to meet me again and I hope I shall be able to arrange it by my letters. I have given him instructions about where to meet me if he can get leave. If all goes well, and my calculations are accurate, we should be able to make it.

Geoffrey is, by the way, in Karachi, but you must not mention it in your letters to him or put it on the envelope. You will be glad to hear he is there for it is a healthy and comparatively cool station and it is far from the fighting zones. He seems quite happy and settled and has plenty of friends. He was expecting to have a very good Christmas according to his last letter.

We had a very good time here. The wards were beautifully decorated and the patients were well provided for. I wish their relatives at home could have seen how well they fared. It would have made them so happy, and would have helped to dispel the rumours that the troops out here need better amenities! They lacked nothing.

You will be interested and glad to hear that I have really made up my mind about joining the Regulars, and my application has gone to HQ. The Principal Matron for this Command has written to say she is pleased I am going to join. I now have to wait for the application forms to be sent to me from Delhi.

I will write again soon dears. Fondest love to you both and Muriel.

Your loving
Vera

❧

No 127 IBGH
India
7.1.45

My Dear Muriel

I am so sorry I have taken a long time to answer your two letters dated 29th November. I was so pleased to have them, and they were so full of news. I hope you will forgive me for keeping you waiting for an answer.

Christmas has come and gone – my sixth one overseas. We had a very good time. The wards were beautifully decorated with streamers, lampshades, and even Christmas trees which were not real fir trees but which took the place of the proper thing very well. The patients had a very good time – plenty of good food and entertainment, such as conjurors and ENSA parties. We sang carols round the wards, there were fifteen wards to visit, and when we had finished we could hardly speak, having sung so heartily for so long.

I was given two nice books by the Sisters. Matron gave me a pretty tablecloth, and I also had another book from one of the Sisters. I received a writing case and a box of handkerchiefs from the mothers of two of our dangerously ill patients. Wasn't that sweet of them.

Matron was delighted with the gift given her by the staff – a black and silver evening bag. I gave her a green leather writing case which she was also very pleased to have. On 23rd December, I had news of my repatriation. It was an order to stand by and be ready to move at short notice. I have not heard any more since then, but must be prepared to go at any time. It is all very exciting and thrilling and I have my luggage almost ready. I have written a letter to Mother and Father since then, telling them to expect a cable soon asking them not to write until they hear from me again. You will know by that that I am on my way! One of the Sisters here is going to write to you after I have gone, which will be a great help in warning you. I don't know what happens at the other end, whether we are allowed to go straight to our homes, or whether we are held up in a transit camp for a time. How awful it would be to have arrived in the country and not be able to get home by the quickest possible train! I will send you a telegram as soon as I arrive anyway.

I do so hope I shall be able to see Geoffrey before going. I have written to give him some warning and hope he will be able to go to Bombay.

As I told Mother and Father in my last letter, I have sent in my application to join the Regulars, and am waiting for the application forms to be sent. If they do not arrive before I go, I will apply again at home. I have definitely decided that it is what I must do, and feel glad I have made up my mind.

I do hope you had a happy Christmas. Lots of love, and God bless you. May we meet soon. Much love to Mother and Father.

Vera

My Dear Mother and Father

I do not know how long this will take to reach you but I hope it will not be long and will be the means of giving you more news of me.

There is not much I can say but I wanted to let you know that I am very well and longing to see you again quite soon now! I am so excited and thrilled about it. I sent you a cable a few days ago from a certain place _____ and I do hope it has reached you safely. It was to tell you how far I was, on my way! I am not allowed to repeat the message here. It was in EFM code. I will send you a telegram when I arrive *there*.

I hope Mrs Greenland's letter arrived safely. She wrote the day I left for Poona, to tell you I had started on my way. I also sent a cable telling you not to write as I had moved.

You may have heard from Geoffrey by now, since we met. I am looking forward to telling you all about it. We had a lovely few days together in Poona and stayed in the same camp. He was so delighted to meet me again, and you can imagine I was too.

My orders came so suddenly that I had to send a series of telegrams to him, first asking him to meet me in Bombay, next, (when I thought I was not going so soon), asking him to come down to Secunderabad, then (when I was sent away suddenly) asking him to meet me in Bombay, again.

When I got to Poona, I arranged to pay a quick visit of a few hours to Bombay to meet him, but just before I left, a telegram came from my unit, to say that Geoff had been there and found I had gone, and was now on the way to Poona. Of course I waited for him instead of going to Bombay and we met. He had not received the telegram asking him not to go to Secunderabad but to wait in Bombay. How we talked! He had travelled a total of 2,400 miles across the country and back, to see me! I must tell you more about it when we meet.

Don't worry about me. I am in good health and in good

hands! We are well protected in every way. The cold weather is terrific already. We know we must expect it much colder before long.

I do hope you are all taking great care of yourselves in this bitter weather at home. I know how quickly you can catch bad colds, you told me in a recent letter that you have all had colds, so do be careful.

Well, my dears, until we meet.

Lots of love to Muriel and to both of you.

God bless you.

Your loving

Vera

FOOTNOTE: I arrived home at last in late February 1945, after a delay of two weeks at Port Said while our ship waited to join a convoy going through the Mediterranean.

Glossary

IBGH	Indian Base General Hospital
QAIMNSR	Queen Alexandra's Imperial Military Nursing Service Reserve
KGH	King George Hospital
GLT	A postal term for a route
NZ	New Zealand
BoC	Burnham on Crouch
Pips	Insignia of rank
IHS	*Iesus Hominum Salvator* (Latin for 'Jesus Saviour of Men')
Bedouin	Nomadic people of the desert
Musso	An army slang name for Mussolini
Pukka	Good

Printed in the United Kingdom
by Lightning Source UK Ltd.
104433UKS00001B/7-21